THE AMERICAN EVOLUTION

HOW AMERICA CAN ADAPT TO THE POLITICAL, ECONOMIC,

AND SOCIAL CHALLENGES OF THE 21ST CENTURY

Matt Harrison

MR. GETUN —
HOPE YOU ENJOY.
BEST,

© 2009 Matt Harrison
Published by The Prometheus Institute Press

Praise for *The American Evolution*

"If America is to overcome its profound geopolitical, economic, and technological challenges, the failed remedies of the past will not work. In their place, Matt Harrison offers his innovative theory of evolutionary choice – merging biology, economics, physics, psychology, and philosophy. The American Evolution is a provocative initiative for troubled times."
- Robert A. Levy, Chairman, Cato Institute

"Harrison has cracked the genetic code of innovation and progress in America. This book celebrates our intrinsic traits of diversity and free choice and creates a roadmap for reviving the American Dream."
- Krisztina "Z" Holly,
Vice Provost for Innovation, University of Southern California,
and Executive Director, USC Stevens Institute for Innovation

"The American Evolution is a powerful guide to the conscious evolution of humanity. By applying his Evolutionary Choice theory to current crises, Matt Harrison dramatically demonstrates how American values of freedom, innovation and entrepreneurship offer the best way forward. This book applies the principles of evolution to foster political, economic and social progress in the 21st century."
- Barbara Marx Hubbard,
Founder, The Foundation for Conscious Evolution, and
former Vice Presidential Candidate for the Democratic Party

"If we know anything by now in social theory it is that recursive systems are superior to static systems, meaning that a system capable of reflecting on itself, and using these reflections to secure higher levels of efficiency and equity, will prevail over its dogmatic rivals. Matt Harrison trades on this maxim by reflecting on the current economic and moral travails of the United States and reminding us of our own best capacities to change, to evolve. This book is an ambitious and creative use of evolutionary choice theory, a happy fusion of natural selection and freedom of choice, as a normative guide to adapting and restoring the best dynamic versions of the American dreams of progress. The book is a provocative summons to rethink our deepest purposes as a nation in a global economic system."
-Fred Frohock, Chair, Department of Political Science, University of Miami

PROMETHEUS INSTITUTE PRESS
Los Angeles, CA

Copyright ©2009 by Matt Harrison
Cover design and illustrations by emKel (emKel.com)
ISBN 13: 978-0-615-28204-6
ISBN 10: 0-615-28204-11

Printed in the United States of America

Visit *The Prometheus Institute* online at www.ReadPI.org

CONTENTS

Author's Introduction

*T*HIS BOOK IS ABOUT EVOLUTION, but not in the narrow biological sense. It's about the progressive adaptation of the ideas, technology, and institutions of the modern world. It's about taking the universal lessons from the science of progress and applying them where progress seems to be the least understood - namely, our complex and fluctuating global economy, government policy, and the break-neck growth of modern technology.

In these difficult times, Americans are wondering whether we can rise out of the many political, economic and social challenges in which we find ourselves. Can we, as a nation, evolve? If so, how? Questions of progressive evolution have never had more relevance to all Americans than now in this 21st century climate of uncertainty and doubt. I simply argue that the science of evolution has profound and essential lessons for American policy.

The American Evolution is not the first book to apply evolutionary theory to social science, but it applies it differently and more comprehensively than any other. Before the knee-jerk reactions come, let me say it is neither the Social Darwinism of the last century, the cold determinism of modern sociobiology, nor the utopianism of evolutionary psychology.

It is about evolutionary choice theory, a new understanding of freedom and progress. Evolutionary choice theory is not concerned with the development of apes and amoebas, but rather of ideas and technology. It does not oppose itself to religion or science, nor does it view the two as mutually exclusive. Instead, it is dedicated to understanding evolution after the advent of humanity, and studying the growth of humanity's ideas, taking us from stone wheels and tribal anarchy to satellites and constitutional government. Put simply, it's not your grandfather's evolution.

With evolutionary choice theory, I synthesize what I see to be the universal lesson in progress as interpreted through evolutionary scientists such as Darwin, Jacob, and Dobzhansky, economists Veblen, Schumpeter and Hayek, physicists Heinsenberg, Einstein and Bohr, philosophers Heraclitus, Hegel and Bergson, and more.

Standing on the shoulders of these giants, I then apply this synthesis to the pressing real-world challenges facing 21st century America today, from economic and social policy to defense policy and constitutional law.

On the 150th anniversary of the publication of *The Origin of Species*, we've witnessed an evolution of the theory of evolution itself, and I hope that evolutionary choice theory can help continue that development. We've argued enough about the origin of humanity, it's about time that we start understanding the evolution of human ideas and institutions.

In these these trying and chaotic times, many Americans are longing for a new perspective. It seems that both sides of the political divide are out of ideas, and are merely resurrecting old arguments from the past. Every passing day is additional testimony to the fact that these old models are failing miserably.

This book is my humble effort to provide a new perspective: an original, independent, and empirically verified framework for progress in human society. I hope I can apply this perspective in a way that helps to move this great nation forward.

If I fail, then I hope this book can be refuted effectively, in a way that will better illuminate policy solutions in the multitude of fields discussed in these chapters. If so, then it's a net victory.

Most of all, I hope *The American Evolution* can transcend the stale old divisions of Left and Right, and hopefully can unite Americans behind a new pursuit of political, economic and social progress.

Thanks for reading.

Matt Harrison
Laguna Beach, California, USA
© MMIX

1

THE AMERICAN WAY FORWARD
Our nation's tried-and-true approach to uncertain times

*W*E AMERICANS ARE FACED with a dirty political truth: a growing number of threats to our democracy, freedom and long-term prosperity. The Government Accountability Office, the independent agency charged with investigating the (in)efficiency of U.S. government programs, recently warned Congress that they had created a "burning platform" of unsustainable policies which had "striking similarities" to those contributing to the fall of the Roman Empire.[1]

How bad is it, really? Our $10 trillion-plus national debt is an obvious start, but it's only the beginning. Our spending on Medicare, Medicaid and Social Security alone is projected to balloon to 20% of GDP by 2075, or in other words, about as much as our entire current federal budget.[2] Our currency and economy are threatened by a persistent and growing financial crisis, despite trillions in bailouts intended to "stabilize" the system. An alarming proliferation of special interest spending, lobbying scandals and political corruption has disgraced our democracy.

We've given out an $8 trillion prescription drug benefit to seniors, our health care spending is already the highest per capita in the developed world, and yet we somehow still have 47 million citizens who lack health insurance.[3] Globalization continues to threaten traditional ways of American life, causing income inequality, an outsourcing of positions in industries across our economy, and the vanquishing of iconic American companies on the sword of cutthroat foreign competition.

Our public education system is failing in many important respects,[4] rendering us ill-equipped to retain our national dominance in today's "knowledge economy."[5] Our highly inconvenient dependence on fossil fuel poses dual environmental and national security threats to our nation's future.

Our security is further compromised by incompetent immigration policies, which have produced 12 million illegal immigrants living in the U.S.,[6] and yet the government has somehow successfully excluded highly skilled immigrants from entry.[7] The threat of terrorism continues to loom large while our nation's critical infrastructure remains at risk. Shall I continue?

In these difficult times, the question we face as a nation is how we can best avoid the tragic decline of great empires past and retain American prosperity in an ever-changing world.

Most of all, it is a question of national evolution: can our nation adapt to the economic, demographic, technological and security challenges of the new century?

Against a backdrop of political failure, it's easy to be cynical and say that our nation is simply doomed to decline in influence. Serious writers are finding increasing parallels between America's current malaise and the death of other great empires, and are publishing books with ominous titles like *The End of America* and *The Post-American World*.

Many observers and lay people alike think America is simply doomed—doomed to lose competitiveness to China and other rising powers, doomed to suffer permanent economic decline and currency crisis, doomed to endless military quagmires around the globe, or doomed to some other fatal failure of our democracy.

Certainly, pessimism is understandable, given the malpractice of our current political leadership. In this poisoned political environment, it's hard to see how a solution will ever emerge.

The American evolution

Let us not forget, however, that our nation has come through much worse. We may be divided now, but remember, we also fought a Civil War which killed an estimated one out of every ten Americans under 40.

The Revolution itself was hardly the swift and unified triumph of American ideals we're taught in school; half of our population opposed declaring independence, and our army lost most of the major battles in the war. Most egregious, even after achieving independence, we enslaved ‹ portion of our population, finding them unfit for citizenship or basic human rights.

Yet we still stayed together to become the most humane superpower the world has ever seen. Knowing this long history of solving intractable disputes on the way to greatness, why should today's Americans doubt our ability to solve new problems?

A sense of optimism about America is not an expression of blind faith; it is a justified interpretation of our national history and the due respect for the potency of our national values. The story of American history is that of overcoming obstacles through innovation, perseverance, and creative compromise. Through civil wars, depressions, and world wars, we made it through - against all odds.

Our scholars and historians rightly credit our founding ideals for our success. But could it be that this great nation's ideals are most successful because they serve to empower political, economic and social evolution?

To this question, I answer yes, and I hope to build that case throughout this book. With the study of the sciences of progress - evolutionary science, quantum mechanics, systems theory, and complexity economics - we can discover a new interpretation of American greatness, and a new roadmap for our uncertain times.

We can then apply this idea to the specific crises facing America, from the economy and social policy to defense and foreign policy, in order to find the real-world policies to best aid our nation's evolution.

While these concepts might represent a substantial departure from the Liberal/Conservative orthodoxy, they also represent a fundamental and unifying American ideal. Just as natural selection fuels the progressive evolution of the natural world, *freedom of choice* fuels the progressive evolution of our political, economic, and social worlds.

> *...could it be that this great nation's ideals are most successful because they serve to empower political, economic and social evolution?*

One of the leading scientists of the modern evolutionary synthesis, Theodocious Dobzhansky, argued that one of the most fundamental characteristics of human evolution is the ability to choose freely between ideas and acts.[8] Echoing similar sentiments, Nobel Laureate scientist François Jacob argued that advanced

systems maximize "choice and freedom of response" in order
 to adapt to future situations.[9]

Just as you don't need a weatherman to tell which way the wind
blows, you don't need an evolutionary scientist to tell you about progress.
You can simply ask the people.

---

*advanced evolutionary systems maximize
"choice and freedom of response."*

The American Way

On the first Fourth of July after 9/11, *Knight Ridder* newspapers
surveyed Americans about what made our nation great. In summarizing the
findings, the paper wrote, "Whether immigrant or native, man or woman,
young or old, their replies expressed one overarching theme: freedom of
choice."[10]

A typical response came from Glenna Fouberg of Aberdeen, South
Dakota. "I can choose to think and believe as I want, and I can choose
to pursue happiness in my own way," Ms. Fouberg said. "I can choose to
persevere or quit, smile or frown, work or be idle, and I can choose any
religion I desire. I can fill my life with experiences or excuses, and I can dare
to dream and take risks. Whatever I make of my life is really up to me."[11]

Or take Shabnam Moshref, a 19-year-old living in Indiana, who emi-
grated from Pakistan with her parents when she was three years old. What
did she think was best about America?

"The freedom of choice," Ms. Moshref proudly asserted. "It's what
makes America unique from other countries."[12]

Ms. Moshref noted that freedom of choice was particularly meaning-
ful to her as an immigrant. "It's especially important to me because I'm from
a Middle Eastern country. I wouldn't be able to do anything I wanted to
there. My parents came here to have the opportunity for a better life...their
choice to want to come here completely changed my life. If I had stayed
where my parents are from...I would be like a servant."

But in America, Ms. Moshref has embraced her new freedoms. "I've chosen to further my education by going to college. Since I'm young, I can choose where my future's headed. My choice to go off to college instead of staying at home has totally changed my perspective of life, of other people, and what I expect."

Without the right to choose, Ms. Moshref said, "I'd probably be in an unfulfilling, boring life. We have the right to say what we say, what we do, what we think. Without that, you would be like a robot. It would be existing, but it wouldn't be like a life, because you wouldn't be happy."

Even psychologists have noted Americans' uniquely strong belief in the value of choice.

In a recent experiment at Stanford University, a group of Indian and American students were asked to select a pen from a set of five—one blue and four red. The Americans consistently chose the unique blue pen while their Indian counterparts consistently chose the common red pen.[13] A demonstration of American individualism? Perhaps.

In a second experiment, the researchers immediately took the pen the student chose and replaced it with an opposite color pen. When asked to rate the pen that was forced upon them by the researcher, the students' reactions were similarly divided. The Indian students couldn't have cared less about their original choice and were just as happy with the replacement. However, the Americans consistently expressed their dissatisfaction and rated the substituted pen lower.

"Taking away their choice threatens their freedom," concluded Hazel Markus, distinguished professor of psychology at Stanford, "and so they devalued the pen the experimenter gave them."[14]

Indeed, freedom of choice is our national pastime, and there's a reason we Americans react with such displeasure to the quashing of our unique self-expression. The American experience is testimony to the lesson that freedom of choice is essential to our nation's evolution.

The unalienable right of choice

"America has believed that in differentiation, not in uniformity, lies the path of progress. It acted on this belief; it has advanced human happiness, and it has prospered."[15] **-- Louis D. Brandeis, Supreme Court Justice**

"My choice is what I choose to do, and if I'm causin' no harm, it shouldn't bother you."[16] **-- Ben Harper, American musician**

Only in America can Supreme Court justices and rock musicians extol the same vaunted metaphysical principle. As students of history know, freedom of choice has defined some of our greatest advancements, from the expansion of voting rights to the expansion of free speech protections.

The American Revolution was a triumph of choice, after all. One can even think of our rejection of taxation without representation as our national demand for choice over the spending of our own money.

But the issue was bigger than money; it was about independence. Despite living under the freest country in the world (England: providers of natural liberty, the Magna Carta, democratic government and a robust legal system), we still threw off the yoke of foreign power, and rightly so. We wanted more. We wanted freedom of choice.

Our Declaration of Independence enshrined, for the first time in the history of the world, the American principle that governments derive their power from the "consent of the governed," and that the choice to put up with governments, or to alter and abolish them, always lies with the people. Our Constitution was the first "law of the land" in the world to be adopted by the choice of the people through popular ratification.[17]

The Constitution's text creates a system of federalism through which states have broad authority over their own affairs and can choose policies to fit their unique needs and requirements. James Madison called this system "a workshop of liberty."[18]

In 1848, the *New York Journal of Commerce* wrote that the biggest factor distinguishing America from Europe was America's belief in "free agency," or the power of individuals to pursue their interests and cultivate their unique talents without outside interference.[19]

Freedom of choice also defines the American approach to the "marketplace of ideas." Our First Amendment protects free speech much more than European countries, which routinely imprison those who perform such obviously repugnant acts as Holocaust denial or the sale of Nazi paraphernalia, for example.[20] But in the land of the free, it is perfectly legal to put swastika doo-rags for sale on eBay and solicit prospective anti-semitic roommates on Craigslist. In America, the choice is yours.

Religion and spirituality provide another excellent example of American pro-choice traditions. While many European countries have official state religions, our First Amendment bans such spiritual favoritism and allows Americans to worship according to their personal spiritual preferences. Even though many of our Founders were Christian, others were not; our Constitution has always preserved the

> *"...evolution acts as a search process for beneficial advancements; and similarly, our free choices act as a search process for beneficial advancements in the realm of our government, economy, and society."*

right to personally dissent from the spiritual orthodoxy.

As we will discuss, evolution acts as a search process for beneficial advancements; and similarly, our free choices act as a search process for beneficial advancements in the realm of our government, economy, and society. Over time, America's culture of freedom has effectively empowered the evolutionary search for life-improving innovations.

Put simply, Americans realize freedom of choice is the key to better living. Thomas Jefferson's Declaration of Independence defined the pursuit of happiness as an inalienable right; and as early as 1789, historian David Ramsay wrote that our new nation was based on a special destiny "to enlarge the happiness of mankind."[21]

The paradise of choice

Freedom of choice has long empowered the American consumer, and while one still can't buy happiness, the marketplace offers a lot of enticing products and services to make one's misery more palatable.

It's hard to deny that consumer choices have proliferated in the modern age. While some of those choices may be tasteless and unnecessary, the trend toward more options is undoubtedly a positive development.

But the difficulty in proving that point affords an opening for demagogy. Some conservatives as well as liberals now argue that this proliferation of choice in the marketplace is really a *bad* thing.[22]

Anyone who thinks that more choice in the marketplace is detrimental should look at Amazon.com, which has over 5 million titles on every subject of human interest—seriously, everything. In fact, Amazon *epitomizes* the concept of "too many choices." No matter who you are, you can go to Amazon.com and find a disturbing plethora of reading material for sale on the subject you find most repugnant to the natural order of humanity, whether it be communism, atheism, fascism or any other "ism."

Amazon's something-for-everyone approach defines a new era in 21st century business called the "long tail" model, by which consumers are no longer subject to one-size-fits-all options, but rather enjoy the near-infinite expression of their individual tastes. The name is taken from the long "tail" on each side of a bell curve graph, representing data well outside the average. In his book *The Long Tail: Why the Future of Business is Selling Less of More*, Chris Anderson explains the effects of this new choice-maximizing business model.[23] Through technological advancements, companies are able to satisfy an ever-increasing diversity of preferences.

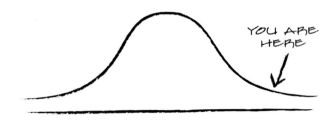

Music is an example of the near-infinite yet ever-controversial value of choice. As we'll discuss in Chapter 6, few areas of human interest are more disputed, arbitrary and personal than the debate over what constitutes "good music." There are those who believe the term should be exclusive to Mozart and the classical giants, others to jazz musicians, and others to contemporary pop stars. There are also those who believe that none of this is music at all, but objectionable "noise" that has negligible social value.[24]

But in the long tail internet age of choice, our music options are endless, and true music fans couldn't be happier. New platinum-selling bands are now discovered through their MySpace pages.[25] Apple's iTunes music store offers a virtual selection that trumps the best record stores, at lower prices and with instant gratification. Ventures such as the Music Genome Project utilize technology to facilitate exposure to new artists, styles and genres.[26] Artists can use widely available yet highly sophisticated equipment to self-broadcast, transcending the narrow-minded dictates of the FCC or

Clear Channel. Musicians have never before had a greater chance to express themselves, or find listeners who will appreciate their own unique talents.

In music and elsewhere, we see the freedom of individual choice creating a better environment for all of us.

Yes, choice is good.

Is there such a thing as too much of it?

Well, you choose.

The punishment of choice

As Aristotle reminds us, there is great value to moderation, and every choice has its saturation point.

Believe it or not, people can even have too much Starbucks. Thanks to low market demand, the chain recently announced that they would be axing hundreds of their under-performing locations.[27] Thus, we see that freedom of choice can even influence Corporate America. Don't want that extra Starbucks on the corner of Main? Then don't buy your coffee there, chap.

Free choice is the enemy of the monopoly. There is a popular conception of American corporations as all-powerful behemoths, but to paraphrase Mark Twain, the reports of their immortality are greatly exaggerated. Take the experience of the Fortune 50 companies of 1980. By 2000, 40 of them were knocked off the list, including eight out of the top ten.[28]

It's quite the paradox, but freedom of choice in the marketplace is the friend of the anti-corporate crowd. In the 21st century, one can vote with the wallet and buy a variety of products to protest Big Industry and their assault on the Common Man, including eco-friendly, organic and locally grown products.

Consumers in California who feel their gigantic corporate grocery store is too intimidating and inhuman can now shop at Fresh and Easy, a new chain offering reduced store sizes, simplified aisles and menus, organic food selections and more.[29] Even Wal-Mart has joined the reduced-selection club with its new Marketplace stores, featuring a similarly simplified shopping environment.[30] A popular new choice for shoppers: less choice.

The market choices for the green-minded citizen are ever expanding as well. Those upset with the use of genetically modified foods can choose to shop at Whole Foods markets. Those terrified of global warming can choose to buy "carbon credits" to offset their greenhouse gas emissions. Now there was no Tree-Hugging Food Amendment in Congress that achieved any of these options; it was merely people choosing to buy something, and companies responding to those demands.

The power of free choice to impact Big Business should not be underestimated. In 1998, Naomi Klein wrote the anti-globalization book *No Logo*, excoriating multinational corporations for, *inter alia*, their complicity in low working standards in third world factories.[31] The book was a bestseller and became the defining text of the anti-globalization movement.

The book was so successful that Nike—the company that Klein's book criticized most—actually *responded* to the book via press release.[32]

Wait, how is this possible? A giant, faceless multinational corporation responding to the critical viewpoint of its actions?

Nike replied because the public relations disaster created by Klein's book threatened the very success of its brand. Brands are only psychological abstractions—their meaning is entirely generated by the perception of the public. The effectiveness of "Nike the brand" is entirely determined by the public's decision to buy Nike shoes. After *No Logo*, the growing unpopularity of the Nike brand concerned the company. Nike had to respond to ensure that people would still choose to support them.

Imagine that. Can you picture the Pentagon responding to a Noam Chomsky book? The IRS responding to a Neal Boortz book? Of course not. Unlike shoe brands, you can't just choose a new defense agency or tax-collecting service.

This example is a wonderful demonstration that the solution to so many difficult political issues is the simple exercise of choice. Want to keep American jobs? Convince people to pay the high prices required to buy goods made in America. Worried about the working conditions in the place that a company gets its goods? Convince people to not buy anything from that company.

Better together

Freedom of choice also helps to facilitate vibrant and dynamic communities. As John Donne famously noted, no man is an island, and much of the value from our lives comes from our community and the relationships we build. For this reason, perhaps the greatest public benefit from free choice is its enhancement of our social and cultural lives.

Nowhere has the social value of choice been better demonstrated than the case of religion in America. Lacking a national religion, Americans have always enjoyed free choice regarding their church attendance and worship practices. Churches that do not attract worshippers are forced to adapt or die away. As *USA Today* wrote:

> American individualism in religion puts pressure on churches to change in ways that can make traditionalists uncomfortable. There is something disquieting about shopping for religion the way one would pick among lattes at Starbucks. But having options makes believers comfortable, not trapped, in their faith. It promotes intellectual exploration and unleashes creativity and outreach, typified by successful megachurches. In religion as in coffee, choice is a critical ingredient — one all too scarce in much of the world.[33]

As Americans recently turned away from church attendance in the latter half of the 20th century, churches were forced to become more competitive in the new age of secular liberalism and skeptical materialism.

The result, as *USA Today* mentioned, was the rise of the "megachurch," offering more contemporary services capable of attracting the cosmopolitan worshipper. Foremost among these is Rick Warren's Saddleback Church, offering espresso selections and closed circuit television for its crowds of Orange County, California suburbanites.

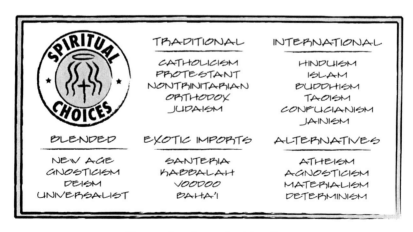

The marketplace of spirituality

In the book *Better Together,* author Robert Putnam uses Saddleback Church as an example of voluntary community associations that have risen to address the problems of our modern age.[34] The choice among people to freely associate encourages the formation of dynamic social groups to create positive change in communities, economies or society at large.

The dynamic formation of social groups has long been a defining feature of America. In 1840, French historian Alexis de Tocqueville wrote, "I met with several kinds of associations in America of which I confess I had no previous notion; and I have often admired the extreme skill with which the inhabitants of the United States succeed in proposing a common object for the exertions of a great many men and in inducing them voluntarily to pursue it."[35]

Thanks to internet technology, it has never been so easy for new communities to organize for common purposes. Online message forums and web groups such as Facebook and MeetUp allow common-interest communities to organize and effect change in pursuit of their shared goals, whether in protesting a company's behavior or organizing boycotts, protests or other grassroots activism.

Riding together

The evolutionary power of choice is even apparent in the world of sports. The history of the sport of snowboarding offers a surprising example of how freedom of choice and the right to dissent from the orthodoxy can create unforeseen benefits for everyone.

Snowboarding is an American invention, first appearing on our ski slopes in the 1980s, as baggy-pant-clad delinquent kids began sliding down mountains on makeshift surfboards, smoking joints on chairlifts, and mostly lying prostrate in the middle of runs due to an unnecessarily high proportion of wipeouts.

At the beginning of the sport, few thought this self-parodying stoner diversion had a future. Some ski patrols often kicked out individual snowboarders, and many resorts banned them entirely. After all, who would want to be a snowboarder?

As it turns out, being different was only part of the appeal of snowboarding. As an avid snowboarder myself, I'll help explain the appeal. Snowboarding enables one to easily jump, spin and stylize tricks in a variety of different terrain conditions. While this feature is understandably appealing to the risk-inclined, I believe it has universal appeal. Few experiences are more exhilarating than floating through the air, suspended in the blissful transcendence of gravity. Moreover, the act of snowboarding is a more fluid and passive activity than skiing, making the act of carving down hills a serene and enlightening experience.

Today, snowboarding is the world's fastest growing winter sport. As millions of kids and adults chose to give the new sport a try, it rapidly gained popularity and mainstream success. New choices created a new community, and now "professional snowboarder" is a legitimate career choice. The sport is constantly televised on ESPN, and hundreds of snowboard companies offer high-tech equipment and fashionable gear for riders of any age, gender and style. Resorts have embraced snowboarding too, providing "terrain features," jumps, rails and other tricks for snowboarders.

The enhanced diversity of clientele—thanks to snowboarding—helped the resort industry avoid a recession. As skiing has declined in popularity, snowboarding has exploded, keeping uncomfortable layoffs at bay. "If it wasn't for snowboarding, the industry would have suffered a major contraction," said Michael Perry, president of the National Ski Areas Association.[36]

"What the hell are those damn hooligans doing, Byron?"

"They're part of our new economic stimulus package, sir."

Recognizing the economic value of this new market, ski resorts now embrace snowboarders with open arms. Most of all, they realize that social differentiation is in their own interest. "Basically, snowboarding has brought more people to the mountains and introduced more people to snow sports," said Kurt Hoy, editor in chief of *TransWorld Snowboarding*.[37]

Thanks to snowboarding, America has won eight Olympic medals. Each provided classic moments of Olympic heroism that graced the covers of Wheaties boxes and inspired little kids at the breakfast table. Snowboarding has also created billions of dollars in economic growth, and those involved continue to hold numerous events to support charity work around the world.

Imagine—all that from a few hellions who chose to buck tradition on the mountain.

The spontaneous order

"Among a free people," Justice Brandeis observed, "there can be no self-constituted body of men possessing the power to decide what the action of the whole people shall be."

This idea has shown itself repeatedly in American history, and the successes of snowboarding, Starbucks, Whole Foods and Saddleback Church are only a few examples. These institutions - social technologies, as we'll call them - represent different lifestyle choices for different goals.

The evolution of these social technologies, as the stories so far have shown, is unpredictable. Only the unrestrained exercise of free choice over time can create this spontaneous social-technological innovation. Someone tried something, everyone else decided they liked it, and somehow, we all ended up with advancements to improve our lives. The true expression of freedom of choice means that inevitably, some people will live differently, think differently and worship differently.

Playing the choice card

Knowing the broad national appeal of freedom of choice, both liberal and conservative politicians give lip service to the principle...when it's politically convenient, of course.

Democrats are most (in)famous for seizing the term to exclusively define their defense of abortion rights. On *Meet the Press*, Democratic Party chairman Howard Dean argued that freedom of choice distinguished the Democratic and Republican views on abortion. "This is an issue about who gets to make up their minds," Dean argued. "Democrats are for the individual. We believe in individual rights. We believe in personal freedom and personal responsibility."[38] Along the same lines, Senator Barbara Boxer warned voters before the 2000 election that a Republican victory would commence a "final assault on the freedom of choice."[39]

But if you ask Democrats how they plan to protect your freedom of choice when it means the ability for workers to save for retirement, the ability for parents to choose their children's school, or the ability for citizens to spend their own money, you'll get nothing but a blank stare.

On those issues, Republicans have seized the moment and played the Choice Card to their political advantage. In the *Washington Post*, Dick Armey argued that Republicans should emphasize their support of freedom of choice on issues like taxes, education, health care and retirement security.[40] In this vein, Republicans excoriated their opponents' health care plans for their abrogation of freedom of choice.[41]

George F. Will, a conservative and America's greatest living political commentator, recently wrote a piece contrasting the liberal and conservative world-views, arguing (surprise) that *conservatism* in fact was defined by freedom of choice.[42]

By contrast, Will argued, "Liberals favor expanding government controls, shrinking the sphere of freedom of choice." Will concluded that liberals implement these choice-limiting programs in order to create "social solidarity" through government.

Even while conservative and liberal politicians claim the title of Defender of Free Choice, both more often spend their time fighting it. Our current leaders are the greatest limitation on Americans' freedom of choice today. Popular targets for decision regulation in Washington include your eating habits, employment decisions, child's education, video games and other entertainment media, personal indulgences, metaphysical beliefs, public utterances of not-politically-correct statements, internet behavior, decisions about your health care, and decisions about your retirement.

Despite all the examples of the spontaneous benefits of human choice, political figures believe that they know enough about us to make those choices for us, thanks to some omniscient grasp of information. And further, despite their rhetoric about "freedom of choice," politicians believe they must spend and save our money, educate our children and make personal choices for us because we wouldn't be able to figure out how to do it on our own.

The resurrection of ourselves

What should we do about our government's un-American assault on freedom of choice? First, we need to put it all in perspective.

Every history student will tell you that the failure of the American government to respect our national ideals is nothing new. With a track record of slavery, segregation, limited suffrage, prohibition, forced internment, military conscription and a host of other affronts to freedom, an unfortunate and jarring dichotomy has always existed between American ideals and American government practice. As political scientist Samuel Huntington put it:

> Being human, Americans have never been able to live up to their ideals; being Americans, they have also been unable to abandon them. They have instead existed in a state of national cognitive dissonance, which they have attempted to relieve through various combinations of moralism, cynicism, complacency and hypocrisy. The 'burr under the saddle' as Robert Penn Warren called it, and the efforts to remove that burr have been central features of American politics.[43]

Indeed. But it is the way we remove that "burr under the saddle" that makes us so unique. Through two millennia of turbulent political change, our ideals are what served as the road map to guide our political progress. On an asymptotic national path toward freedom, our ideals have defined our greatest political achievements.

At the heart of our evolution is the expansion of freedom of choice, for all Americans. The civil rights movements gave women, minorities and youth the right to choose their elected leaders. When Martin Luther King quoted Thomas Jefferson's declaration that "all men are created equal," he defined the American ideal of equality: that the worth of a man is not determined by the features over which he has no control, such as the color of his skin, but rather by the content of his character, manifested by his own choices.

Today, American values are still coterminous with the golden standard and can still serve as the inspirational fire of political change. Americans should feel extremely confident facing the challenges of the 21st century.

Even though our politicians' hostility toward choice comprises many of our political failures, there is reason for optimism. More than any other country in the world, our national ideal remains the key to our future success.

This national ideal is now being confirmed with the most modern of sciences, from evolutionary science itself to quantum mechanics and systems theory. As it turns out, evolutionary systems adapt to uncertainty the same way the American system does: by maximizing individuals' freedom of choice.

Over the next few chapters, we will be taking lessons from the sciences of progress, and applying their lessons to address pressing policy questions of the modern age. These discoveries, constituting the leading principles of evolutionary choice theory, can give us new insights to aid progressive adaptation in the 21st century.

As we'll discuss, the true understanding of evolution gives a whole different perspective on the world, one that transcends the traditional ideological dichotomies of Left/Right, liberal/conservative, or individualist/communitarian.

If there is one lesson that *The American Evolution* imparts, it is that while we are dedicated to the concept of "freedom of choice", our version differs greatly from the current mainstream conception. The freedom of choice in evolutionary choice theory bears little or no resemblance to the static mathematics of what is called "choice theory"; or the weak-kneed nihilist relativism that rejects all forms of moral authority.

Evolutionary choice theory is about *evolition*: the choices made that constitute social progress. Evolition is invention, creating the alternatives that were heretofore impossible. It does not assume the static permanence of choices between A and B; it is dedicated to the *creation* of choices C, D, and E. Evolition is progress in action, and is represented by the advent of progressive innovations that few people saw coming. Snowboarding, Saddleback Church, computer technology, and the many other examples in this book are examples of evolition in the modern world. Evolition is the way of progress, and evolutionary choice theory is the study of the elements of this progress.

Over the next two chapters, I'll try to synthesize the main elements of the evolutionary perspective of progress, and explain how it revolutionizes the popular political, economic, and philosophical ideas of the day.

This might seem technical at times, but I beg your patience through the journey. The background is essential in order to illuminate the framework through which we'll be analyzing the specific political, economic and social problems facing America. In order to figure out how our nation can evolve, we must first figure out how evolution works.

2

IMPOSSIBLE IS NOTHING
Evolution, technology, and the new story of human progress

*F*OR THE VAST MAJORITY of our existence, humans have lived a life best described by philosopher Thomas Hobbes as "nasty, brutish and short."[44] Rampant disease, warfare, famine and the constant toil at a subsistence level were the norm. The Greek historian Thucydides wrote that early humans "could never rise above nomadic life," and "without commerce, without freedom of communication either by land or sea, cultivating no more of their territory than the exigencies of life required," they "neither built large cities, nor attained to any other form of greatness."[45] Harsh.

Gradually, humans began to gain access to new technologies, although the process was an excruciatingly slow one. It took 12,000 years to go from the primitive tribe/hunter-gatherer society (with an economy producing an average $90 per capita) to the economy of Thucydides in ancient Greece (estimated at only $150 per capita GDP).[46]

Life remained nasty, brutish and short, and all but the most powerful rulers and social elites lived at a subsistence level. By the time of the Roman Empire, life expectancy was still a paltry 22,[47] and this dismal state of affairs continued into the mid-eighteenth century.

Then suddenly, the rules changed. The divine right of kings gave way to the rights of man. Religious superstition gave way to scientific inquiry. Laws began to encourage free trade and commerce among all people. Expanding global trade gave consumers around the world even more choices and access to new technologies. Secured property rights for all citizens helped encourage trust and cooperation for mutual gain. Through the 20th century, America and other Western nations expanded the protections of freedom to more people, and more developing nations implemented institutions of freedom in their own lands.

As freedom began to take root around the world, choices in the marketplace expanded (of products as well as ideas), and technological growth boomed.

By the turn of the 21st century, average per-person GDP on Earth had increased 37 fold from 1750, to its current level of $6,600. In the U.S., it currently stands at a world-leading $45,000. We can now expect to live well past 70.[48]

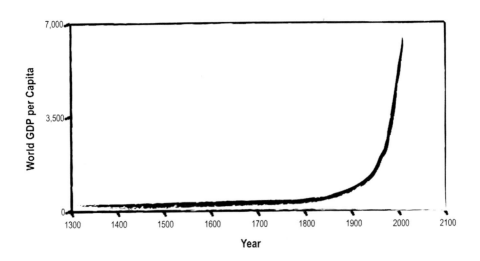

The technological evolution

It is hard to see the breakneck growth of human capacity as anything else but evolution in action. How have we managed to go from stone wheels to carbon-fiber aircraft, from clay tablets to touchscreen PDAs, from smoke signals to wireless internet, or from mud huts to solar-powered glass skyscrapers, all from basically the same endowment of natural materials?

To me, the answer is quite simple: it is evolution. It is evolution of human ideas, figuring out how to use people and the earth's resources in progressively more useful ways. It is the discovery of Good Tricks for survival and better living, just as the story of biological evolution is the discovery of Good Tricks for survival and better living.

One need not believe that man and apes evolved from a common ancestor to realize that man's ideas have evolved from his inception to the present day. By focusing the debate on evolution after the advent of *homo sapiens* - whether you think that period lasted only 10,000 years or 200,000 years - we can help transcend the narrow cultural wars of the past in pursuit of a greater understanding of the future.

No one can deny that evolution in some form impacts the natural world. (If not, try to explain why the flu virus mutates to adapt to each season's vaccine.)[49] Given this fact, I simply argue that no one should dispute that evolution in some form impacts our political, economic and social worlds as well.

Moreover, if that same force of evolution can take us from stone wheels and tribal anarchy to satellites and constitutional government, then surely it can also help us get through our current political, economic, and social crises. The rest of this book is about figuring out exactly how this human evolution occurs.

Obviously, this evolution takes the form of new technologies. But the technological advancements that drive growth include more than traditional *physical* technology, such as computers, automobiles and the tools of modern medicine.

In fact, as Richard Nelson of Columbia University notes, there is a second category of technologies—*social technologies*—that may be even more important in the creation of value-added growth.[50] Eric Beinhocker of the McKinsey Institute defines social technologies as "methods and designs for organizing people in pursuit of a goal or goals."[51] Social technologies include organizations, institutions, laws, rules, norms, and other methods of organizing human behavior for a specific goal. By improving the effectiveness of collaboration, such technologies help us better harness human knowledge for social benefit.

> *By focusing the debate on evolution after the advent of homo sapiens, we can help transcend the narrow cultural wars of the past in pursuit of a greater understanding of the future.*

Last chapter, we touched on a number of social technologies and how they've evolved to improve our lives. The long tail model of business is a hugely significant social technology, empowering access to knowledge, communication tools and other avenues of personal satisfaction.

Business models are social technologies as well. Starbucks offers patrons a comfortable neighborhood gathering place for good coffee, social interaction, exposure to new kinds of good music, and even a safe (if cliché) spot for a first date or a reunion with friends. Whole Foods or Fresh and Easy offers shopping experiences to satisfy the unique identity preferences of environmentalists, vegans and other green-minded shoppers. Online social technologies, such as Facebook and other internet forums, help us communicate, plan events, share information and express ourselves in new ways.

Sports, music and film are also social technologies. Each are classic examples of organizing people for entertainment, and are also well known for vocal purists who insist on stagnation in a changing world. But our example of snowboarding's evolution shows that tradition and modernity are not always mutually exclusive when it comes to social technologies.

Before you think social technologies exclusively pursue frivolous diversions, think again. Social technologies are also organized in pursuit of much higher goals.

Religion is perhaps the oldest, most popular and most powerful social technology, helping billions of humans understand the metaphysical meaning of life and death. We've already seen its evolution, allowing contemporary Christians to sip their lattes as they take in the Sunday's digital sermon at Saddleback.

Whether choosing a church or a cappuccino, our choices represent an evaluation of competing social technologies. All social technologies, like physical technologies, attempt to make our lives better in different ways, whether they're entertaining us, expanding our knowledge, enhancing our communication or even encouraging political activism.

Our government is a social technology as well, although it has rather noticeably lagged behind the development of most other modern technologies. From our burning platform of unsustainable policies, complete with widespread bureaucracy, inefficiency and corruption to our divisive and destructive political debate, the social technology we call our civil society

Social technologies: Ideas or designs in pursuit of a goal

appears to be rusting, crumbling and increasingly obsolete.

Over the rest of this book, we'll be studying the elements of technological evolution, in order to empower the progressive adaptation to our current crises.

Athwart history, yelling Stop

But wait a second—who says we should evolve? There are many in politics and economics who think my viewpoints are reversed, that it is the physical and social technologies that have progressed too far, and that government is needed to restrain the socially-damaging progress of business, technology, entertainment or other social institutions.

Even with our fantastic rise from brutally short living to enjoyably comfortable living, brilliant minds question the progress of physical and social technology. Why, the critics charge, should we trust the fact that technology will keep getting better? What if we've come as far as we should come? What if our innovations turn out to be for the worse? Why should we not decide to, in William F. Buckley's famous words, stand athwart history, yelling Stop?

Others question whether we *can* evolve. The icon of unbelief in technological progress is the economist Thomas Robert Malthus. Back in 1798, Malthus wrote that the growth of population was "indefinitely greater than the power in the earth to produce subsistence for man."[52] Malthus' argument was forever enshrined in the concept called the "Malthusian Trap," or the view that the world's population will eventually grow to a level that will outstrip the world's supply of life-sustaining natural resources. Malthus, in his foresight, predicted this would happen some time in the mid-1800s.

But today, we know that technological change has rendered Malthus' objections—however well reasoned at the time—to be patently false. With advancements in agriculture, trade, communications and even genetic modification, we continually find ways to evolve our environment and expand the ability for the human community to flourish. With every year of increasing per capita GDP, we find ways to produce more with the same people.

But the unfortunate belief that we've come as far as we'll ever come has never been limited to economists. In 1885, Lord Kelvin, the president of the Royal Society, Britain's leading scientific society, argued that "heavier than air flying machines are impossible."

In 1923, Robert Millikan, the Nobel Prize winning physicist, wrote that there is "no likelihood that man will ever tap the power of the atom."[53]

Interesting. How can all these brilliant people make such utterly false predictions?

Stumbling toward ecstasy

The answer is the unpredictability of evolution. Growth has become an enigma among historians, economists, sociologists and other "experts" because most important advances were completely unforeseen, to even the most intelligent observers, before their invention. If there's one thing we know, it's that the path of technological advancement is uncertain, capricious and unpredictable.

There is no magic or metaphysical profundity to the development process of technology. It is simply a trial-and-error process of fitness. We try new technologies and keep what works well. This process is random, complex, radical and often uncomfortable—but it's also the only thing that works.

It's easy to doubt the future development of technology. In fact, given its unforeseeable development, doubts are understandable. But history has also shown that despite how smart we think we are at a given time, the cycle keeps moving forward. Pat Michaels of the Cato Institute put it well:

> For an interesting thought experiment, consider the energy and technology world of 1900, and a vision of the future. 'Scientists will discover a new element called plutonium,' some placard-carrying crackpot on the horse-infested streets of New York might say, 'and if we compress a few pounds of it, almost all the buildings on Manhattan will be destroyed, along with their inhabitants.' What a wacko! And that's nothing, compared with his assertion that, by 1975, people would fly from New York to London in a little over three hours, 65,000 feet in the air, or that all of the information in all the libraries of the Earth could be on everyone's desktop by 2000.[54]

As Mr. Michaels aptly notes, technology replaces old methods of living in ways that we could never have imagined at the time.

By the 1990s, IBM had established itself as the world's leading computer company, with massive market power and a substantial team of genius engineers and computer scientists to match. Yet by the turn of the century, Big Blue was knocked entirely out of the personal computer market, vanquished by the brainchild of a 19-year-old whiz kid named Michael Dell.

It turned out that all of the money and brains at IBM couldn't figure out that allowing consumers to custom-order their own computer would be a good idea. Dell did, though, and within a few short years of starting a computer company in his garage, the company was near the top of the Fortune 500.

The IBM-Dell story is most interesting because Dell's success had less to do with the physical technology of its computers (PCs operate on highly similar infrastructures), and much more to do with the social technology of their business model—viz., custom-ordered computers delivered direct to each consumer.

Technology moves in mysterious ways. Often times, evolutionary advancements don't come from an ambitious rogue entrepreneur, but are discovered entirely by accident. Many people know that the antibiotic penicillin, so indispensable in aiding human health and fighting disease, was an accidental discovery from mold. Many people also know that the inventor of Kellogg's Corn Flakes discovered his famous recipe by screwing up a recipe for corn gruel. The list goes on, and includes some of humanity's most beneficial and popular innovations—microwaves, champagne, Post-it notes and the pacemaker—that were invented entirely by accident.[55]

Effort, intelligence or good intentions may be important in helping create market success. But the presence of these traits doesn't guarantee that a socially beneficial innovation will be created. Usually, it's just dumb luck.

Most of the time, the touchstone of technological progress is not ethical or intellectual, but rather functional. There is one main question that matters: does the innovation *work*?

That question can only be answered by the free choices of individuals.

But to many experts, this is still unsatisfactory. Shouldn't there be a way to predict these advancements? How do we know freedom of choice won't destroy society? How do we know Saddleback Church is not blasphemous sacrilege? How do we know kids won't start killing people after they play these realistic video games like *Grand Theft Auto*? How do we know all of these new complex financial instruments won't bring our economy to a screeching halt? *Ad nauseum.*

The answer is, we don't know, and we never will. The only thing we can do is create as many choices as possible to best find new innovations, and let the people choose what works.

Evolutionary processes discover "black swans," or events that seem to be impossible before their occurrence. The term comes from the fact that black swans were not discovered by Europeans until the end of the eighteenth century. But before that point, it was perfectly rational and logically accurate to say that black swans don't exist. Similarly, evolutionary systems unleash innovations - like the airplane, automobile, and computer - that seem completely impossible prior to their invention.

Freedom of choice is the lesson of evolution, because as Dobzhansky and Jacob both noted in Chapter 1, individual choice allows progressive adaptation in even the most uncertain climates.

Evolutionary destruction

So where do all these ideas about evolution and technology come from? A rapidly expanding academic field has dedicated itself to studying technological innovation and social growth as an evolutionary process. Leading this field is a maverick group of economists in the *evolutionary economics* community, who seek to understand the processes behind social-technological and physical-technological progress.[56]

As an aside, it's important to reiterate that this field has nothing to do with the controversial questions of biological evolution, specifically whether evolution is universally responsible for the creation of man, the creation of life, the complexity of life, or any other currently unanswerable questions. Thus, it's unnecessary to discuss these specific issues any further.

The understanding of evolution has moved beyond the narrow conception of biology or genetics, to the general study of the spontaneous creation of progressive growth.[57] A leading evolutionary theorist defined evolution as a process of "increasing differentiation and complexity of an organization which endows the organism, social system or *whatever the unit in question may be* with greater capacity to adapt to its environment than its less complex ancestors."[58] Or in the words of famed evolutionary scientist R.A. Fisher, "Evolution is progressive adaptation...and nothing else."[59]

Evolutionary understandings of human progress have several advantages. First, they best explain the random and unpredictable path of human progress.[60] Second, they recognize market competition as the continual process of fitness selection, or in other words, testing which

> *"Evolution is progressive adaptation... and nothing else."*

technological resources work to make us better off as a people. Third, they recognize and embrace the constant change that drives our world. Fourth, and perhaps most importantly, evolutionary theory gives us a robust, comprehensive, and empirically verified conceptual framework for how progress occurs.

Adam Smith, considered to be the father of modern economics, observed that individual decision-making in the marketplace, subject to certain rules, created social progress.[61] Smith was also the first to note how specialization and division of labor were social technologies that encouraged such innovation.[62] Unfortunately, Smith gave little in the way of a rigorous scientific explanation of the dynamic process that allowed self-interested indivduals to somehow achieve the public good. Instead, Smith relied on a metaphysical concept, the "Invisible Hand."

In 1898, an economist named Thorstein Veblen made the bold first attempt to explain economic growth within an evolutionary framework. In an article with the no-nonsense title "Why is Economics not an evolutionary science?", Veblen argued that economic growth resembled the random process of evolution, and economists should recognize it as such. [63]

Veblen's critique turned out to be an important one. How else does one explain the manipulation of natural resources into physical and social technologies of much greater value than the original resources? Something out of nothing? Or evolution?

The evolutionary explanation of economics got another boost when Joseph Schumpeter became the first major economist to incorporate evolutionary ideas into mainstream economic thought. "In dealing with capitalism," Schumpeter wrote, "we are dealing with an evolutionary process."[64]

Schumpeter argued that market evolution derived fundamentally from the innovations of entrepreneurs. By their introduction of novel social and physical technologies into the marketplace, Schumpeter believed, entrepreneurs created better ways of life at the expense of the old ways of doing business. Schumpeter used the phrase "gales of creative destruction" to

Adam Smith, holding his invisible hand to the camera

describe the process by which entrepreneurial innovation helped revolution-ize the economic landscape and help our society move forward.

Others would seize on Schumpeter's ideas and expand the study of intersections between evolution and economic growth, including the evolution of market structure and business strategy.[65] Other evolutionary economics pioneers include Kenneth Boulding's 1981 *Evolutionary Economics*, Richard Nelson and Sidney Winter's 1986 *An Evolutionary Theory of Economic Change*, and the 1991 establishment of the *Journal of Evolutionary Economics*.

The economic study of evolution has never been limited to the mar-ketplace, however.

Nobel Laureate Friedrich Hayek is considered another forefather of evolutionary economics, specifically in the context of evolved social tech-nologies. Hayek believed that the norms, rules and institutions that guide our behavior in modern society are all part of an evolved "spontaneous order" which encourages better living.[66]

"Our institutions of property, freedom and justice," Hayek argued, "are not a creation of man's reason but a distinct second endowment con-ferred on him by *cultural evolution*." Hayek believed that "rules of human conduct that gradually evolved (especially those dealing with several prop-erty, honesty, contract, exchange, trade, competition, gain, and privacy)" were "chiefly responsible for having generated this extraordinary [social] order, and the existence of mankind in its present size and structure."[67]

Taking a similar perspective, the philosopher David Hume argued that rules of property and other legal principles were conventions that evolved spontaneously.[68] Other great thinkers from sociology to anthropol-ogy, including Carl Menger and Adam Ferguson, have also applied evolu-tionary ideas to explain the emergence and growth of political institutions,[69] money,[70] the common law,[71] language,[72] constitutional structure,[73] and even human culture itself.[74]

Most comprehensively (and controversially), the German philoso-pher G.W.F. Hegel applied evolutionary ideas to the development of human knowledge itself, as an "organic process in which the contributions of [the people] converge toward the common goal, albeit dimly perceived or even altogether unknown to them."[75]

Thus, evolutionary perspectives regarding political, economic and social progress have a long and distinguished history. Most of all, we've seen how the complexity, unpredictability, and chaotic changes of the modern

EVOLUTION OF ECONOMIC MAN

HOMO SUBJECTUS

HOMO AGRICULTURUS

HOMO LABORIOUS

HOMO QUANTIFACATUS

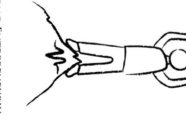

HOMO ENTREPRENEURIUS

world closely resemble the models of evolutionary science.

Given the fact that adaptation in the natural world abides by the laws of the evolutionary synthesis, in my view, the burden of proof should be on opponents of evolutionary theory to explain why the adaptation of human technology would not abide by the laws of evolution as well.

How well does the social science establishment carry this burden? Let's find out.

The old school

Mainstream economists heavily criticize evolutionary explanations of growth. Nobel economics laureate and *New York Times* columnist Paul Krugman, for one, calls them "biobabble."[76]

Old school economists such as Krugman prefer to explain human economic behavior not as a dynamic and evolutionary process, but rather a static and linear one. This view follows the intellectual tradition of Marie-Esprit-Léon Walras, who is credited with founding the mainstream, or "neo-classical" study of economics.

Walras created the "general equilibrium theory," which held that economic interactions between people tend to settle into a stable, static allocation of resources, called an equilibrium. He used mathematics to explain this process, by which perfectly rational economic actors trade resources to arrive at an optimal equilibrium distribution.[77]

Anyone who has struggled through an economics course in high school or college likely wants to curse Marie-Esprit-Léon Walras; it was Walras who introduced the use of complex mathematical formulae in economics.

Walras was able to confine human decisions to math and graphs through his ingenious adoption of unrealistic assumptions about behavior, such as humans possessing perfect rationality and experiencing no transaction costs.[78]

These assumptions were essential in order to ram his static mathematical model onto the dynamic progress of the economy, but at the cost of real-world accuracy.

It makes one wonder, when progress is defined by equilibrium-shattering change, what good is a discipline that explains behavior as a static and steady state of affairs? One cannot confine human idiosyncrasy and free choice to a set of mathematical formulae, no matter how ingeniously complex.

"The question," as Veblen pointed out, "is not how things stabilize themselves in a 'static state,' but how they endlessly grow and change."[79]

"Man is not simply a bundle of desires that are to be saturated by being placed in the path of the forces of the environment," Veblen continued, "but rather a coherent structure of propensities and habits which seeks realization and expression in an *unfolding* activity."[80]

Friedrich Hayek notably despised the quantitative trends in economics because he recognized that static thinking had no place in economics. "Economic problems," Hayek noted, "arise always and only in consequence of change."[81]

Certainly, it's easy to understand why neoclassical economists like their static equilibrium model. It's devilishly easy to predict. Find Point A: where we are now. Then find Point B: where we want to go. Plot it on a graph, crunch the numbers, and voila! A perfect Walrasian prediction of human behavior!

"Nobel Prize-winning foresight"

But we've just seen how growth itself is unpredictable and techno-logical changes are surprisingly diverse. The static model ignores the real question—the problem is finding Point B. Where do we want to go exactly, and how do we get there?

Thanks to their self-installed Walrasian blinders, economists have the worst track record of prediction outside of television weathermen. As a direct result of using static and mathematical models to explain dynamic and unpredictable behavior, neoclassical economics can't even predict the very progress it purports to study.[82] This explains why economists like Malthus could think that population growth would outstrip technological growth before the year 1900.

Our current financial crisis is exposing neoclassical economics for its deep and pervasive flaws. Economists who can't even successfully predict the next month's unemployment numbers are now opining on how many years our recession will last. It is time for the charade to stop.

Before I get buckets of hate mail from aggrieved economists, let me state that neoclassical economics has absolutely aided the advancement of human knowledge. Classical economics has taught us many lessons, such as the value of competition, importance of incentives, the necessity of price signals and more. These lessons, much like the Newtonian mechanics on which they are conceptually based, are essential for advancing scientific understanding and helpful in explaining certain aspects of the world. In fact, we'll be relying on many of these lessons throughout this book.

But just as quantum mechanics is reinterpreting the Newtonian paradigm, the foundations of economic thought

> *Our current financial crisis is exposing neoclassical economics for its deep and pervasive flaws.*

are being similarly revolutionized in favor of a more dynamic and complex model of reality.[83]

Quantum mechanics has shattered the classical assumptions of a static, predictable, and deterministic universe. As physicists perform experiments on the subatomic scale, they discovered that particles do not behave in a perfectly predictable manner, but rather exhibit "genuine ontological chance."[84] As a result, quantum mechanics teaches that at the most basic level of the universe, uncertainty is simply part of the "fabric of nature", and that the behavior of the universe cannot be predicted exactly, but only with a probability.[85]

Some quantum theorists argue that quantum uncertainty can "percolate up" into the level of biological populations, creating a "genuinely indeterministic" evolutionary trajectory.[86] Encapsulating the quantum perspective as applied to evolutionary theory is Nobel laureate Jacques Monod, who argued that "chance alone is at the source of every innovation...[and] at the very root of the stupendous edifice of evolution."[87]

The dynamic models of evolutionary science and quantum mechanics give a powerful indication that freedom of choice may be the essential creative force behind progressive change.[88] Quantum mechanics allows for the type of rule-breaking leaps of creativity that are foreclosed by neoclassical economics.

Given these developments, evolutionary perspectives represent a conceptual paradigm that better integrates the contemporary understandings of modern science. They give a much better understanding of progress, simply because the field is dedicated to accurately understanding the nature of change. Thus, it is the most powerful tool to solve questions of progress and growth in human society.

> *The dynamic models of evolutionary science and quantum mechanics give a powerful indication that freedom of choice may be the essential creative force behind progressive change.*

As a result, it's appropriate to question whether it remains a good idea for economics to rely on static equilibrium assumptions that not only don't exist in the real world, but constitute the precise opposite of real-world progress.[89]

The evolutionary elements

In the landmark book *The Origin of Wealth*, Eric Beinhocker outlined the major discoveries of evolutionary theory as applied to the phenomenon of economic growth. Beinhocker's main thesis was that the market, in effect, performed a "search function" for useful social and physical technologies, and that such discovery helped empower us with the knowledge to achieve our goals and live better lives. As we choose ideas that work well, Beinhocker concluded, we are selecting evolved technologies.

Beinhocker's simple conclusion regarding the nature of economic growth was, "Wealth is knowledge and its origin is evolution."[90] Therefore, evolved social technologies represent advanced ideas to empower us to achieve our goals.[91]

Evolution follows a universal three-step process of *differentiation, selection and amplification*.[92] Beinhocker argued that the same three-step process defined the evolution of social and physical technology.[93] In an evolutionary system, prospective technologies are differentiated, the technology that works best is selected, and the selected technology is amplified *vis-a-vis* other options.

The three steps of evolution are essential to the thesis of this book, so let's analyze each step in turn.

Step 1: Differentiation[94]

Differentiation is simply the creation of multiple options, allowing the creation and evaluation of experimental new technologies.[95]

Differentiation in the marketplace encourages freedom of market entry, allowing companies to compete openly and offer alternative options to the consumer. Differentiation thus explains the success of snowboarding and Whole Foods, as they provide selections for unique tastes.

Differentiation also explains the value of the traditional economic concepts such as Adam Smith's division of labor and David Ricardo's comparative advantage;[96] the idea is that we all benefit most from doing the different and unique things that we do best.

Applied to the marketplace of ideas, differentiation involves an active intellectual debate to constantly challenge existing assumptions and propose new solutions. The evolutionary value of differentiation helps explain the argument by John Stuart Mill, that open debate and discussion benefit all ideas,[97] as more ideas increase the odds of discovering the right idea.

Put simply, differentiation is essential in order to better find the next new, unforeseen social or physical technology. Differentiation is part of the entrepreneurial discovery process that creates economic evolution.

In the biological context, scientists recognize that genetic differentiation helps to improve the evolutionary process. Researchers have discovered a DNA-synthesizing enzyme, called Polymerase IV, which generates mutations under conditions of stress. The creation of more mutations, the scientists hypothesize, creates a higher probability of finding a source of successful evolution.[98] Thus in nature, as in human technology, more options help encourage progress.

Step 2: Selection

Selection is the most important step in the evolutionary process. Natural selection, the conceptual cornerstone of modern evolutionary theory, is defined simply as "differential reproduction", or some biological variations surviving while others do not.[99]

Though the concept of natural selection, in varying forms, has been hinted at by thinkers dating back to Empedocles of ancient Greece,[100] it was Darwin's progressive version of the idea that touched off the scientific revolution. Darwin's unique perspective, as evolutionary theorist Stephen Jay Gould explains, was to highlight selection not as a negative force, merely eliminating the "unfit", but rather as a *positive* and *creative* force of evolutionary change.[101] As some variations die, the more evolved variations can better develop.

> **Selection in the human context is performed by the free exercise of choice.**

Selection in the human context is performed by the free exercise of choice.[102] Selection is the positive result of the evolutionary fitness test and is the people's answer to the question: which technology works best for me?

In evolution, selection takes place at the individual level; biologists call this concept phenotypic selection.[103] In the human context, selection is similarly phenotypic: the decision of whether a given social technology is worthwhile can only be accurately made at the individual level.

Selection isn't about picking one best technology for everyone, but letting everyone pick the best technology for them. Nearly every technology—physical and social—has its useful and damaging applications. Some people use the internet to communicate with friends and family or educate themselves; others use it to steal identities. Some people use religion as a tool for spiritual discovery, others as a means for social exclusion. Some people find rap music an enjoyable diversion or inspiring art form;[104] others use it as a soundtrack for armed robbery. Some people like McDonalds, Starbucks or foreign cars; others like vegan food, green tea and bicycles. Some people use guns to commit crimes; others use them for self-defense. You get the picture.

The fitness test for each of these prospective social technologies, in every conceivable human endeavor, remains free choice. The evolutionary system works only when people can select the social technologies that make their life better, not when their choices are stifled in the paternalistic assumption that they'll choose to make their lives worse.

But still, critics of choice are skeptical. Can you *really* make choices, comrade, or are you just a tool of the Big Corporate Media?

While community and media certainly play a role in influencing decisions, the final volitional authority does lie with the individual.

Evolutionary theorists have noted a feedback process that may interfere with the selection process. In the words of evolutionary scholar J.S. Metcalfe, "Variety drives selection while positive and negative feedback processes mean that the development of variety is shaped by the process of selection."[105] What this means is while our choices may be difficult, they still can impact the world around us.

There's a certain paradox of the evolutionary selection process. Just like every death in nature is not necessarily the true verdict of natural selection, neither is every person's choice the true verdict of social-technological selection. The point is that the aggregated choices over time create the evolutionary wisdom.

Step 3: Amplification

Amplification is the final step of the evolutionary process, where a selected technology becomes widely adopted among society. Amplification is essential to maximizing the benefit of a given technology. Amplification is an emergent property (a concept we'll discuss later in this chapter) of the evolutionary selection process, and is exemplified by the type of dynamic social phenomena that drive our modern age.

Though the first two steps involve individual action, amplification manifests itself in public action. As a result, amplification is perhaps the most paradoxical step in the evolutionary process. Individualism is essential for effective selection, but society is essential for effective amplification.

Though amplification processes serve to benefit everyone, they often appear uneven and unfair to those on the wrong side of a given amplification. As an inevitable *yin* and *yang* of progress, the amplification of one technology results in the diminution or elimination of another. Cell phones replace pagers. Computers replace typewriters. Cars replace trains. Services replace products. Computer programmers replace stagecoach repairmen. *Et cetera.*

The complex division of labor means that different people will be engaged in different trades. Since the selection and amplification process will favor certain technologies over others at any given time, income inequality often results, especially during large-scale technological changes.

However, the point is that in the long run, the process works to the advantage of everyone. The most important part about innovations isn't the compensation given to the innovator; it's the compensation the innovation gives to society through the process of amplification.[106] Rich people die, but their technological contributions to society, if any, live on.

Evolutionary scientists, from Jean-Baptiste Lamarck to Charles Darwin, have long recognized that evolutionary amplification requires some form of multiplication through inheritance.[107] The social-technological equivalent of evolutionary "inheritance" is essential to the complete understanding of amplification.

Inheritance occurs as we learn new ways of doing things and educate our successors in the useful methods of organization and production we have learned. Even the most radical innovations are built upon the innovations that have come before; the most revolutionary thinkers still rely on the knowledge and ideas of those who come before them. As we'll discuss in the next chapter, technological evolution allows us to harness the knowledge of others, past and present, in unprecedented ways. With the amplification of beneficial technologies, innovations can grow to benefit all people. Inherited social technologies are very similar to the concept of Richard Dawkins' concept of "memes," or the replicating units of social evolution.[108]

When social technologies become sufficiently amplified—that is, they work well enough to become universally adopted—they are inherited by new generations in the form of rules, norms and laws.[109] Like any other social technology, our evolved social rules perform the same function: helping us live better. As Friedrich Hayek noted,

> Rules [of morality, freedom and justice] are handed on by tradition, teaching and imitation, rather than by instinct, and largely consist of prohibitions ('shalt not's') that designate adjustable domains for individual decisions. Mankind achieved civilization by developing and learning to follow rules (first in territorial tribes and then over broader reaches) that often forbade him to

do what his instincts demanded.[110]

As we understand the equal importance of individualism and community in the evolutionary process, we can better understand the dynamic process with which they operate. Individual choice helps to discover socially beneficial technologies, which then get distributed to society at large, until individual choice again discovers new technologies to start the process over. Thus, freedom of choice is not a panacea in itself, but rather an essential element for the discovery of beneficial advancements.

Now we've got the basics down. The idea we've been discussing so far—that free choice is a necessary condition for the spontaneous value-added evolution of social and physical technologies—we'll call evolutionary choice theory.

As a review, here are the basic elements of evolutionary choice theory:

Characteristics of evolutionary progress: Dynamic, complex and exponential

Purpose: Search process for useful life-improving social and physical technologies

Evolutionary process: Differentiation, selection and amplification

Human element for differentiation: Freedom of expression/freedom of market entry

Human element for selection: Freedom of choice

Human element for amplification/inheritance: Freedom of association

3

JOIN THE EVOLUTION

**The cooperative venture of evolution, and what
it means for our politics, economics and society**

*I*MMEDIATELY, I'M SURE SOME READERS RECOIL at the thought
of using evolution to explain human progress. I can see it now: *You pig! You
support Social Darwinism, that disgusting and repugnant ideology that views
market outcomes as a demonstration of moral superiority?*

This just isn't the case.

Evolutionary choice theory thoroughly obliterates Social Darwinism
as a legitimate social theory.[111]   Our advanced understanding of evolution
puts such exclusionary views to rest.

An important distinction between Social Darwinism and evolutionary choice theory is that under the latter, "survival of the fittest" applies only
to *businesses*, not people.   In the words of Eric Beinhocker, "Businesses
are the grist for the evolutionary mill."   In other words, businesses are the
vehicles through which new social and physical technologies are tested, and
it is businesses that must attempt to survive in the open marketplace.

 Differentiation is thus essential to distinguish the fate of a given business from the fate of people themselves.[112] It is the unfit technologies and the
firms promoting them that die out.   Precisely because they do, individuals
are left with better options for sustaining ever-richer lives.[113] With the selection and amplification of new technologies, the evolutionary process creates
greater value for all humans.

A similar duality explains evolution in the marketplace of ideas. As
philosopher Karl Popper argued, the evolution of human thought is distinct

from the evolution of animals because humans have the ability to distinguish their ideas from their actual existence. Popper argued that humans uniquely recognize each competing idea as a separate object to "consciously investigate and criticize for mistakes,"[114] and thus can uniquely "destroy [a] hypothesis through criticism without [the human] perishing with it."[115] Hence, social technologies live and die for the evolutionary pursuit of greater knowledge.

> **"Businesses are the grist for the evolutionary mill."**

As Dobzhansky notes, the problem with "survival of the fittest" applied to people's lives is that it's more inefficient than an inclusive policy of reciprocity.[116] Selection is most efficient and creative when individuals are exposed to the largest possible variety of environments, which in the human context involves encouraging transitions into new enterprises when one's current endeavor becomes grist for the evolutionary mill.

Because everyone else's choices are part of the fitness selection process for new technologies, evolutionary choice theory views choice as a *cooperative venture*, one that benefits from maximum public participation at all times. The more people involved in the choice-based selection process, the more effective that process becomes. It's a radical conclusion, but individual choice is most valuable as a *public* benefit, namely performing an evolutionary search function for new socially beneficial technologies.

Evolutionary economists recognize the unique symbiosis between individual choice and the public good. Friedrich Hayek argued that individual liberty is the means to the collective end of progress because individualism was essential to secure the "unforeseeable and unpredictable" benefits of the evolutionary order. Therefore, Hayek claimed, "True individualism is the only theory which can claim to make the formation of spontaneous social products intelligible."[117]

Despite his reputation as an anti-government radical, Hayek criticized the concept of *laissez-faire*, arguing that government must provide the structure and resources to enhance people's ability to choose.[118] With programs such as publicly funded education, safety regulation and disclosure laws, as well as some form of basic assistance for those who needed backing in employment transitions, Hayek believed such interventions "certainly assisted intelligent choice" and sometimes may be "indispensable" for it.[119]

The result may be counter-intuitive, but the formula is simple: more individuals choosing independently creates a better social product. There may be such a thing as a public good, but it's only found through the independent expression of individuals.[120]

As you can tell, this concept shatters the Left/Right philosophic mold. If it all sounds strange to you, you're not alone: the principle is a great paradox of evolution.

The wisdom of crowds

In his book *The Wisdom of Crowds*, James Surowiecki explains how the aggregated decisions of regular people in large groups can make better decisions than any individual "expert," no matter how educated the expert or how difficult the decision. Surowiecki's book offers a fascinating demonstration of the cooperative nature of social evolution, as well as how selection and amplification processes create a public benefit.

Whether guessing the weight of an ox at a county fair, regulating traffic, making market decisions or even solving mysteries, Surowiecki explains how groups can exhibit a form of collective knowledge that is more accurate than a single individual. While the recognition of group wisdom has been around at least since Aristotle,[121] Surowiecki's work stands out for its rigorous analysis of the phenomenon, from performing information evaluation to achieving value-added cooperation.

If Surowiecki's thesis that groups can be smarter than individuals sounds counterintuitive, it's because it is yet another example of the evolutionary paradox.

But Surowiecki emphasizes that it is not all groups that demonstrate such wisdom, but only those which exhibit certain qualities. Those qualities, which the reader will notice are mighty similar to the main elements of evolution, are *diversity* of opinion (similar to differentiation), *independent* and *decentralized* decision-making (similar to selection), and some form of *aggregation* of those preferences (similar to amplification).[122] When all elements are present, Surowiecki explains, group decision-making can avoid the hazards of groupthink, as well as preventing the opposite effect, of anarchic and chaotic individualism.[123]

In the 21st century, the wisdom of crowds is increasingly directing the evolution of some of the world's most innovative technology companies. The archetype, of course, is Wikipedia, the user-driven online encyclopedia, that allows anyone to create or edit entries on any subject of relevant interest, and is regulated only by the spontaneous order of its users.

Crowd-driven collaborative approaches are also behind the booming growth of "open source" software that any developer can modify and improve, as well as "crowd sourcing" as a business tool for research and development. As the crown prince of open-source innovation, the Apple iPhone App Store offers an amazing and ever-expanding array of mobile technological wizardry, from UrbanSpoon, which displays all restaurants near your current location, to the Ocarina, which turns the iPhone into a fully-functional wind instrument and global concert producer. In the modern age, the wisdom of crowds has never looked so smart.

The interdependence of choice

"Nothing in the world is single,
All things by a law divine
In one another's being mingle
Why not I with thine?"
-- P. B. Shelley[124]

The advancement of social technologies has yielded a mind-boggling interdependence between humans in society. Captured by the popular "six degrees of separation" concept, the social networks of modern society create an unprecedented amount of P.B. Shelley's "mingling."

Evolutionary economics recognizes the interdependence and complexities of advanced social technologies. It also realizes that interdependence is beneficial, allowing humans to dynamically access the knowledge of more individuals than previously possible. Nearly every technology in modern society is connected to, or in some way built upon, ideas spanning across centuries and around the globe.

Take the seemingly simple technology known as the pencil. Leonard Read beautifully pointed out the extended "family tree" of this writing instrument. Writing as an individual pencil, Read articulates his ancestry:

"I, Pencil, am a complex combination of miracles: a tree, zinc, copper, graphite, and so on. But to these miracles which manifest themselves in Nature an even more extraordinary miracle has been added: the configuration of creative human energies—millions of tiny know-hows configurating naturally and spontaneously...in the absence of any human master-minding!

Man can no more direct these millions of know-hows to bring me into being than he can put molecules together to create a tree.

My family tree begins with what in fact is a tree, a cedar of straight grain that grows in Northern California and Oregon. Now contemplate all the saws and trucks and rope and the countless other gear used in harvesting and carting the cedar logs to the railroad siding. Think of all the persons and the numberless skills that went into their fabrication...

The logs are shipped to a mill in San Leandro, California. Can you imagine the individuals who make flat cars and rails and railroad engines and who construct and install the communication systems incidental thereto? How many skills went into the making of the tint and the kilns, into supplying the heat, the light and power, the belts, motors, and all the other things a mill requires?...

My 'lead' itself—it contains no lead at all—is complex. The graphite is mined in Ceylon. Consider these miners and those who make their many tools and the makers of the paper sacks in which the graphite is shipped and those who make the string that ties the sacks and those who put them aboard ships and those who make the ships. Even the lighthouse keepers along the way assisted in my birth—and the harbor pilots.

The graphite is mixed with clay from Mississippi in which ammonium hydroxide is used in the refining process... To increase their strength and smoothness the leads are then treated with a hot mixture which includes candelilla wax from Mexico, paraffin wax, and hydrogenated natural fats....An ingredient called 'factice' is what does the erasing. It is a rubber-like product made by reacting rape-seed oil from the Dutch East Indies with sulfur chloride....The pumice comes from Italy; and the pigment which gives 'the plug' its color is cadmium sulfide.

Does anyone wish to challenge my earlier assertion that no single person on the face of this earth knows how to make me?"[125]

Read's essay was penned in 1959, but the essential truth of his writing is even more applicable today. Given the inability of a single person in 1959 to know how to build a pencil, the inability of a single person in the 21st century to build other modern technologies—physical or social—is glaringly apparent.

Read's essay teaches an important lesson about the cooperative nature of market innovation. Technologies, no matter how innovative, are never the exclusive product of a single mind; rather, they build upon the work of innumerable other minds over time. A strictly individualist economic philosophy misses the essential fact that every social technology in existence was created by someone else.

In this way, it's easy to see our social and physical technologies as networks of ideas, harnessing the collective power of human intellect for the greater good.

Much like modern technology, networks only become useful with large numbers of participants. Metcalfe's Law (named after Bob Metcalfe, the inventor of ethernet) explains that the value of a network is proportional to the number of users squared. A classic example of Metcalfe's Law is the telephone; just one phone is useless; the incredible social value of the technology only comes when most of the population has one.

I, Network

Networks, defined, are systems that are organized according to behavior rules called *schemata*. Schemata are thus akin to the blueprints of human technology, and adaptive networks evolve by evaluating, modifying or discarding schemata according to their real-world fitness.

We can thus think of our social technologies as a giant Boolean network, that is, a network operating off of binary (0 or 1) commands regarding various schemata. Our decisions as individual "nodes" in our social networks – yes/no, or 1/0 – governs the adoption of various ideas and concepts. Just as individual transistors in a computer can render amazing effects from such a simple binary algorithm, the collection of free choices in modern society can create a similarly adaptive and beautiful structure.

All of this sounds like a bunch of technobabble, but it's actually quite relevant. Thanks to advanced computer technology, the behavior of adaptive

JOIN THE EVOLUTION

networked systems can be studied as never before. These experiments - lead by the scientists at the Santa Fe Institute - are providing new insights on how evolution really works, from the biological world to the economic world.

The most important discovery of these experiments is the understanding of complexity. Complexity is not just a lazy concession of humans' limited intellect, but a feature of all adaptive systems.

Complex systems don't evolve in a comfortable or predictable manner; they suffer from distorting phenomena such as noise and feedback loops, which can create uncertainty and fluctuating performance. Examples of phenomena in modern economic networks include stocks and flows, informational asymmetry, currency "panics," the distorting effects of investment speculation, transportation gridlock, and the volatile undulations of booms and busts. These systems are distinct from the closed and mathematically-driven system of neoclassical economics, as they are open, dynamic, unpredictable, prone to error and do not settle in equilibrium. Complex systems demonstrate pervasive randomness, which means their future behavior cannot be predicted from past events, and they are incompressible, which means they can't be reduced to simple mathematical formulas.[126]

Far from the linear models of neoclassical economics, adaptive correction is far from seamless or predictable. In fact, complexity theorists argue that this adaptation is highly error-prone and tends to emerge only when a system is on the edge of chaos.[127]

Network complexity, even while it is undoubtedly intimidating, operates to the advantage of everyone. In the words of evolutionary scientist Geerat J. Vermeij, "Each transition in complexity - from prokaryote to eukaryote to multicellular organism to society - is accompanied by greater adaptability... The culmination of this trend is human culture, which for better or worse has given humans an ability to modify, control and respond to the environment as no preceding biological entity has been able to do."

Complex systems adapt through the creation of *emergent properties*, that is, properties that represent more than the sum of their parts.[128] Emergence spontaneously arises from complex individual interactions, creating a value-added property at a certain "tipping point" or critical mass within a network. Emergence is the magic of evolution[129], and it occurs whenever individual interactions create value greater than themselves.

adaptation is highly error-prone and tends to emerge only when a system is on the edge of chaos.

Oft-cited examples of emergence are a whirlpool or a symphony, but other instances abound in our daily lives. All technologies demonstrate emergence. Leonard Read's simple pencil is an emergent property of wood, graphite, and other natural materials, representing a writing instrument far more valuable than any of the ingredients in themselves. The modern computer takes emergence to a new level by creating a staggering amount of computational power derived from ingenius combinations of silicon, metal and plastic.

Social technologies are no exception: Adam Smith's division of labor is emergence; our example of snowboarding is prosperity and Olympic success emerging from a few kids who decided to slide down a mountain on a modified surfboard.

The concept of emergence is important because it is the source of evolutionary growth. As theoretical physicist Lee Smolin notes, the shared lesson of complex systems, evolution, and quantum mechanics is that they all describe systems that are capable of spontaneous emergent self-organization.[130] So, how does this emergence occur?

An early founder of complexity theory was Nobel laureate Ilya

---

Emergence: *The spontaneous creation of value greater than the sum of a network's parts*

Prigogine, who studied spontaneous emergence in chemical and physical systems. Prigogine argued that as complex systems drifted toward disequilibrium states, they would reach a certain level of disorder, called a "bifurcation point", at which the system could freely "choose" among various pathways of development. This choice, Prigogine argued, caused an emergent phase transition that represented the time-dependent concepts of invention, progress, and evolution. [130.5]

Complex systems tend to move in cycles. They alternate between emergent innovation and structured consolidation, or what Stephen Jay Gould called "punctuated equilibrium".

Network growth follows a continual three step process. The first is a *random* phase, where a network experiments with different structures for different tasks. The second step is a *growth* phase, where certain efficient network structures are selected. These successful networks inspire a positive feedback loop of emergent innovation, change and growth. Finally, the third step is an *organized* phase, where the major changes are consolidated and the network becomes highly structured again. This process repeats itself as the next innovation is discovered.

Network theorists understand that highly structured networks (called "lattice" networks) are important for facilitating efficient information sharing. But they also understand that unstructured ("random") networks are important for breaking through the inevitable gridlock created in highly structured lattice networks. As a result, many successful networks exhibit both lattice and random features.

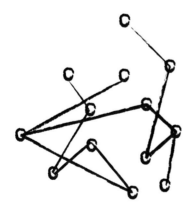

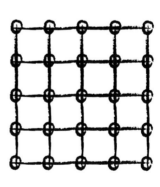

RANDOM   LATTICE

Evolution is fueled by an intricate interplay between order through laws and novelty through chance.[131] Evolutionary systems are neither chaotic anarchy nor rigid structure, but evince elements of both.

A balancing act

Now we can better understand the evolution of our social institutions. In organized phases, we can choose to conform and strengthen traditional communities, or in growth phases, we can create new discoveries that will eventually become new social institutions.

But it's best to combine the two. Like Saddleback Church, we can expand the modern appeal of ancient faith, or like consumers who drive their hybrids to purchase organic food and fans who download classic music, we can use technology to empower retro lifestyles.

In *The Wisdom of Crowds*, Surowiecki confirms this phenomenon in the human context. Surowiecki argues that imitation is a "rational response to our own limits," and that relying on others' behavior is often an efficient way to evaluate an option of uncertain value.[132]   However, while group choice aids evaluation, Surowiecki maintains that decentralized individual choice is still required for innovation.[133]

Should we continue to use an established technology or adopt a new one? Shall we conform to tradition or blaze new trails? Follow the crowd or rebel?

As we choose among varying combinations of traditional structure and rebellious innovation, we are able to find the syntheses that work best. By modulating religion versus materialism, or community versus commerce, we can modify the fitness function to work better for us.

The power of the community and the power of the individual are both useful tools. The key is letting them both operate freely within an environment of free choice.

Please please me

The continual battle between structure and innovation is the very competitive pressure that creates emergent growth in our economy. [134]

In their book *Good Capitalism, Bad Capitalism*, authors William Baumol, Robert Litan and Carl Schramm explain that American capitalism works successfully as a hybrid of two business forms. The first form is called "entrepreneurial capitalism," where a new idea comes along that transforms a given industry. People begin to choose the new idea, supporting the entrepreneur, and the companies that used the old idea are forced out of business. The second form is called "big firm capitalism," where the massive resources of corporations are used to more efficiently distribute the new idea, thus further empowering people's choices, even if it puts the original entrepreneur out of business.[135]

Big corporations and small business entrepreneurs are both essential to good quality in the American marketplace.[136] Entrepreneurial capitalism is essential to selecting new variations of technologies in the random/growth phase. Big firm capitalism is essential to amplifying and multiplying them in the structured phase.

As network theory would predict, most of America's hugely successful companies—such as Nike, GE, Apple and Microsoft, to name a few— combine structural "big firm" features with dynamic "entrepreneurial" features.

We need the innovations of the entrepreneur and the mass-produced efficiency of the Big Corporation, but most of all, we need the ability to choose between the two. Corporate giants like McDonalds, Nike and IBM are only as good as the extent to which we want to buy their mass-produced products. Similarly, the entrepreneurial Davids taking on the corporate Goliaths are themselves only as good as the extent to which we find their innovations useful.

As author and blogger Seth Godin observed, "where there is competition, there is evolution."[137] The ability to select each competing institution is the key to the effectiveness of this pressure. That's how our ability to choose alternative shoe companies makes Nike responsive

> *The continual battle between structure and innovation is the very competitive pressure that creates emergent growth in our economy.*

to *No Logo*, while our inability to choose an alternative courier for first-class mail makes the Postal Service responsive to, well, practically no one.

In the words of an evolutionary historian, "We have more than just a few little hints that, for Darwin, the driving force behind all sorts of evolutionary change, including progress, is the sort of competition that goes on in the natural economy and the political economy alike."[138]

The pressure to satisfy the choices of the people on a large scale (or otherwise perish) translates into incentives for useful and efficient production. Economists may misunderstand the predictability or rationality of these choices, but they are right about the fact that such choices are the driving force behind efficient capitalist production. This constant economic competition pushes businesses to the edge of chaos where they can better learn and adapt.

In the book *The Affluent Society*, the late economist John Kenneth Galbraith noted the wide disparity between the lavish opulence of goods provided in the private sector—homes, cars and "handsomely packaged products"—and government-controlled services—schools, roads and parks—that were poorly maintained. Galbraith called this disparity "an atmosphere of private opulence and public squalor," but it just shows that with more competition, the quality of choices tends to be better as a result.

I always laugh at the claim that "markets don't work." I am writing this on an Apple MacBook Pro, synched with my Apple iPhone, which together give me communication and research abilities that never used to be possessed by humans. I can even get my most basic necessities delivered online, from food to clothing, right to my door. Or, I can take my car to an ever-increasing number of retailers for an ever-increasing number of life-improving products. Anywhere I go, I have a plastic card that vouches for my bank account and lets me buy anything I want without ever paying cash.

Now, I'm not rich. I'm just part of the evolution. So we all are.

One of my best friends justifies her redistributionist political views with the clever maxim, "I believe in none with cake until all have bread." What my good friend misses, however, is that the pursuit of cake is the most efficient bread-making system in history.

The humanity of choice

In his book, *Darwin Day in America: How Our Politics and Culture Have Been Dehumanized in the Name of Science*, John C. Gray gives exhaustive evidence of how "evolutionary" perspectives have mostly viewed humans as mere cogs in the evolutionary machine, with no more consciousness than amoeba. Determinists deny the existence of free will, and view the whole concept of conscious choice as an illusion.

Given their unsavory association with biological determinists, evolutionary explanations of progress have understandably been unpopular. Many misguided pseudo-scientists have used evolutionary science to justify the "natural" presence of poverty, inferiority or inability in certain individuals, and deny the ability of humans to change these putative "biological" realities.

From Herbert Spencer and the aforementioned Social Darwinists to Ivan Pavlov and the disgusting eugenics movement of the 19th and 20th centuries, many sociobiological studies of human society have, to date, largely espoused a version of determinism that treats humans as mere automatons shaped wholly by their environment.

Encapsulating this dismally anti-human perspective, the psychologist B.F. Skinner argued, "A scientific analysis of behavior, must, I believe, assume that a person's behavior is controlled by his genetic and environmental histories rather than by the person himself as an initiating, creative agent."[139]

However, simply because some some scientists have tried to deny freedom in the past does not mean that all must always do so. Given the pro-freedom views of the evolutionary giants Dobzhansky and Jacob, there is plenty of evidence that biological determinism, in addtion to being the wrong philosophical interpretation, could be the wrong *scientific* interpretation of evolution as well.[140]

As biologist S.A. Barnett points out, "The attempt to interpret human actions and feelings by a simple [determinist] principle fails in the face of our diversity and readiness to change our behavior - our adaptability... [which depends] greatly on our previous experiences, and also on conscious *choice.*"[141]

Or as P.L. van den Berghe puts it, "The ultimate challenge of humanity is to prove sociobiology wrong...through self-conscious changes in our behavior."[142]

The philosophy of evolution

In understanding the value of freedom in evolution, it helps to briefly mention the philosophers who have touched on some of those fundamental ideas.

Unlike the static philosophies of Plato and Aristotle, Heraclitus

HERACLITVS FLORVIT OLIMP. 89
Verba sibilinus uitam grauis omnia plorans.
Heraclitus eram, cui genus ex Epheso.

Embrace change, saith Heraclitus

(530-470 BC) saw the universe as in a state of continual flux and perpetual change.[143] "Everything flows," Heraclitus taught, and "nothing stands still." Heraclitus saw the universe as undergoing an "eternal transformation," through which conflict and strife created unity and progress; in his aphoristic style, he noted that "the mixture which is not shaken decomposes."[144]

Epicurus (342-270 BC), with insights that would predate quantum mechanics by millennia, argued that atoms did not move predictably, but rather with a certain "swerve" that created the fact of contingency in the natural world. Epicurus further believed that this "swerve", in its unpredictability, created the physical and metaphysical foundations for free will.[145]

Philosopher G.W.F. Hegel (1770-1831) is credited with being the "first and most successful philosopher [to view] civil society as a theory of a highly differentiated and complex social order."[146] His thought centers around the idea of dialectic, through which opposing ideas become challenged, evaluated and eventually synthesized into a greater truth. Hegel's philosophy gives us a new perspective on the necessity of both freedom and community in the evolutionary growth process.

Channeling Heraclitus[147], Hegel argued that the conflict of opposing ideas yielded a "mediated synthesis"—in essence, an emergent property—between ideas previously thought as incompatible.[148] Hegel believed that the dialectic created an "indwelling tendency" to discover greater knowledge.[149]

Hegel thus viewed the dialectic as a process of progressive evolution. His dialectical process contains a unique concept known as "differentiated unity," by which ostensible incompatibility is harmonized in pursuit of greater truth.[150] In one of Hegel's more lucid passages, he uses nature as a metaphor for the concept:

> The bud disappears in the bursting-forth of the blossom, and one might say that the former is refuted by the latter; similarly, when the fruit appears, the blossom is shown up in its turn as a false manifestation of the plant, and the fruit now emerges as the truth of it instead. These forms are not just distinguished from one another, they also supplant one another as mutually incompatible. Yet at the same time their fluid nature makes them moments of an organic unity in which they not only do not conflict, but in which each is necessary as the other.[151]

"The key to Hegel's dialectic," argues Hegel scholar Renato Cristi, "lies in the spontaneous order that springs naturally from the self-seeking behavior of free individuals." According to Cristi, Hegel believed that this cooperative venture of choice effectively "safeguards the freedom of individuals and, at the same time, disciplines and reconciles their divergent aims."[152]

It is not surprising that Hegel recognized a dynamic synthesis between structure and individualism. Hegel believed that the highest form of freedom emerged as a synthesis of "subjective freedom," or the personal choices of individuals, and "objective freedom," or the social good; this created the ultimate emergent form that he called "absolute freedom," maximizing *both* subjective and objective freedom.[153]

Hegel used the German term *Aufheben* to describe his dialectical process. *Aufheben*, a term that has no direct English translation, is defined simultaneously as "preserving", "cancelling", and "lifting up", and perfectly encapsulates the evolutionary paradox.

As we mentioned in Chapter 2, the creative power of evolutionary selection was Darwin's unique philosophical contribution. This concept also exemplifies a Hegelian dialectic, in that it produces a positive synthesis from something negative. Because of the conceptual similarities between the Hegelian dialectic and the evolutionary paradox, Friedrich Nietzsche observed, "without Hegel, there could have been no Darwin."[154]

Some Hegelian Dialectics		
Thesis —> Antithesis	—>	Synthesis
Being —> Nothingness	—>	Becoming
Hope —> Frustration	—>	Opportunity
Life —> Death	—>	Evolution

Hegel even delivered a defense of the American Revolution, arguing that our essential grievances were not based on economic particularities, but our legitimate desire for greater freedom:

"The duties which the English Parliament imposed on tea imported into America were extremely light; but what caused the American Revolution was the feeling of the Americans that with this totally insignificant sum, which the duties would have cost them, they would have lost their most important right."[155]

Hegel believed that freedom flourishes best within a society where there is "free play for every idiosyncrasy, every talent, every accident of birth and fortune," and where "the waves of passion continually gush forth," regulated only by "reason glinting through them."[156]

Now, it must be said that Hegel's philosophy is much more complex, nuanced and varied than I could ever present here.[157] However, his ideas still help to powerfully defend the principle that complex differentiation, free selection and social amplification represent a dynamic process that serves to benefit all in society.

Nobel Laureate biologist and philosopher Henri Bergson (1859-1941) is arguably the modern founder of evolutionary choice theory. Bergson did much to continue the legacy of Hegel,

Bergson: Evolution through choice, et le élan vital

combining philosophy and science into a comprehensive philosophical system of creative evolution. Simliar to Hegel's dialectic, Bergson viewed evolution as a process by which "continuous phases penetrate one another by a kind of internal growth" and "an unfurling whose distinct parts are placed in juxtaposition to one another."[158]

Given the uncertainty, contingency and seeming contradiction of the evolutionary process, Bergson believed that evolution implies the necessity of choice. "Life," Bergson argued, "implies at least a rudiment of choice...an anticipatory idea of several possible actions."[159]

In his work, *Creative Evolution*, Bergson defends freedom of choice as humanity's essential tool for mastering the evolutionary process. Bergson believed that humans, as part of the evolutionary unfolding process, had gained the essential power of consciousness, which he defined as "synonymous with invention and freedom" and "corresponding exactly to a living being's power of choice."[160]

The true understanding of evolution, Bergson argued, shows that the nature of progress is "quite different from the realization of a program," as the biologicial determinists would like to think. Instead, "the gates of the future open wide" when "freedom is offered an unlimited field."[161]

In my view, the contemporary philosopher best representing the evolutionary perspective is Robert M. Pirsig (1928 -), author of *Lila* and *Zen and the Art of Motorcycle Maintenance*. Pirsig's evolution represents the progressive expansion of a sweeping metaphysical concept he calls Quality, a concept with no precise definition, but subsuming traditionally separate ideas of knowledge, truth, happiness, morality and the Good.

Echoing many of the ideas of this chapter, Pirsig argues that Quality manifests itself in a dynamic form and a static form. Static quality represents the preservation of successful methods of the past, and contributes useful structure on which to build. But static quality always "emerges in the wake of Dynamic Quality", because the latter is necessary for continual growth, progressive creativity, and evolutionary adaptation.

Dynamic Quality is the force of change, progress and growth. Pirsig argues that life itself "is a migration of static quality patterns toward Dynamic Quality," and that "natural selection is Dynamic Quality at work." Pirsig argues that Dynamic Quality is unleashed by the values of freedom, diversity, competition, and choice. Furthermore, he argues that the successful growth of numerous social technologies, such as cities, democracies, the free market system, free speech, the scientific method, and ultimately, ethics, all rely on the continual progressive discovery of Dynamic Quality. [161.5]

America, the evolved

Our commitment to freedom of choice has caused the discovery of technologies that help our economy, culture and even legal system adapt to changing times.

Our discussion of evolutionary choice theory thus far has shown an entirely new perspective on the history of our great nation. Our commitment to freedom of choice has caused the discovery of technologies that help our economy, culture and even legal system adapt to changing times.

The institution of American capitalism, ensuring an open marketplace and free choice, has helped unleash myriad evolutionary innovations to improve our lives and create economic growth. The French may boast a traditional way of life, but America is the unquestioned global home of innovation. Yankee ingenuity continues to lead the 21st century world in the technological, intellectual, business and entertainment fields. Our social technologies are superior as a result.

American society is a testament to the cooperative nature of evolutionary choice theory. As we mentioned, Alexis de Tocqueville recognized Americans' unique ability to evolve new social technologies for a variety of purposes,[162] and the American evolution has continually extended freedom of choice to include new groups, viewpoints and nationalities. Our open system of immigration and civil rights movements expanded the cultural menu of citizenship, and our open market system expanded the menu of technological innovation.

The advanced understanding of evolutionary choice theory gives us the ability to articulate defined policy solutions that modernize our political institutions, in order to help lead America into the 21st century. The rest of this book is concerned with outlining specific and positive policy solutions toward that end.

The general lesson is that we should maximize free choice for as many people as possible in order to empower the differentiation, selection and amplification of new social innovations. This principle offers an intuitive guide to policy decisions that perfectly explains the failures of our current leaders and defines the road map to our success.

The only way to evaluate each policy is through a framework of differentiation, selection and amplification. This requires a process similar to the way we test all other social and physical technologies for fitness, but as we'll see, the current political system fails to offer these tests.[163]

Some may doubt our nation's ability to rise to the challenges of the new age, but in the 21st century, the outlook for the American evolution is exceptionally positive. We'll be applying evolutionary choice theory to pressing issues facing America including globalization, trade, education, social policy, foreign and defense policy, Constitutional law and more. Through all of these issues, evolutionary choice theory prescribes the same approach: more choices for people, and institutions to empower smarter choices.

Now, let's get down to the details.

4

THE INDUSTRIAL EVOLUTION
How the economy really works, and how to make it work better

SO FAR, WE'VE TALKED MUCH about the value-added results from technological evolution. But in reality, it's much easier to notice the manifold instances where social and physical technologies fail to evolve. Think of the underpaid jobs that drain the productive energies and emotional inspiration of Americans. Or corporations that seem to rake in billions, no matter how low-quality their product or service becomes.

These stagnating institutions are cited as conspicuous examples of "market failure," and to the pessimistic observer in the age of corporate malfeasance, the economy's "evolution" seems impossible to envision. Encapsulating this view, Barbara Ehrenreich, author of *Nickel and Dimed: On (Not) Getting By in America*,[164] articulates a grim vision of the American economic underclass: suffering poor treatment, difficulty finding employment, poor benefits and other maladies. One can see Ms. Ehrenreich's riposte to this book so far: where is the evolution in her life, or in the lives of so many of these workers?

The uncomfortable answer is that Ms. Ehrenreich finds herself in failing social technologies. Sadly, many Americans today find themselves stuck in jobs that demoralize them, squander their talents or pay them less than what they're worth. Among the discrete set of job options that many Americans face, choice seems to be worthless.

The road to success is paved with failure

Evolutionary choice theory is familiar with this fact. It recognizes that the market works, but also, and *far more often*, the market fails. Ask anyone with a dead-end job, any victim of corporate fraud, or anyone who reads the *Huffington Post*, Salon.com, or other serial exponents of corporate failure. Common failure is the inevitable result of any experimental process, as the market is.

Failing social technologies are everywhere, and it's not just limited to the marketplace. Take a look around. How about the atrociously bad music that's played both on the radio and by aspiring musicians in your local dive bar? How about the atrociously bad writing that poisons the op-ed sections of our newspapers and the shelves of our bookstores?

Evolutionary scientists recognize the inevitability of such failure. As Stephen Jay Gould explains, evolutionary processes do not produce beneficial results at all times.[165] In fact, evolution is an experimental process that often produces degeneration instead of progress.[166] Gould calls the belief in linear, mathematical and inevitable progress the "Panglossian fallacy."[167]

Confirming the fact that evolution fails, paleontologist David Raup estimates that while the Earth currently supports anywhere from ten to one hundred million species, the number of extinct species is ten to one hundred *billion*.[168] This makes an evolutionary success rate of less than one percent. Charles Darwin called this phenomenon *superfecundity*, or the creation of more life than could be sustained by a given environment.[169]

Similarly, James Surowiecki noted that despite the accuracy of the "wisdom of crowds" in many aggregated group decisions, a substantial portion of the individual guesses that comprise each group decision are terribly inaccurate.[170] And, Hayek admitted that despite the advantages of the spontaneous order, there was no guarantee that "the new state [of affairs] will give us more satisfaction than the old."[171]

The diversity of human opinion makes universal agreement quite rare, and so the effort to give something to everyone creates a panoply of undesirable options. As sociologist Niklas Luhmann noted, even while

Superfecundity: More life than can be sustained by a given environment

modern society provides ever-increasing opportunities, for every given choice, more "noes" must accompany every single "yes."[172]

Furthermore, even as Chris Anderson argued that the long tail model of business was remarkably beneficial, he also bluntly conceded that "the long tail is full of crap." Anderson cited Sturgeon's Law, which is defined as, "90% of everything is full of crud."

Despite its vulgar definition, Sturgeon's Law has a somewhat credible empirical foundation, being more scientifically established by economist Vilfredo Pareto, as the "law of the vital few." Known popularly as the "80-20" rule, the law of the vital few establishes that 80% of results arise from 20% (or less) of the causes.

The law of the vital few shows itself in the fact of income inequality. Mathematician A.Y. Abul-Magd has found that income distributions have followed a rough Pareto distribution—80% of wealth generated by about 20% of the population—from Egyptian society through the present day.[173] This rule has also found its way into business management; renowned leadership consultant John Maxwell and other eminent figures advise clients to recognize that 80% of value-added effort often arises from 20% or less of an organization's staff.

The black swan

**The black swan:
Doing the impossible since 1790**

A twist on the "law of the vital few" is that when differentiation and amplification increase within a given network, the statistical distribution of quality and garbage gets even more skewed. As a result, the 80-20 rule increasingly resembles a "power law," featuring an exponential disparity between the tiny minority of successful options and the huge majority of flotsam.[174] Power laws are most common in the growth phases of networks.

When power laws govern, black swan events tend to become amplified. In *The Black Swan: The Impact of the Highly Improbable*, Nassim Nicholas Taleb explains that such unforeseeable events—terrorist attacks, financial crises, scientific or technological breakthroughs, etc.—are increasing in the highly differentiated and complex networks that define the modern world.[175] As our social technologies grow more complex, the percentage of significant information for a given purpose becomes infinitesimally small and impossible for a single mind to recognize. But when that significant information is eventually discovered, it often has an exponential impact.

One implication of proliferation of black swan events is the obliteration of any single human being's ability to effectively "direct" American progress in the 21st century. As Chris Anderson notes, a single individual's knowledge is wholly inadequate to accurately predict even the 20% of Pareto's 80-20 distribution, let alone to forecast success in the exponentially skewed power law distributions that govern the modern world.[176] As we've seen, the only effective tool humanity has developed for such discovery is the wisdom of crowds, essentially reliant on individual freedom of choice writ large.

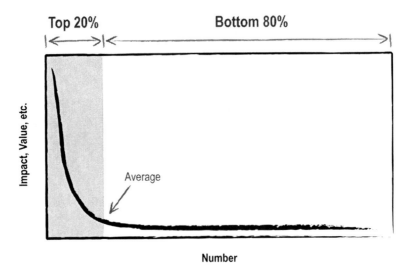

A Power Law Distribution

> *Law of the Vital Few:* Establishes that 80% (or more) of results arise from 20% (or less) of the causes

A second implication of black swan events is to undermine the neoclassical economic assumption that people possess the perfect rationality necessary to pick each optimal product or service. Evolutionary theorist Richard Nelson argues that a central premise of evolutionary economics, unlike neoclassical economics, is that "the cognitive capacities of humans and organizations are very limited compared with the actual complexity of the contexts in which they operate. Hence, one cannot presume that they actually see or think their way through to an 'optimal' behavior and then adopt it."[177]

The neoclassical fantasy of ultra-rational actors making deliberate choices toward defined ends with rational certainty is wholly repudiated by the reality of human decisions within the complex social networks we live in. As Hayek put it, "The solution of the economic problem of society...is always a voyage of exploration into the unknown, an attempt to discover new ways of doing things better than they have been done before."[178]

Or, as Hayek said it another way, "*If* we possess all the relevant information, if we can start out from a given system of preferences, and if we command complete knowledge of available means, the problem which remains is purely one of logic...This, however, is emphatically not the economic problem which society faces...The reason for this is that the 'data' from which the economic calculus starts are never for the whole society 'given' to a single mind which could work out the implications and can never be so given."[179]

Quantum physicists recognize Hayekian uncertainty in the form of Heisenberg's Uncertainty Principle, which holds that one cannot know the value of conjugate variables (such as position and momentum) with certainty, because as one knows more about one, the other becomes more uncertain.[180] In the social science context, the Uncertainty Principle means that one cannot gain an exact grasp of current facts without losing the understanding of future changes.

As our social and physical technologies probe the limits of the unknown, there are going to be some casualties.

Chaos theory

It's important to understand market adjustments as inevitable during social-technological evolution. Due to the inability of rational individuals to accurately predict the vagaries of the complex global economy, many get it wrong. When individuals are wrong in the context of business strategy, the result is bankruptcy. With the additional volatility and interdependence present in complex networks, such bankruptcy can often translate into systemic economic calamities.

A recent example of such a correction is the current global financial crisis in reaction to the collapse of the mortgage-backed securities market, which followed a precipitous decline in housing prices. The problem began with the Federal Reserve's artificial lowering of interest rates, which made debt cheaper and encouraged speculation.[181] This economic and political climate encouraged excessive lending to financially-questionable mortgage borrowers, supported by a blind faith in the continuing ascent of property values. As those values finally began to decline, the economic ripple effect was devastating. Some of America's largest and most respected financial institutions, through exposure to such risks by complex risk-spreading mechanisms known as "credit default swaps" and "over the counter" derivatives, found themselves bankrupt. The problem was so interconnected that no single business model, strategy or other market-based social technology found itself unscathed.

The bubble was fueled by a lack of adequate information in the marketplace. At the time of this writing, there is still no knowledge of the exact extent of the derivatives market—what Warren Buffett called "financial weapons of mass destruction"—or of their total economic impact. Government must now bring transparency in the notoriously opaque derivatives market, so that investors can make informed choices as to the risk they are exposing themselves to. Moody's estimates that a central clearinghouse, allowing free yet fully transparent derivative transactions similar to the stock market, would have reduced the damage from the collapse of Lehman Brothers, the investment bank, by two-thirds.[182]

In the meantime, economic evolution can only occur through collapse of the companies that took excessive risks in the sub-prime feeding frenzy, as a result of failed risk-management technologies.

Catastrophe and success are both effective teachers, and their lessons are essential to social growth. Government, in quashing the evaluative verdict of either, is only inhibiting the development of human understanding. The "stability" of the financial system may sound like a noble goal, but when stability is achieved at the cost of understanding, no one benefits in the long run.

To interfere with the market's evaluation process serves only to deny opportunity for new, more enlightened financial institutions to arise. The growth process of the economy ensures that as unsuccessful social technologies fall, more evolved social technologies will rise to the opportunity.

In the case of the credit crunch, more evolved social technologies will be those whose risk-management was prudent, responsible and leery of the excessive leverage that doomed others.[183] To keep the reckless financial industry afloat is to effectively enforce a monopoly that denies the equal opportunity for more responsible institutions to gain access to the market. We all lose in the end.

Many of the financial institutions currently receiving taxpayer bailouts are the ones who have slavishly obeyed the very technocratic philosophies that evolutionary choice theory repudiates. As long our government continues to subsidize these terrible business models in their current form, it inhibits our financial system from evolving.

Catastrophe and success are both effective teachers, and their lessons are essential to social growth. Government, in quashing the evaluative verdict of either, is only inhibiting the development of human understanding.

As the market punishes and expunges reckless business strategies, the evolutionary process creates opportunity to discover superior strategies. In this sense, one can even think of "market failure" as "market success," as long as the failing business technologies are eliminated from the marketplace and replaced with effective ones.

As long as borrower deposits are insured and government helps to facilitate orderly private buy-outs of banks that go under, there is little reason for additional government protection. For example, my personal bank, Washington Mutual, was a casualty of the credit crunch of 2008, thanks to its toxic mortgage portfolio. But since WaMu has other efficient social technologies within its business model—above-average customer service, free checking and other convenient banking features—it was quickly purchased by the well-capitalized JPMorgan Chase. As a customer, I didn't notice a single change except for a letter telling me I'd be receiving a new JPMorgan Chase-branded debit card in the mail; even my account numbers and online banking logins stayed the same. Such an experience highlights the essential difference between protecting people (an essential job of government) and protecting social technologies in the marketplace (absolutely *not* the job of government).

This process could have continued to resolve the issues plaguing the financial system, although it certainly would have resulted in numerous bankruptcies. But because Congress hasn't read this book, they obeyed the neoclassical technocrats and their professional agitators and forked over a trillion dollars (at current count) to save reckless banks from their own bad decisions.

Not surprisingly, the plan backfired. Stocks continued to tumble, and the bailed-out companies, such as AIG, continued to fail.[184] To make it worse, banks took such advantage of taxpayer largesse that private credit markets lent even less money after the bailout.[185]

Put simply, the financial crisis is a problem that Uncle Sam alone can't solve. The Treasury's effort to shower the stinking corpses of failed social technologies with government cash is a clever sleight of balance sheet that only shifts the problem to future generations. This soak-the-grandchildren scheme might please Wall Street or current politicians, but it does nothing to help our nation's financial system evolve.

Recall the example in the first chapter of the Fortune 50, as well as the aforementioned evolutionary principles of superfecundity and the fact that 99% of species are extinct. Evolution is messy, and it involves selecting a ridiculously small amount of quality out of a ridiculously large amount of failure.

The "too big to fail" concept is antithetical to evolution. No corporate fat cats are too rich to have to stay competitive, and the American people have nothing to lose from a well-regulated bankruptcy proceeding. Bankruptcy is a helpful and necessary tool of restructuring, but shoveling cash at stagnant, inefficient or otherwise uncompetitive corporations helps no one. Washington Mutual was the largest bank failure in U.S. history, and I'm still checking my online bank account at Wamu.com without losing a dime. The market is remarkably adaptive when governments provide the structural conditions for its growth. It's a shame our current leaders appear hell-bent on doing the precise opposite.

Instead, our politicians congratulate themselves on saving the financial system, but they don't really mean the financial system. They mean the pet corporations that have been arbitrarily chosen to exist at this point in time because they make enough profits to be crowned "too big to fail" by some pundit.

The "too big to fail" concept is further repugnant to American ideals. While millions of entrepreneurs toil endlessly in order to make it with their fledgling small businesses, our politicians decide that corporations that had once made a lot of money previously should continue to do so simply because the politicians say so.

Banks don't need more taxpayer capital; they need to start making better decisions. Washington, in keeping alive the corrupt, bureaucratic, and reckless corporations that the market's evolutionary process is trying to *kill*, only ensures that the virus that actually caused the financial crisis remains alive and well. By saving the fates of Citigroup, AIG, Goldman Sachs, General Motors and their idiot CEOs from the lessons of their own bad decisions,

"Because your business models have been proven clearly ineffective, we are hereby giving you one trillion dollars so that you can stay in business."

CITI   AIG   GM

CORPORATE JUSTICE
CENTER

politicians keep the economic virus festering in the United States economy as a whole.

To make it even worse, politicians paired the bailout with a dollop of regulation that has the noble intention to prevent such complex market corrections in the future. But the whole problem isn't preventing this type of correction; it's preventing a future correction that current regulators are even less able to predict or foresee. It's easy to say things like "smart regulation" and "necessary oversight" on a campaign trail, but in the real world, they mean absolutely nothing. These are merely hubristic assertions of foresight that individuals do not and cannot possess.

As *Financial Times* columnist John Kay put it:

> It is easy to assert that the solution to any market failure is better regulation. If regulators were all-knowing and all-powerful; if they were wiser than the chief executives but willing to do the job for a fraction of the remuneration awarded to such execu-tives...then banking regulation could protect us against financial instability. But such a world does not exist. Market economies outperform planned economies not because business people are smarter than civil servants – sometimes they are, sometimes not. But no one has enough information or foresight to understand the changing environment, so the market's messy processes of

experiment and correction yield better results than a regulator's analysis.[186]

The problem is that the cause of market failures—namely, the fallibility of humans—also applies to politicians' efforts to correct market failures.

Fixing financial crises isn't as easy as haughtily pronouncing the obvious fact that markets are imperfect. Unfortunately, one must actually enact rules to *fix* it. But therein lies the rub. It turns out that the wisdom of the market mechanism, in its most complex and evolved form, can still outwit the smartest economists and policy wonks.

In fact, there was a whole government agency already appointed to overseeing the failed mortgage giants, Fannie Mae and Freddie Mac. Yet it was precisely the profligate lending of those two institutions—encouraged by a direct Congressional mandate to lend to lower-income borrowers—that fueled much of the shoddy lending practices that sparked the crisis. As *The Economist* argued, "Much though people now blame deregulation, flawed regulation was more of a problem."[187]

The bugbears of the moment - high leverage, complex financial instruments, and short selling - are just social technologies. They are just methods in pursuit of goals, and can have a positive or negative impact depending on the goals they pursue. Leverage can help companies or individuals gain early capital that they wouldn't be able to obtain otherwise, thus empowering new ventures that could, in the long run, make a positive economic impact. Complex financial instruments help build wealth in the economy as a whole, and can provide a much more effective "stimulus" than any plan cooked up in Congress. Short selling helps bring information to the marketplace, which keeps the marketplace operating efficiently.

Banning any of these technologies, or setting arbitrary limits on them, only inhibits their positive usage and only prolongs the downturn. The last thing we want to do is keep new and innovative companies from being created simply because of some overzealous attraction to the empty concept of regulation.

Because social-technological and physical-technological progress is spontaneous and unpredictable, we cannot foresee specific solutions to every given quandary. We can only prescribe the necessary elements to create an environment under which our complex networks can positively adapt in the future—even if none of us could see it coming.

Markets, like all complex adaptive systems, self-regulate. Most of the time, they self-regulate by expunging the firms that can't, won't, or don't effectively self-regulate on their own. Through superfecundity and selection, creative destruction aids adaptation.

In the evolutionary recovery process, the wisdom lies in crowds; not in Washington.

This complex feedback process creates network effects, which explains why it occurs in such a chaotic, nonlinear, and volatile way. But self-correction still occurs, and most of all, it works best when authority is decentralized and choice is maximized. The same feedback effects that create calamitous downturns also create widely shared prosperity when new innovations are created.

In the evolutionary recovery process, the wisdom lies in crowds; not in Washington.

An evolutionary case study

The evolutionary chemist Leslie Orgel is especially known for his Second Rule of Evolution, defined simply as "evolution is smarter than you are." Orgel's Second Rule is a pithy yet profound confirmation of the spontaneous intelligence generated by evolutionary processes, specifically in the generation of unforeseen benefits in an environment of ostensible hopelessness.

There's a problem with unforeseen benefits, especially when they're buried in a long tail of metaphorical garbage. Given the inability of individuals to predict such advances, it's awfully easy to take a Malthusian view of the future and rationally doubt the existence of a solution to any given current problem.

Even Joseph Schumpeter, the economist who did more than any other to promote the free market's creation of progressive growth, wrote in the 1950s that he thought American capitalism had almost reached its creative limit and would basically cease to evolve.[188] Schumpeter wrote this a whole half-century before the information technology revolution.

In the 1990s, William F. Buckley, Jr., the greatest political commentator of the 20th century and another passionate free-market advocate, frowned

Orgel's Second Rule of Evolution: *Evolution is smarter than you are*

with Malthusian pessimism at the advent of the internet. In 1996, Buckley wrote a column[189] in which he conceded that the social potential for the internet was profound but faced a potentially fatal roadblock. Back in the pre-Google days, the internet had yet to devise a way to help you effectively find something on the information superhighway.

Buckley related a recent attempt at finding the years Thomas Jefferson spent in Paris as ambassador on the internet; he searched for hours in vain to no avail. Buckley eventually found it, but only through the assistance of a man who had just taken a 16 hour course on the internet.

Buckley's pessimism seems pretty understandable under the circumstances, but to us children of the new millenium, it's hard to stifle our laughter at the story. Today, the two step process for finding such information is first, accessing google.com, and second, typing "jefferson paris years." Then, all that's left is reading the answer right off the page. Information discovery on the internet is perhaps the web's most potent feature today, with Google and Wikipedia organizing the world's information in a way that must have thoroughly boggled Buckley. (R.I.P.)

But Google has now solved the world's internet searching difficulties. As a result, it's filthy rich. As a result of it being filthy rich (and also being run by brilliant visionaries), Google offers its over 16,000 employees perhaps the most enticing employment experience known to mankind. Google jobs are as far removed from the ones in *Nickle and Dimed* as William F. Buckley is removed from Bill O'Reilly.

In the words of *Fortune* magazine, as they crowned Google, for the second year in a row, the Best Company to Work For:

> At Google you can do your laundry; drop off your dry cleaning; get an oil change, then have your car washed; work out in the gym; attend subsidized exercise classes; get a massage; study Mandarin, Japanese, Spanish, and French; and ask a personal concierge to arrange dinner reservations. Naturally you can get haircuts onsite. Want to buy a hybrid car? The company will give you $5,000 toward that environmentally friendly end. Care to refer a friend to work at Google? Google would like that too,

and it'll give you a $2,000 reward. Just have a new baby? Congratulations! Your employer will reimburse you for up to $500 in takeout food to ease your first four weeks at home. Looking to make new friends? Attend a weekly TGIF party, where there's usually a band playing. Five onsite doctors are available to give you a checkup, free of charge.[190]

Google's 16,000 employees don't seem like much compared to many companies' workforces. But like many evolutionary achievements, there's more than what meets the eye. The full impact of Google's technological innovation reverberates across the global economy, spawning the $4 billion search engine optimization (SEO) market, where firms specialize in providing various schemes to move a client's website as high as possible in Google's rankings. Even the SEO example isn't the full story; the economic side effects of Google's rise have created unprecedented economic opportunity for a technology that's barely ten years old.

Other tech innovations have arguably had even more impressive impacts on the American employment landscape. Take eBay for instance, which has allowed over 750,000 people to make a profit from selling their old stuff, or Craigslist, another online empowerment of community-based commerce. These highly complex technologies have evolved to serve as striking examples of Orgel's Second Rule.

Google's own success has been aided by spontaneous evolution. The company requires its employees to spend 20% of their time on personal projects that they think will eventually help the company, outside of their specific assignments. Some of Google's most popular features, such as Google News, Gmail and Google Finance, were the brainchildren of these spontaneous idea sessions.

Google's founders may be unquestioned geniuses, but they still don't have all the good ideas. Evolution is even smarter than they are.

The call of the entrepreneur

Entrepreneurs are the primary source of evolutionary innovation in the capitalist economy. In this new century, entrepreneurship is even more essential to provide the necessary know-how to cope with a changing world.[191]

From 1980-2005, firms less than five years old accounted for all net job growth in the United States; and more than one-third of total job creation is due to the entry of new businesses.[192] Around the world, studies have found that nations which encourage entrepreneurship have lower rates of unemployment than ones where the political, legal or cultural climate is less supportive of entrepreneurs.[193]

Without entrepreneurial innovation, pessimist economists like Thomas Malthus would be correct that population growth will eventually be unsustainable. It is only through technological advance that economies can adapt to changing times, growing populations and new challenges. Most importantly, it is only through entrepreneurship that we discover such technological advances. Unfortunately, economists (with a few exceptions) have been slow to embrace entrepreneurship as the driving force behind growth.[194]

Entrepreneurship can take many forms, shapes, sizes and colors, from the traditional business owner to the self-employed musician, and from nonprofits to for-profits.[195] As Carl J. Schramm rightly notes, the entrepreneurial imperative is America's greatest asset, and is now more than ever, the competitive advantage that will ensure our rise in the 21st century.[196]

However, as an evolutionary process, entrepreneurship is not predictable, even by the most intelligent economists and policy analysts. Prior to Google, the neoclassical economic projection models could not have included Google or the $4 billion search engine optimization market that it spawned. Prior to snowboarding, the neoclassical economic projection models had the ski industry heading for calamitous decline; certainly, none had the now-thriving snowboard industry.

The point of these examples is not simply to belabor the haughty fecklessness of economists and policy analysts. It is to recognize the unpredictability of the evolutionary process, especially regarding the spontaneous innovations that employ us, inspire us and improve our world.

Entrepreneurs are the primary source of evolutionary innovation in the capitalist economy.

Microsoft, MTV, CNN, FedEx, Intel, Hewlett-Packard, Burger King, Disney, McDonald's, Southwest Airlines, and Johnson & Johnson are just a few examples of great companies formed during recessions. These companies are powerful real-world demonstrations of how evolutionary innovation often occurs on the edge of chaos.

Given these facts, the ill-advised bailout looks even more repugnant. Who is the next great Microsoft, MTV, Disney, or Intel that will be founded in this recession? Sadly, we'll never know, since entrepreneurial growth is continually stunted by the government's artificial resuscitation of existing corporations.

Entrepreneurship is a form of ad hoc experimentation, "tinkering" in Francois Jacob's words,[197] that is essential to the evolutionary process. I mean entrepreneurship in the broadest possible term, as one who "goes out where there is no rule book, and creates," in the words of Ann Reyes-Robbins, my professor at USC.

We should embrace the entrepreneur as the evolutionary spark and maximize his or her opportunity. The call of the entrepreneur should be America's national mission, encouraging every man, woman and child to pursue one's independent calling.

Echoing Jacob, Nassim Taleb argues that "random tinkering is the path to success." The reason American free enterprise works, Taleb argues, is that it allows entrepreneurs to translate the randomness of our environment into innovative knowledge. As he states further, "We need more tinkering: Uninhibited, aggressive, proud tinkering. We need to make our own luck. We can be scared and worried about the future, or we can look at it as a collection of happy surprises that lie outside the path of our imagination."[197.5]

How to escape the grind

Jobs are created by entrepreneurs, but they also are created by "labor entrepreneurs", workers who find new positions that better utilize their talents and respect their contributions.

The evolution of the labor market requires gales of creative job destruction. The U.S. economy is constantly churning out new jobs,[198] and on first glance, the constant job cutting and creating might appear to be replacing one person's job with another, a zero-sum example of economic homicide. But in the modern economy, employment differentiation is increasing and the quality is rising. As the *New York Times* noted, "In the past, menial and unskilled occupations were usually the ones predicted to grow the fastest. Now the growing importance of technology means that the fastest-growing jobs are also among the highest-paying."[199]

Though we have lost about 3 million manufacturing jobs in this century so far, we have gained 11 million in sectors where the average wage is *higher* than manufacturing.[200] Another emerging trend has been the growth of "green collar" jobs, dedicated to environmental sustainability and including both white and blue collar jobs, ranging from fuel cell design and production to solar panel installation.

> *The evolution of the labor market requires gales of creative job destruction.*

Back in the beginning of this country, over 80% of Americans spent their days working on a farm. Today, less than 2% do. That's bad news if you're a farmer, but good news if you're someone who'd prefer to avoid manual labor.

From the company man, we have evolved to the self-made millionaire, and from the 60-hour workweek of manual labor, we've evolved to the four-hour workweek.[201]

In the complex network of our economy, jobs evolve as unpredictably as any other prospective social technology. Bad jobs abound, and quality varies widely within industries. Some nannies, for example, enjoy a comfortable and lavish lifestyle; others face abuse and shockingly low pay. Some Starbucks baristas find the company culture, benefits and opportunity for advancement to be exceptional; others complain to Naomi Klein about how much they hate their jobs.[202]

Politicians fall over themselves promising to create new jobs, but yet are powerless to understand or predict—let alone control—the evolutionary trends that actually create them. Politicians had nothing to do with the evolution of Google's enlightened human resources philosophy, nor eBay's empowerment of entrepreneurship, nor snowboarding's economic rescue of the ski industry; neither can they decree such evolution in the future.

We can encourage the evolutionary process by encouraging mobility between jobs, so people can find better options to fit their lives.

Labor mobility can help turn the bankruptcy of one's boss into a better opportunity to be one's own boss. Just as the case with financial firms, every case of employer misconduct is an opportunity for creative destruction at the hands of a new, more enlightened business social technology. As Hayek aphoristically noted, "It is only because we are free in the choice of our means that we are also free in the choice of our ends."[203]

Entrepreneurship is about more than macroeconomics; it is about self-expression and the pursuit of happiness through one's chosen calling. Entrepreneurship allows individuals to live out their own unique purpose, analogous to the concept psychologist Abraham Maslow called "self-actualization." Maslow believed self-actualization was the highest source of motivation, and represented the last step in the hierarchy of human needs.[204]

> **Entrepreneurship is about more than macroeconomics; it is about self-expression and the pursuit of happiness through one's chosen calling.**

The advanced social and physical technologies in the modern world are granting entrepreneurial self-actualization on a scale never before seen. It is time that our laws finally catch up. Unfortunately, the average American business takes weeks of red-tape-jumping to start, a bureaucratic hurdle that only inhibits the spontaneous generation of evolutionary advancements.

Policy should be dedicated to enabling a system where everyone can freely choose their calling and have the necessary opportunity to pursue it.

Working man blues

A popular hobby of politicians and pundits in these dark economic days is designing grand job-creation schemes to "put America back to work." These noble but misguided programs, much like the New Deal efforts from which they are inspired, will do precisely what they did then: prolong the economic downturn while inhibiting the correction of the root economic problems.[205]

Such programs don't fail because of lack of willpower or fiscal expenditure, but because their design is violative of evolutionary principles. Unemployment is not simply a number to be played around with by mischievous econometricians: it represents a complex reality and is created by a multitude of causes. To think economists know what the "natural" rate of unemployment should be, or that politicians know how to "jump start" an economy, is to believe in the mystical powers of bureaucrats.

The economists' quantitative concepts miss an essential qualitative distinction that no regression analysis can calculate. That fact is that things change, and that frustration from one perspective can constitute opportunity from another. Employment in a bad job is *unemployment* in a good job, although the economists wouldn't know the difference and would think everything is fine. Some people leave jobs to start their own businesses and struggle for an initial period of time, although if enough people did it, economists would fret that unemployment is rising and the American economic system is collapsing. Growth is determined by the value of one's production, which as I hope I've proven, is an eminently subjective concept fueled by the type of black swan events that no economist can predict.

For an amusing thought experiment, imagine your favorite local econo-shaman advising ski resorts on their economic difficulties a few decades ago. Our friendly econo-shaman might even have noticed the growing unemployment and stagnation in the sector, so what would he propose in response? From the proposals of most "experts", we can guess that after consulting his crystal calculator, he might propose some sort of stimulus package for skiers, or perhaps a "shovel-ready" community labor effort like filling empty chair lifts with well-sculptured snowmen clad in locally-made ski gear. There's no limit to any of the shaman's ideas, but as we know, none of them would have actually done anything to fix the problem.

The real solution came from a group of people that skiers and ski resorts then despised - a long-haired and tattooed motley crew of fledgling entrepreneurs who would soon evolve into the billion-dollar snowboarding industry. Nobody saw it coming, and as we know now, the real solution was not listening to some expert's predictions, but rather by empowering freedom of choice.

But empowering freedom of choice doesn't win economists Nobel Prizes anymore, apparently, and although economists' methods would have blinded them to the evolutionary path of the snowboarding industry, they now smugly assure us that their methods will somehow illuminate the evolutionary path of the entire economy.

Let us be clear. Technological evolution, not the schemes of politicians or policy experts, creates jobs. Electricians are employed because of the spontaneous genius of Thomas Edison and his ilk, not because anyone voted for a job-creation package regarding electrical currents. Take the most life-changing technological innovations - from the wheel to the automobile - and you'll see that first the technology evolved, second the industry was exploited, and third, the state came in to regulate.[206] The cycle works dialectically because first the technology must expand the range of the possible, then it must be exploited to determine the outer limit of the socially permissible, and then the state must balance the two principles.

Unfortunately, confusing this order of operations is the current fad in Washington, with politicians' fantasy plans of "shovel-ready" infrastructure projects.

Technological evolution, not the schemes of politicians or policy experts, creates jobs.

Will the plans work? Well, it depends on what you mean by "work." Such employee-wards of the state might have a meal ticket, and they might not register as technically "unemployed", but their employment is scarcely more rewarding than prisoners who stamp license plates or pick up trash on the side of a freeway. One can give a man a job, but only he can give himself a career.

Psychology since Maslow has confirmed the fact that job satisfaction arises from a sense of identification with the work, and a belief that one is producing something of value. This value is internal and varies from person to person. Grand "shovel-ready" federal projects might succeed in lowering the gross unemployment rate, but does nothing to dent the problem of stagnating economic institutions and the absence of quality choice. A citizen unemployed in transition to a fulfilling, rewarding job that maximizes his or her talents is much better off than a citizen employed in a position that demeans his or her sense of self. One should not seek to flatter the macro-economists of the world at the expense of the people who really matter.

The artificiality of such one-size-fits-all programs crashes down upon the very people it is designed to help. Either the program eventually runs out of bridges to build (although, knowing Congress and its penchant for financing bridges to nowhere, such a situation is highly unlikely), or, if it continues, the program perpetually advances toward irrelevance, with ever more citizens stuck in demeaning and value-less work.

The government effort should be to empower every citizen's own pursuit of happiness, not to assume that a politician already knows the destination. We are all unique, and the American Dream is about following these special paths. The holy grail lies in the entrepreneurial initiative of the American people, not the quantitative creativity of the world's economists. As the snowboarders of the world can attest, the key to the American evolution lies in the entrepreneurial imperative.

President Obama is right to suggest that the economic recovery will require government action. It will require government action in removing the many real-world barriers to entrepreneurship in America. These barriers abound in economic policy: high tax rates, burdensome regulations, corporate bailouts, archaic pension and health policy. As we'll see in Chapter 6, they also exist in social policy, which is failing to develop the entrepreneurial spirit, by deluding children with rote memorization of useless facts in school rather than practical knowledge and belief in personal agency. Recognizing this, policy should seek to lower the numerous real-world barriers to the American Dream, not erect billion-dollar monuments to the egos of overweening number-crunchers.

President Obama is right to suggest that the economic recovery will require government action. It will require government action in removing the many real-world barriers to entrepreneurship in America.

You, Inc.

Some barriers to labor mobility are inevitable—physically moving to a new job is usually difficult. However, there's another force that inhibits labor mobility in America, and that's people's attachment to their health and retirement benefits. This benefit-induced ball and chain is encouraged by current tax policy in the United States because it gives a deduction to employers who provide health insurance to their employees. Laws in some states like California even require employers to provide insurance.

Requiring employers to provide health insurance may have worked well in the Company Man days of the 1950s, but in the age of labor mobility and spontaneous mid-life entrepreneurship, relying on one's employer for benefits is as anachronistic as *Amos 'n Andy*.

As an initial matter, it's difficult to understand what expertise an employer would have in selecting an insurance policy *for you*. When did we appoint General Motors as physician and retirement consultant *de facto* for its 100k plus workers?

Instead, imagine a health care system where employers simply *contributed* a specific and negotiable percentage of money to a personal health care fund, tax-free, and workers could then select the health care plans of their choice to apply the money towards.

For employers, it would cost the same and would be one less thing to worry about. For workers, it would be a revolution. The power of the system would lie in the effective maximization of freedom of choice in health care, allowing people to select from a smorgasbord of health care technologies—independent of their employer.

Personal health care funds would thus take employers out of the picture entirely. As the employer contribution to the fund would be wholly controlled by workers, fears about stingy bosses would be a thing of the past. Even if you lose your job, you would keep your health care. Why lobby Wal-Mart to increase health benefits when we can implement a system that lets workers do it themselves?

State governments could supplement these funds according to criteria they find necessary, thus helping the needy but without thrusting one-size-fits-all health care technologies on a diverse public. The virtue of American federalism, as we will discuss in Chapter 7, is that individual states can experiment with these and other policies to help assist their citizens.

Most importantly, the fund would involve every worker in the cooperative venture of choosing health insurance, which would create strong incentives for quality in that industry.

Under our current employer-driven system, most health insurance decisions are made by companies, not by individual workers. Given such a stifling choice, we now know why our health insurance system is so abysmal; the system needs active individual choice among the public at large, wielding the wisdom of crowds to drive higher quality selections.

Personal health funds would do something no other program would do—they would simultaneously address problems with medical entitlements and the unemployed middle class, as well as enhance the dynamic innovation of American health care. Put another way, they would effectively maximize the evolution of all our social and physical technologies dedicated to preserving human health.

How to escape depressions

A similar idea can be applied to retirement benefits, another currently employer-and-government-controlled provision. We can reform

Social Security to divert existing FICA payroll taxes, along with a worker's 401(k), into a personal retirement account. Letting all workers choose their investment options not only encourages labor mobility, but also creates market pressure to help more Americans plan for their retirement and live a more prosperous future.

Social Security is a noble attempt to design a universal social technology in order to provide a secure financial future for all. But unfortunately, politicians are incapable of designing such a system, and seventy-plus years after its introduction, Social Security's lack of evolution is manifest. Due to an antiquated and arbitrary funding system—paying for the benefits of current retirees with the taxes of current workers—Social Security faces a $26 trillion unfunded liability, and rising. Thanks to an influx of Baby Boomer retirees, by 2030, it is expected that only 2 workers will be paying for every one person collecting Social Security, which will be down from 16 workers paying for every recipient back in 1950. Addressing the financial gap will require an estimated 50% increase in Social Security taxes or a 27% cut in benefits.[207]

Such budget difficulties inevitably arise when government attempts to mandate a single social technology in a complex environment. Rather, Social Security should enhance personal choice. Current Social Security taxes should be divided: half paying for recipients in the current system, and half controlled by each individual taxpayer in a highly diversified personal retirement account.[208] This way, we can upgrade the social technology of Social Security without harming the people themselves.

Furthermore, in giving citizens legal control over the disposition of funds, the system would facilitate greater financial freedom. Citizens could withdraw funds to cover unexpected expenses, invest in new businesses, bequeath them to family and more, all of which would yield an extra layer of financial protection. In providing more social-technological options with the same funds, private accounts could harness evolutionary processes to create greater prosperity.

Despite the punctuated occurrence of recessions and large-scale economic calamities, differentiation in the marketplace is an effective hedge against disaster. In investment jargon, differentiation is called "diversification," and it has been shown to substantially reduce one's exposure to economic loss. Studies show that global diversification can result in a 60% reduction in volatility and an 80% reduction in maximum loss, as well as an improvement in portfolio returns.[209] If financial institutions were not allowed to diversify their holdings, for example, the negative impact of the 2008 credit crunch would likely have been even worse.

Evolutionary choice theory wholly concurs with the cliched injunction against putting one's eggs in one basket. Diversification allows investors to free themselves from the vagaries of cutthroat free market capitalism. Differentiation helps cushion shocks, even when things don't work out like we (or your local economists) predict they will. Even if a worker had started investing strictly in diversified blue-chip stocks (i.e. the Dow Jones Industrial Average) at the beginning of his career, and then retired the very day of the 2008 stock collapse, he still would have made over seven times what he had started with.[210]

Those still averse to such investment could place their savings in government bonds or stable commodities such as gold, and avoid much of the volatility of the stock market; there is a strong argument for making this a default option.

Though Americans currently hold the lowest personal savings rate in the industrialized world,[211] there's no reason why this must be the case. In fact, one great advantage of private accounts is that they would save money *automatically*. Think of it as armchair investing; a true boon to us lazy Americans.

Now, given that over 48 million Americans regularly draw from Social Security, personal accounts would help more Americans achieve more comfortable, secure and prosperous retirements, or in other words, live the American Dream. And isn't that what it's all about?

Quite simply, the private accounts system would return the selection process to retirement funds. Social Security, IRAs, 401(k)s all have severe flaws because of their restriction on free choice, but freedom and competition can help develop better options.

The greatest advantage of bringing choice into the retirement issue means letting the people decide how their money can be spent. It's difficult to argue that this would not be vastly superior to our current system of voodoo economics, which lets politicians spend the money of people who haven't even been born yet.

So there's two ideas to aid the evolution of some traditional social technologies. Had they been in place, Ms. Ehrenreich would have been building a nest egg and enjoying consistent health benefits, even if she still couldn't find a job she liked. Sounds like a win to me.

The paradox of choice

Still, there's a problem. To many of us, the thought of picking among so many prospective insurance companies, HMOs, 501(k)s and mutual funds simply makes our heads spin. Do we really want all that choice? How would one know quality in such a complex differentiated environment? Do we really want to be our own bosses, after all?

Psychologist Barry Schwartz dedicates a whole book to such difficulties. With a combination of convenient anecdotes and a sporadic citation of research, Schwartz's book, called *The Paradox of Choice*, bemoans the proliferation of decision options in the 21st century. He's particularly critical of the idea that choice over important matters such as health care or retirement savings is a good thing.

To prove his point, Schwartz cites an experiment in which researchers presented various selections of fruit jams to participants. The researchers found that as participants were offered more varieties of jams, they eventually became less satisfied with their choices as a result.

Schwartz complains, "We can imagine a point at which the options would be so copious that even the world's most ardent supporters of freedom of choice would say 'enough already.' Unfortunately, that point of revulsion seems to recede endlessly into the future."

Au contraire, Monsieur, we ardent supporters of freedom of choice constantly recognize the fact that one can have too many choices. However, that point varies from person to person, and thus freedom of choice is still required to find it. As we mentioned in Chapter 1, free choice is essential as a tool to narrow our menu of options. There's no saying "big box" supermarkets—literally or figuratively—are for everyone. Specialization, niche marketing and other useful social technologies we've mentioned so far actually serve to limit choices.

Even Amazon, with its millions of choices, is successful at giving the perception of many *fewer* choices. When one accesses Amazon.com, 5 million books are not displayed. Rather, the site automatically filters its many choices into a few recommended selections displayed on each page that are directly related to a user's demonstrated preferences, as manifested by search, link selection or past purchasing behavior.

Starbucks may intimidate some with its 17,000 selections of international coffee. But ordering at Starbucks is still much easier than sifting through the hundred million bags of coffee produced around the world ourselves; one can buy coffee from Ethiopia without even having to leave the country.

Having many choices doesn't mean you have to necessarily choose all of them. The point of differentiation is not that more is *always* good; differentiation is often essential in order to *reduce* complexity.[212] Chris Anderson explains this process through the creation of "filters," by which choices are made more easily.

A fact Schwartz ignores is that all choices are not created equal. Obvious to anyone who has visited a supermarket in the past ten years, choice in jam is actually something consumers want on a fairly regular basis, unlike what scientists found in the jam experiment. This is likely because curious academics looking for research fodder, instead of businesses subject to market forces, selected the "choices" for the experiment.

Sheena Iyengar, a researcher on the jam study, has conceded the overwhelming psychological literature confirms the benefits of choice. In fact, she wrote, "Despite the detriments associated with choice overload, consumers want choice and they want a lot of it."[213]

An entire industry has sprung up to deal with the paradox of choice: the burgeoning personal organization industry, offering choice-overwhelmed citizens everything from administrative services and time-management consulting to closet organization and *feng shui* analysis.[214]

Even though Schwartz is quite concerned about the outbreak of abulia in the modern age, his fear is overstated. (abulia, n., an inability to make choices or decisions.)

Consumers suffering from abulia don't bring corporations any money, so there is a strong incentive for companies to make it as easy as *possible* for consumers to choose. This is why Starbucks offers its products on a nice-looking menu, and why the DMV, ever indifferent to the preferences of its consumers, offers its services on hundreds of different yet equally incomprehensible alphanumeric-named forms.

If Schwartz is right about one thing, it's that there are detriments to choice. What are those detriments? Well, we already know—there's a lot of crap in the long tail, and it's occasionally difficult to pick out something that you actually want when there are so many options.

In the end, Schwartz' supposed indictment of free choice is nothing new. He merely proves Sturgeon's Law, the 80-20 rule, the law of the vital few, and all the other aforementioned instances noting a surprisingly robust eruption of inferior options. But he misses the other point of those discoveries, namely the futility in implying universality from a few instances of failure.

Keep on truckin'

In the complex network of the global economy, the fate of a given industry is subject to forces beyond a single worker's control. As such, no-fault economic calamities are common place. Think of the hardworking GM factory workers who have no ability to change the fact that the company bosses keep designing hideous, soulless and unreliable automobiles. Or the Kansas wheat farmer who can't stop developing world competition from undercutting him. In many unfortunate cases, the evolutionary process that benefits all of society happens to harm the prospects of certain individuals. As Hayek pointed out, "In a spontaneous order, undeserved disappointments cannot be avoided."[215]

Oftentimes, what represents progress for the people at large is not good for a given industry, or the people who work in it. For example, take the telephone industry. In 1970, there were 421,000 switchboard operators and Americans were making about 10 billion long-distance calls a year. By 1994, Americans were making over 80 billion long-distance calls a year, but new technology allowed telephone companies to downsize to only 176,000 operators.[216] Many might see 245,000 job losses as calamitous; but they would miss the point. Without the boost in technological efficiency, today's volume of long-distance traffic would require us to employ nearly 4 million operators, or 3% of our labor force, instead of the 0.1% it now takes.[217]

While unemployment is inevitable, there is no shortage of policy options to aid displaced workers as they find new jobs in the dynamic modern economy. Privately-run transition programs, which take payments from the welfare system in exchange for successfully training unemployed workers for new careers, can experiment with novel approaches to help individual workers find gainful employment. Furthermore, a negative income tax (in essence, a subsidy paid through the tax system) provided by the states can provide displaced workers with a temporary level of income while they seek new jobs, without unnecessarily restricting one's financial choices. Unemployment compensation aids social justice by differentiating between economic and family life, thus preventing every fluctuation in the economy

Though we mourn the death of our beloved Idea, we take solace in the fact that we survive together...

from having a devastating effect on a person's life outside the workplace.[218]

Of course, it's easy to see job losses, industry evaporation and widespread outsourcing, and angrily curse Adam Smith and everything he stood for. If it were all just lost jobs and lost wages, the anti-capitalism crowd would have a great point.

But that's *not* all it is. We put up with the messy and uncomfortable evolutionary process not because it's messy and uncomfortable, but because it has gotten us as far as it has. If it weren't for the billions of value-added technological advancements that enrich our lives as a result of the evolutionary process, the whole thing would arguably be a big waste of time. Yet it is the search of something better, the calm assurance of progress and adaptation even in our darkest hour, that drives us forward.

The evolutionary search process is more than imperfect; as we mentioned, its average rate of success is low enough to be statistically insignificant.[219] And as was mentioned last chapter, system theorists have found that complex networks tend to evolve, not in a linear or predictable fashion, but only when the system is on the edge of collapsing into chaos.

These facts might shatter the utopian dreams of neoclassical technocrats and paternalist policy wonks alike. They might be uncomfortable for all of us when we're stuck with bad choices, have few options or low quality options. But the point of the evolutionary process isn't its batting average. The point is that evolution remains the only method known to humanity that can successfully discover and develop the unforeseen advancements that drive human progress and prosperity.

The inevitable disappointments of the evolutionary order can best be appreciated as part of a Hegelian dialectic, through which they constitute an opportunity for future advancement, an antithesis to eventually create a synthesis, and part of the unfolding process toward absolute freedom.

It's awfully easy to take the Malthusian approach and doubt our progress. But we must not, in the aphoristic words of economist Jagdish Bhagwati, "confuse inertia for rigor mortis."[220] Instead, we should recognize the power of evolutionary adaptation to improve our lives in ways which we previously thought impossible.

5

THE GREAT DIFFERENTIATION
The evolutionary benefits of diversity and freedom

*B*ECAUSE SO MANY evolutionary advancements come from an unlikely source, differentiation is essential to help find adaptive solutions to pressing challenges. Like Polymerase IV, the enzyme that encourages evolution through genetic experimentation, or snowboarding saving the ski slope from economic catastrophe, differentiation has been shown to aid adaptation and the discovery of life-improving technologies.

This chapter will explore the numerous ways that differentiation supports the evolutionary adaptation of social and physical technologies.

America, the differentiated

The progressive value of differentiation has continually demonstrated itself throughout history. The first trading tribes were found with tools made from resources not found in their local area, allowing them to use the diverse skills and resources of foreigners to better survive.[221] The correlation between peaceful commerce and technological growth has always persisted, and as tribes began to trade, early humans could specialize, diversify and create better tools for their own survival. Some historians argue that the link between merchant trading and scientific progress has existed since prior to the Renaissance, and even prior to the scientific philosophy of Francis Bacon.[222] The evolutionary process is about discovering ideas to live better, and open trade is essential to that process.

International trade remains a powerful source of differentiation, enabling American consumers to import an ever-expanding menu of choices. As the technological capacity of global trade has expanded, the variety of goods imported into America has tripled in the last quarter century.[223]

American industry has created innumerable value-added technologies, but it has not and will never create all of them. Instead, the American economy thrives on the principle of comparative advantage, which holds that countries are better off doing only the things that they're best at, and importing everything else from other countries.

In the cooperative venture of the global economy, more participation works to the benefit of all participants. This principle was established well by Frederic Bastiat:

"In virtue of Free Trade we enjoy the sun of Portugal like the Portuguese themselves. The inhabitants of Havre and the citizens of London are put in possession, and on the same conditions, of all the mineral resources which nature has bestowed on Newcastle."[224]

As a pro-globalization writer noted in *Newsweek* more recently,

> Globalization is nothing more (or less) than the accretion of countless millions of individual acts by people who have availed themselves of the potential granted them by technologies that shrink the planet. Our humanity is enriched when we do the mundane things that are now possible--eat new foods, cheer sports heroes from unlikely places, visit towns and villages that but a generation away seemed as close as the far side of the moon, understand at least the surface of unfamiliar faiths. Looked at in that way, globalization is not something of which one should despair; but rather an excuse for celebration.[225]

American tourists may be derided for their bumbling indifference to European norms, but we certainly know all about Italian fashion, French wine and German beer. We might not be able to locate Switzerland on a map, but we'll buy their best watches, cheese and chocolates with distinction. Despite Lou Dobbs' protestations to the contrary, this process works great for Americans. For example, we used to make great cars, and now, with a few exceptions that we'll mention later, we really don't. But Americans still buy great cars from companies around the world.

The differentiated global menu of choices is becoming increasingly apparent everywhere in the 21st century, from finding fresh Chilean salmon in your local grocery store to hiring remote personal assistants in India.

The global multinational corporation is a triumph of differentiation. Sharing human and capital resources with other nations allows multinational firms to have greater understanding of their markets, achieve dynamic service delivery and benefit from an infusion of new ideas. Similarly today, foreign

> *In the cooperative venture of the global economy, more participation works to the benefit of all participants.*

investment is providing our economy with the necessary capital that our country is not currently able to provide itself, allowing our nation to help lessen the severity of economic downturns. In these dark economic times, turning our back on the world will only inhibit future evolution.

¡Viva la evolución!

America is a nation of immigrants. Ever since about 1860, a year before the Civil War, approximately one out of every seven Americans has been foreign born.[226] Immigrant communities throughout American history included the Dutch minorities in the early American colonies, 19th century waves of Scots-Irish and Germans, 20th century immigration from Southern Europe and Asia, all the way through the 21st century waves from Latin America.[227]

American immigrants have been the greatest geniuses and achievers the world has known, including such luminaries as Albert Einstein, Joseph Pulitzer, Rudolph Valentino, John Muir, Madeleine Albright, Elie Wiesel, Bob Hope, John Lennon, Google founder Sergey Brin, and my Governator, Arnold Schwarzenegger, just to name a few. All of them were once working for their home countries, before they brought their peerless talents to America.

However, our history has demonstrated a popular opposition to much of the immigration waves. Benjamin Franklin famously complained about German immigrants in Pennsylvania who, to him, seemed incapable of learning English or assimilating into American society.[228] Each time, immigrant communities were initially sequestered in poor ethnocentric neighborhoods and their people commonly thought to be poor, chronically lazy, incapable of assimilating into American culture, religiously subversive or a variety of other offenses.

American immigrants have been the greatest geniuses and achievers the world has known...

But each immigrant group brought its own unique social technologies to our nation, and the value-added contributions of immigrants abound in modern America. In addition to providing us with economic growth and cultural diversity, immigrants' labor differentiation has helped cities avoid prolonged economic downturns.

There are the criminal immigrants as well, as the inevitable examples of Sturgeon's Law. But studies have found that immigration, *ipso facto*, does not contribute to a socioeconomic underclass. Immigrants just tend to start out in it.[229] Studies also show that immigrants start businesses at a higher rate than natives, which makes perfect sense given the discussion about job evolution. Faced with limited opportunity and discriminatory attitudes in many workplaces, immigrants must pursue independent paths in order to succeed. As it turns out, immigrants have founded more than half of all Silicon Valley start-ups in the past ten years. Immigrant-led tech firms, nationwide, created more than 450,000 jobs and grossed $52 billion in 2005.[229.5]

The Olympics offer a quadrennial testament to America's dynamic social evolution. American gymnastics gold medalist Nastia Liukin, for example, is the daughter of former Soviet Union gymnast Valeri Liukin. The elder Liukin moved to the U.S. in the eighties to live the American Dream, and now bestows on America the gymnastics genius that was once exclusively behind the Iron Curtain.[230] Similarly, Liukin's fellow U.S. gymnastics star, Shawn Johnson, is coached by former Chinese national hero Liang Chow. Our importation of the world's best and brightest is our greatest advantage; while Europeans continue to fall ever further off the medal platform, American social differentiation continues to dominate the Games.

Unfortunately, all is not copacetic in the American melting pot. Thanks to incompetent immigration policy, the American government has lost control over its own borders.

America's current policy uses a complicated and arbitrary set of factors to allow entry into the country, such as the country of origin and family ties to existing American immigrants. But as we mentioned in Chapter

1, this arbitrary policy has backfired, leaving our nation facing a drought of high-skilled workers. As long as hard working immigrants can't get in the country because of the bureaucratic ineptitude by the Department of Homeland Security, Immigrations and Customs Enforcement (or The Bureaucrats Formerly Named the Immigration and Naturalizations Service), illegal immigration becomes an economic inevitability.

To effectively differentiate among immigrants, it would be far better to institute a system of employment-based immigration, facilitating the documented entry of willing workers who have secure offers of employment. That way, those who come for productive purposes can be easily tracked and distinguished. Meanwhile, comprehensive border security would need to exclude criminal or other undesirable elements. It's a solution that can maximize economic growth as well as national security. It's a solution that maximizes freedom of choice.

Stop that advancement!

Unfortunately, many see global differentiation not as a benign force aiding our nation's evolution, but rather a seditious trend causing social unrest and economic decline. Whenever trade or immigration threatens domestic industries, there is an inevitable backlash, and cries of foreigners "stealing" American jobs become commonplace.

Critics have objections to the exciting new global bazaar, mainly the increase of what neoclassical economists call a "trade deficit." What's a trade deficit? It's the measure of how much we imported from the rest of the world versus the *separate* goods or services we exported. In response, nativists often urge Congress to implement tariffs, duties, subsidies and other trade barriers intended to "protect" American business by artificially making foreign goods more expensive.

But imports in themselves aren't necessarily a bad thing—they are arguably good when they deliver more choices for American consumers. The data agree: the American economy has a higher rate of growth in years with the highest "trade deficits."[231]

Barriers to trade only inhibit differentiation, and thus inhibit Americans' access to more advanced social technologies. Artificial barriers to trade have been shown to raise Americans' cost of food by a staggering $16.2 billion annually, which translates to $146 extra paid by every American.[232]

How does it help Americans to prevent them from purchasing food at the grocery store for less money?

Despite its rhetorical popularity, the concept of wealth as a "fixed pie" is absolutely false. Economic growth is not zero-sum, meaning that as one person makes money it must be taken from someone else. Rather, this growth is *value-added*, meaning that the global collection of wealth *increases* as humanity discovers new social technologies. Remember, evolutionary amplification processes create emergent properties as a *positive-sum* synthesis.

Recall Beinhocker's conclusion, mentioned in Chapter 2, that "wealth is knowledge." Similarly, economist Paul Romer has argued that ideas are a factor of economic production as important as labor or capital.[233] Relying on Romer's insights, writer Thomas Homer-Dixon further argues that the most essential asset in the 21st century economy is *ingenuity*, or "sets of instructions that tell us how to arrange the constituent parts of our social and physical worlds in ways that help us achieve our goals."[234]

Thus, the economic question we face today is not a zero-sum battle against invading foreigners, but rather a cooperative pursuit of the next great idea. The only thing protectionism protects Americans from is the valuable knowledge of others.

"I'm sorry, Mr. Good Idea, given your origin in a country with which we have political disagreements, I cannot let you enter."

Testing, 1-2-3

Restriction of the free choice of the people, in the assumption that a given politician or "expert" knows how to develop new social technologies better, is inevitably bound to fail. This is the case because of the extraordinary complexity of the marketplace and society, and the inevitability of change. Even the best laid social plans, with the best of intentions, have the same fatal flaw: the unavoidable ignorance of the designer.

Even if a given social technology is undoubtedly beneficial—take public transportation, for example—there is still no guarantee that a specific state-provided instance is more beneficial than the other social technologies comparatively sacrificed by politicians' well-meaning subsidization.

In a 1959 debate, William F. Buckley, Jr. delivered a damning critique of the freedom-restricting effect of government intervention, specifically regarding a proposed New York State subsidy of New York City subways:

> [The program] involves... a net imposition on non—subway riders, for the benefit of subway riders. So be it. If all goes according to plan, Cayuga County apple pickers will soon be making it possible for Manhattan elevator operators to ride to work for 15 cents even though it costs the Transit Authority 20 cents to provide the service. In due course, the political representatives of Cayuga County will appeal for increased off-season benefits for apple pickers, whereupon it becomes necessary to increase the taxes of subway riders. Keep this up, and the skies are black with crisscrossing dollars... What is wrong with the economy of the crisscrossing dollar? Well, for one thing, there is the well-known fact that any time a Cayugan sends a dollar down to New York City, it is going to stop at Albany for an expensive night out on the town. But aside from the leakage, what is wrong with the political economy of liberalism, in which dollars are exchanged by political negotiation? What is principally wrong is that it is an economics of illusion. What is secondarily wrong is that the system permits profiteering by politically mobilized groups. The third way in which it is wrong is that it diminishes the influence of the individual in the marketplace, transferring the lost power to politicians and the ideologues who stir them up.[235]

Indeed, Mr. Buckley. The flaw in such top-down approaches is not their goals but their execution: they inevitably squelch the kind of bottom-up innovation that is essential to true progress.

Governments can boost the prospects of hugely popular social technologies, of course, and such efforts are immensely popular among voters, politicians, pundits and the policy wonks who arrogate to themselves the ability to create human progress.

A great example of government aiding technological growth is the internet, which began as a Department of Defense project. This confirms the fact that the government can successfully spearhead new research areas. However, what also cannot be doubted is the eventual necessity of differentiation and privatization. As a government project, the internet had no conceivable use for civil society. The internet didn't revolutionize our lives until its development was decentralized, first by differentiated private entities and now, through the use of open-source technology, *by literally everyone.*

Because the evolutionary process is unpredictable, it's impossible to foresee specific maladies that government-fostered uniformity will create. The only certainty is that the absence of differentiation eventually takes its toll.

As usual, history provides an interesting compass. John F. Kennedy's support of the space program in the 1960s is often cited as another grand project that proves government's ability to foster the growth of successful social technologies. It is true that NASA—the government agency with the exclusive right to pursue space travel—got America to the moon before the Soviet Union did.

The internet didn't revolutionize our lives until its development was decentralized, first by differentiated private entities and now, through the use of open-source technology, by literally everyone.

But NASA is no longer a shining example of progress. Its monopolistic control of American space flight is its greatest competitive disadvantage. The Space Shuttle's woefully outdated technology has recently caused the *Columbia* disaster as well as numerous delays and technical glitches.

Another putative success story of grand government projects is the Interstate Highway System, our impressive network of roads that connect our major cities. But yet again, the absence of evolution proved fatal to progress; due to an outdated design from the 1960s, a bridge on Interstate 35 in Minneapolis recently collapsed, killing 13 people.[236]

The irony of "public" projects is they too often silence the voices of the public itself. When the government creates a monopoly over a given social technology, the result might not be immediately calamitous, but the inhibition of evolution eventually has a cost.

The problem isn't the presence of government, *ipso facto*, but rather the absence of differentiation over time. As we mentioned, governments play an essential role in fostering early development in industries that require it for some reason, such as military defense, science and other essential technologies.

The solution is to simply allow differentiation and experimentation with new technologies. All government investment need not be abandoned immediately; the effort should be to gradually inject free choice into the existing programs. Examples would be encouraging private space travel, in order to unleash the technological innovation that has created *SpaceshipOne* and Richard Bronson's Virgin Galactic; and semi-private toll roads, such as the Orange County, CA toll roads which successfully avoid the gridlock of the Interstate, providing superior road quality for a nominal fee.

Another evolutionary case study

Once upon a time, American automobiles were the pinnacle of excellence. Whether one was seeking performance, luxury or convenience, the best choice was to buy domestic. An example of such innovation was the 1957 Cadillac Eldorado Brougham: a 345 horsepower luxury sedan with air ride suspension, automatic transmission, power windows, power doors, six-way power seats, power brakes, air conditioning, radio, cruise control, memory seats and electric clocks in the back seats. Its industry-first quad headlights were capable of automatically dimming so they wouldn't blind passerby on a mountain incline as well as automatically turning on at night. All this in 1957.

Today, however, the domestic options are far inferior. The American automotive industry is largely in shambles, with General Motors continuously teetering on the edge of bankruptcy, and often joined on the verge of corporate death by Ford and Chrysler. Faced with sagging profits, spiraling costs and cutthroat foreign competition, American car companies seem to face a very dark future.

Why the dim outlook? Well for one, American carmakers harbor a supremely inefficient business model, one dedicated to the very type of lavish Company Man benefit packages that, as we mentioned last chapter, serve to inhibit free choice in the marketplace and hamper development.

If that weren't enough, American car companies also face the further predicament of peddling a product that most people just don't want. In contrast to their glorious past, U.S. automakers now excrete a soulless amalgam of inferior-quality vehicles, and in most relevant categories are currently being flogged by Japanese and European competition.

For that reason, American buyers have demonstrated a strong inclination toward foreign automakers, whose cars happen to provide more useful technologies. This competition, while it certainly causes some heartburn in Motor City, gives fantastic options to the consumer: from the reliability and usability of Honda Accords and Toyota Camrys, to the unmatched performance capabilities of the Nissan GT-R or BMW M5, just to name a few.

But there are glimmers of hope in the landscape of American engineering. The Corvette Z06, Cadillac CTS-V, and the Saleen S7 are some examples of dominant American vehicles that remain not only competitive, but actually turn heads. These shining examples arose, as one might expect, not because of protectionist support, but rather competitive Yankee innovation.

For example, Cadillac's new CTS-V was developed and tuned on the Nurburgring, a German race track. The Nurburgring had long been the home testing ground for BMW's M-division sports cars, a fact which BMW smugly argued contributed to the Bavarian company's competitive advantage. But Cadillac wised up and went to Germany to engage in extensive testing and modification of their new sports sedan on the 'Ring. After it was released, the CTS-V achieved a Nurburgring lap time that beat BMW's iconic sports car, the (much more expensive) M5. That's what I call evolution in action.

If the Big Three want to stay in the game, they need to step up their performance. It's time to demolish the Studebaker factories in Flint, Michigan, and replace them with factories capable of building twenty-first century vehicles. Of course 1950s-era factories are boarded up. That's like complaining about the lack of demand for a telegraph repair business.

Nostalgia is understandable, but it's not cause for inaction or conscious stagnation. In Downtown Los Angeles, an area experiencing the type of urban renaissance that defines American federalism at its best, its once-common ghost towns are slowly disappearing. One can still visit the

1930s-era hotels and factories that once stood here. But only the buildings remain, for in them are gorgeous renovated luxury lofts, housing lawyers and artists alike, generating millions for the local economy and revitalizing the downtown neighborhood.[237]

The principle of differentiation should ensure that as GM undergoes distress-induced restructuring, its few profitable technologies will find buyers. The few glimmers of hope in Detroit—the aforementioned CTS-V, or the concept plug-in Chevy Volt—do not justify the rescue of the entire corporate behemoth. Just as JP Morgan's bank customers preserved their WaMu account features after bankruptcy, GM's corporate successors have every incentive to preserve the great ideas (if any) that are left in the Detroit Rust Belt.

A California start up company, Fisker Automotive, offers an electric hybrid called the Karma that looks (and performs) more like a Porsche than a Prius. Such a car, exhibited at the recent Detroit auto show, offers glimmers of hope for the future of the American auto industry. And in an amazing tribute to American entrepreneurial ingenuity, the Karma went "from the first idea to the market in 24 months," according to founder Henrik Fisker.[238]

Now, by what ethical principle of fairness do our leaders take our money from us, spend it on the wheezing and incontinent corporate behemoth that is General Motors, while innovative American companies such as

this are competing for our dollar? What an outrage.

Despite the attempt of the American car lobby to convince us otherwise, the laws of the universe apply to them as much as everyone else. The evolutionary selection process of the marketplace must be heeded. To survive, Detroit doesn't need the sympathy of patriotic Americans or the fiscal coddling of Congress. They just need to make good cars again.

I am a proud and patriotic American who has consciously expressed the preference to not buy an American vehicle until it becomes something I truly desire to drive. Millions of my fellow countrymen feel the same. It is a gross injustice that this expression - our freedom of choice - is cruelly censored and denigrated by a taxpayer bailout. With our tax dollars, Representatives have patronized the companies that we have gone out of our way *not* to patronize. This shameful policy only inhibits the selection process and further stifles the evolution of the once-glorious American car industry.

Can't buy me love

In this state of financial turmoil, many Americans are rightly concerned with the fate of the U.S. Dollar. In addition to its bubble-inducing interest rate policy, the Federal Reserve's monopolistic control of American currency unfortunately inhibits the evolution of our monetary system. Though our leaders assure us that the Fed's arbitrary manipulation of the money supply is based on sound economics, readers of this book confidently know that no such sound economics exists. Rather, our central bankers are shooting from the hip, and experimenting blindly with a complex and dangerous commodity.

The theory behind the Fed's decision-making is that well-timed interest rate manipulations can spur economic growth. Unfortunately, that policy in practice is the economic equivalent of trying to carve the statue of David with a Howitzer. By arbitrarily modifying the complex and fundamental social technologies of the modern economy, the Fed's policy unleashes a myriad of unintended (and sometimes catastrophic) circumstances.

The Fed's interest rate cuts were lauded for their alleged impact in helping America avoid a more severe recession post-9/11. But that artificial boom came at a substantial cost, spurring a speculative debt bubble that substantially contributed to the current economic crisis.

Macroeconomic social engineering by government severely distorts the market signals that underpin effective economic choice. These distortions cripple the evolutionary selection process, blurring the essential distinctions between the vital few good ideas in the marketplace and the excrement-filled majority.

Of course, being wholly immune to any form of political feedback, the Federal Reserve's activities will likely continue apace, no matter what we do. But there is a way to protect the American people from this Frankensteinian financial experimentation.

The legal tender laws should be interpreted to allow the creation and development of alternative currencies. These alternative currencies would aid the evolution of the American economy by providing a number of benefits that our current system does not.

First, it will allow Americans to back their currencies in a real and tangible commodity, such as gold. While the arguments for and against the gold standard are too nuanced and complicated to be entered into here, the point is that there are strong arguments for a gold standard. But there is no need to convince the U.S. Treasury. Rather, the American people, in their capacity as free and independent citizens, should be allowed to make the decisions for themselves.

Second, the system will hasten the discovery of effective monetary structures. Instead of relying on the Federal Reserve to get it right (an unlikely and undemocratic proposition), people would be free to find currencies that fit their needs. As long as all currencies are backed with another currency or solid commodity, consumers could be protected while we are spared the drastic consequence of the Federal Reserve's contemporary attempt at social engineering.

Third, 21st century technology should allow a more seamless transition to alternative currencies than would have been possible in the past. Today, nearly all business establishments accept credit cards. A competing currency need simply be added into the credit card database, which would allow any customer to use the currency at millions of point-of-sale transactions. Even if the individual business owner wouldn't have the time, resources, or interest to exchange a particular paper currency, the customer could pay with their competing currency card while the proprietor would instantly receive the money in their preferred currency.

Such a policy would be a very effective hedge against uncertainty in these uncertain times, as well as a fertile ground for progressive growth in financial technology. Another win-win evolutionary policy proposal.

The silver bullet

Today, another hot topic is global climate change (no pun intended), and the pursuit of a suite of technologies that can substantially reduce greenhouse gas emissions. Rather than encourage the evolutionary process of development, however, pundits and politicians claim the impossible: that they have all of the technological answers.

It's too bad our current suite of technologies is wholly incapable of solving our problems, though. According to eminent experts Robert Sokolow and Jeffrey Greenblatt, et al., keeping global emissions *constant* during the next half-century will require—got a pen?—a doubling in average fuel economy for all vehicles, doubling the global stock of nuclear power plants (that's 700 new plants), creation of new wind power farms the size of Wyoming, solar panels spread out over an area the size of New Jersey, new ethanol farms the size of India, a 100-fold increase in underground CO_2 injection, *AND* a worldwide moratorium on deforestation. Not surprisingly, the scholars didn't put a price tag on their prescriptions.

President Obama promises to transcend our technological incapacity by "fast tracking" alternative fuels. But the problem is there is no one alternative fuel to fast track. We need innovation, which requires differentiation and selection, not lavishing tax dollars on every idea that purports to be an "alternative fuel."

Hydrogen cars, for example, have been dreamt about since the writings of Jules Verne in the 19th century. GM boasted in 1998 that they planned to release a hydrogen vehicle by 2004, but that didn't happen. Despite billions of dollars spent by governments in order to "fast track" this admittedly exciting technology, progress is slow. GM now expects its hydrogen vehicles to reach production capacity within the next few decades. But will they? No one knows—not even President Obama.

Undeterred, Obama believes he can "get 1 million 150-mpg plug-in hybrids on our roads within six years." In the scathing response of George Will:

> This [president], who has never run so much as a Dairy Queen, is going to get a huge, complex industry to produce, and is going to get a million consumers to buy, these cars. How? Almost certainly by federal financial incentives for both – billions of dollars of tax subsidies for automakers and billions more to

bribe customers to buy these cars they otherwise would spurn. Conservatives are sometimes justly accused of ascribing magic powers to money and markets: Increase the monetary demand for anything, and the supply will expand. But it is liberals like Obama who think that any new technological marvel or other social delight can be summoned into existence by a sufficient [government] appropriation.[239]

Indeed; it takes a special kind of arrogance to assume that politicians can foresee, facilitate and evaluate the kind of technological progress that is impossible for any single human being to foresee, facilitate and evaluate.

The hazards of misplaced government intervention are clear. Equal funding for prospective alternative technologies fails to aid the essential discovery of the vital few. Worse than the waste of funds, subsidies inhibit the development of new technologies by keeping its inferior competitors alive and on even footing.

The solution, however, is as simple as empowering differentiation, selection and amplification. Given that no individual knows with certainty which alternative fuel(s) will usher in the low-carbon future, the opportunity for new fuels should be maximized, as well as the opportunity for public evaluation in the marketplace. While government investment is essential, the free choice of the people should be maximized as much as possible.

Given that no individual knows with certainty which alternative fuel(s) will usher in the low-carbon future, the opportunity for new fuels should be maximized, as well as the opportunity for public evaluation in the marketplace.

Traditional economic theory gives a useful approximation for public goods, or goods that government must provide because markets will not provide them efficiently. According to economists, public goods are those goods that are *nonrival*, meaning that one person's use does not diminish the ability for another to acquire it, and *non-excludable*, meaning that it is impossible (or near-impossible) to prevent individuals from enjoying the good. Such principles fit nicely into evolutionary choice theory; public goods are those goods in which differentiation is impossible. Thus, differentiation should still always be the goal of government investment.

Unfortunately, interference with differentiation is commonplace, with well-meaning regulators possessing their own arbitrary ideas of what alternative fuels should look like. Such regulations only squelch technological experimentation and freedom of choice. A recent report by the Business Roundtable identified 38 separate regulatory barriers to the development of new low-carbon alternative fuels.[240] The report featured such experiences as:

"A large manufacturing company reported that it wanted to convert several plants from burning coal and oil in its powerhouses to less carbon- intensive natural gas. Even though coal emits three times the NOx of natural gas and oil emits two-and-a-half times, it took the company almost two- and-a-half years to convince EPA that this change should not trigger the Clean Air Act's New Source Review permitting process and additional control technology review."

"A 1997 U.S. Department of Energy (DOE) report found that two-thirds of all [hydroelectric energy] projects relicensed since 1986 lost generation capacity as a result of the [Department's] relicensing process. In another DOE report, five U.S. national laboratories found that relicensing results in an average loss of 8 percent in hydropower generation capacity [due to the licensing process]."

"Federal and state regulations of motor vehicle emissions consist of conflicting standards that impede the development of more energy-efficient and environmentally superior technologies. These regulations also fail to account for the inherent trade-off between safety and fuel economy. Fuel economy standards encourage vehicle downsizing and the substitution of lighter weight materials...[but] lean-burn direct injection gasoline engines and compression ignition direct injection (CIDI), or diesel engines, offer substantial fuel economy improvements without compromising auto safety and still offer the customer the performance and utility needed. Yet, because these engines fall slightly short of current emissions requirements for NOxand particulates, they face a daunting challenge under EPA's recently announced Tier 2 standards and an almost insurmountable challenge under standards recently announced by the California Air Resources Board (CARB)."[241]

Such examples are only a few of the ways that governments can interfere with necessary differentiation. Amazingly, these laws that the Business Roundtable cites are actually trying to *encourage* the development of alternative fuels. It's not that politicians and their bureaucrat partners are trying to inhibit progress. The problem is that they don't know what progress looks like.

The true challenge we face as a nation in the 21st century isn't a lack of political willpower; it's a lack of know-how, and the politician-bureaucrats have none of it. The best thing they can do is not stand in the way of the innovators.

Risk entrepreneurs

Another essential fact about technological evolution is that new advancements are adopted through an extremely delicate and complex process. History is full of brilliant technologies that were universally spurned upon their introduction, with tiny but fatal flaws, only to be resurrected in similar or identical form, years or even decades later.

The reason for such seemingly inexplicable difficulties is the complex adaptive networks in which such technologies operate. Any computer user who has installed a software "update" that wreaked havoc with an otherwise functional (if nominally outdated) version of the software is aware of such difficulties.

The same risk of incompatibility applies to the development of new social technologies; few good ideas are immune from bad implementation. For a few examples, one can read about "shock therapy" privatization in the former Soviet Union, which was intended to increase consumer choice but ended up causing widespread corruption and recession; or green-minded government investment in America, intended to encourage ethanol and other biofuels but instead raised the global price of food and lavished billions on inefficient corporations.

Differentiation can take two major forms. The first type is through piecemeal improvements; biologists have long noted that gradual mutation is at the heart of natural evolution. The second type of differentiation is the creation of wholly new technologies, represented by the type of quantum-leap black swan innovations that radically expand the realm of the possible. Technological evolution combines both features, and finding the dynamic balance between the two requires free choice.

Put simply, most new technologies are too risky for immediate wide-spread adoption. Marketing experts are familiar with the "product lifecycle," by which a new product becomes adopted through a process of stages. At the beginning, only the risk-inclined (called "innovators" or "early adopters") take a chance on the new offering. These individuals evaluate the product, which often can lead to valuable feedback allowing the company to refine and improve the item. Finally, the product becomes sufficiently developed to be adopted by the mainstream consumer, and eventually the risk-averse "late adopters" and "laggards."

New technologies must be tested, refined and modified. Many of the innovators and early adopters in an economy are the ones who have the means to take such risks. Air conditioning and the automobile, for instance, were once considered mere toys of the rich, so lavish and impractical to never be capable of mainstream adoption. But as the technologies evolved, they became staples of the middle class.

Rich entrepreneurs

In a society of people with varying talents and ideas with varying value, inequality is inevitable. Evolutionary theory as well as systems theory have confirmed the endogenous creation of inequity in adaptive network growth.

Economic differentiation is essential to evolution. As we've seen, the rich perform an important function in the adaptive network of the economy by taking on the risk of new innovations in order that they may eventually become ready for mainstream adoption.

Again, Mr. Buckley:

> The function of the rich as risk capitalists is so childishly easy to understand as to escape the attention of people who can think only in ideologized ellipses.... Let the rich be, is my motto. It is no more my burden to defend the rich than to excuse the poor. Some people *will* be rich. Some people *will* be poor... what should be the point is that the rich are a natural state of affairs, a healthy state of affairs, and we should carefully scruti-nize our deeper motives when we talk about the buffoonery of

H.L. Hunt or the Medicean gall of Nelson Rockefeller. Surely if we can survive free speech, which means Wayne Morse, and a free press, which means the *New York Times* editorials, we can survive Mr. Hunt's self-subsidizing utopianism, and Mr. Rockefeller's flotillas of self-concern, which bombard our political defenses from time to time... There are the deserving rich, and the undeserving rich, and we should as individuals treat them individually rather than as a class.[242]

People will always have varying degrees of success in the marketplace, but that's not something to be upset about. The interdependence of modern economies means that prosperity spreads over time.

The discussion of network growth in Chapter 3 is relevant to these issues. In growth phases of networks, resource distributions become extremely skewed, creating great inequity. But in structured phases, the system eventually self-corrects, consolidating gains and more equally distributing resources. It is thus important to see aggregate distributions of income not as permanent indicators of some underlying economic reality, but rather temporary signals of economic change.

John F. Kennedy famously remarked that "a rising tide lifts all boats," referring to the fact that economic growth in a society benefits even its poorest members. Well before Kennedy, Adam Smith remarked that when society is "advancing to further acquisition...the condition of the laboring poor, of the great body of the people, seems to be the happiest."[243]

Economic differentiation is an essential force behind the gains of globalization. Today, stories abound of poor people around the world harnessing modern physical and social technologies to aid their development. As one example, Kenya's largest publicly traded company, Safaricom—with an $800 million IPO—has nothing to do with diamonds, but cell phones instead. Globalization is not simply a race for cheap resources; it is a discovery process for life-improving technologies.

In recognizing differentiation as the key to evolutionary progress, we can arrive at a whole new perspective on economic issues. Instead of fighting aggregate income inequality, we should concentrate on improving individual welfare and maximizing opportunity. Instead of seeking to preserve old business models or industries, we should maximize competition and aid transitions to new endeavors. Instead of seeking to shut out the world, we should embrace the new ideas that emerge from the global marketplace.

The other side of the coin

Globalization is often accused of causing a culturally bland world. But in fact, it enhances differentiation and allows diverse societies to flourish. As Tyler Cowen put it:

> Around the world, growing numbers of niche consumers are pursuing a fantastic variety of cultural interests and passions, from Indonesian gamelan music to African cinema to the post-colonial fiction of Third World writers. The array of cultural choices available to a person in a single book or CD superstore would have been beyond the imagining of anybody living a century ago. The world has more experts who know more about a greater number of cultural phenomena than ever before. Even the most obscure corners of global culture have their partisans, who study and appreciate them with great fervor, often aided by the Internet and other new technologies....The flowering of various folk arts -- from Haitian naive painting to Tuvan throat singing in Mongolia -- during the past few decades has been driven largely by Western demand, materials and technologies of production. Canada's Inuit, for example, did not practice sculpture on a large scale until an outsider introduced them to soapstone carving in 1948. Since then, sculpture has flourished among the Inuit, and they have developed other arts, enjoying an artistic and commercial success that has allowed them to maintain many of their traditional ways of life.[244]

Far from turning the world into a homogenous culture, globalization enhances social diversity. Take the experience of McDonalds in France. Despite claims that the fast food company is on an international warpath dedicated to creating a bland and homogenous McWorld, freedom of choice has proven to be quite the effective shield:

> In France...[McDonald's] franchisees face increasing competition from fast baguettes. Half of this nation's 932 McDonalds outlets have been upgraded to a level that would make them almost unrecognizable to an American. Far from being cookie-cutter copies, each of the remodeled restaurants features one of at least eight different themes - such as "mountain", complete

with a wood-beam ceiling reminiscent of a ski chalet. The company has even begun to replace its traditional red and yellow signs with signs in muted tones of maroon and mustard. And while the basic burger offerings remain the same, there is espresso and brioche.[245]

And with that question of culture, on to the next chapter we go...

6

THE CULTURAL EVOLUTION
Solving the contentious social issues that divide America

CULTURAL AND SOCIAL ISSUES are among the most contentious disputes in contemporary American politics, but evolutionary choice theory can help explain why such a hostile *Kulturkampf* is unnecessary. Social-technological evolution occurs in a way that neither the Right nor the Left seems to fully appreciate.

Carry on tradition

Dobzhansky argued that "the biological uniqueness of man" lies in the fact that the human species alone has evolved culture.[246] As we mentioned in Chapter 3, there is great value in network structure; society's reliance on tradition, history and collective norms is well-placed. As James Surowiecki argued, given the limitations of individual rationality, reliance on the insights learned by others can be an effective way of gathering information. Similarly, Hayek believed that tradition is "in some respects superior to, or 'wiser' than human reason."[247]

Of course, while some traditions can be beneficial, not all traditions are. This point needs no further explanation, other than the citation of slavery, feudalism, imperialism and segregation, as just a few examples of time-honored institutions that were later repudiated.

The associative decisions of a free people remain the ultimate arbiter of a tradition's beneficial relevance. Traditions face a unique selection process of *group selection*, through which adherents adjudicate the fitness of a given tradition in achieving long-term social goals. Group selection, a process by which groups compete with each other, explains the slow yet important evolution of social cues, group sanction and other collective norms.

This evaluative process, however, still requires free choice. Hayek writes, "It is only where the individual has choice, and its inherent responsibility, that he has occasion to affirm existing values, to contribute to their further growth, and to earn moral merit."[248]

Hayek continues, "Most of the steps in the evolution of culture were made possible by some individuals breaking some traditional rules and practicing new forms of conduct—not because they understood them to be better, but because the groups which acted upon them prospered more than others and grew."[249]

The philosopher Rudolf Steiner echoed similar sentiments, arguing, "[A]ll...objectively ethical laws...sprang from the intuitions of free spirits. There is no law enforced by family authority that was not once intuitively conceived and formulated as such by an ancestor. Even the conventional laws of morality are first established by specific persons."[250]

Or as Karl Popper put it, "The authoritarian will in general select those who obey, who believe, and who respond to his influence. But in doing so, he is bound to select mediocrities. For he excludes those who revolt, who doubt, and who dare to resist his influence."[251]

Granted, the idea of such cultural evolution still sounds controversial, especially to those social Luddites who think social norms should simply stay the same, and perhaps equally to those social anarchists who think traditions are all worthless. But both objections are misplaced. As sociologist Emile Durkheim recognized, the growth of complexity is the main index of progress;[252] and complex social evolution, despite its occasional discomfort, works to *everyone's* benefit.

So, how does any of this help address so many of the intractable and divisive social issues of the day? Let's find out.

Do this in remembrance of Me

Christian traditionalists, such as James Dobson's Focus on the Family, argue that government effort is needed to preserve the social technology of Christianity in the modern world. But their position defeats their whole argument. Whence the insufficiency of volition?

Christianity long flourished when it was illegal (and its worship punished by death) in a large portion of the world. Yet, we are to believe government coddling is necessary in order to save the faith. Scholars have long noted a correlation between the presence of Judeo-Christian value systems and socio-economic prosperity.[253] Yet we are to believe people are incapable of discovering the correlation themselves. The empirical benefits of marriage are well documented; yet, we are told the institution is under attack, particularly by same-sex couples who seek to experience said benefits.

Apocalyptic evangelicals embarrass themselves in their rigid opposition to social change because the evolution of Christian doctrines over time is self-evident. Take Martin Luther's theological rebellion, as he dared to question various time-honored Christian practices. Luther's views got him arrested and indicted for heresy at the time, but through decades and centuries of debate, discussion, revolutions and excommunications, the Protestant mentality flourished as an accepted brand of Christian hermeneutics. This doctrinal schism is directly responsible for the growth of the modern evangelical movement, and therefore, directly responsible for giving James Dobson a job.

Christianity may arguably be waning in cultural popularity in the 21st century, but such trends are not more threatening than anything the faith has faced and overcome previously through its intrinsic power. Were evangelicals to recognize their true mission of choice—that is, to persuade the world to voluntarily adopt Christian doctrines as the superior mode of living—their effectiveness would be greatly enhanced. It is true that Christian ethics have formed the bedrock of Western civilization, but it is also true that the applied ethics have evolved and changed over centuries.

> *Christianity may arguably be waning in cultural popularity in the 21st century, but such trends are not more threatening than anything the faith has faced and overcome previously through its intrinsic power.*

Yet instead of recognizing their own failures, many seek objects to blame, such as Enemy #1, America's lascivious culture. One conservative writer recently complained that evangelicals' pious messages were "getting hard to hear in a prurient culture obsessed with youth and selfish pleasure."[254] Yes. Let's blame our unpopularity on our own unpopularity, shall we? The problem is that culture is created by the free associative decisions of the people within that culture, and no one else.

The "marketing" of religion—the usage of persuasive outreach to attract worshippers to a given cause—is one of the distinguishing features of American religion.[255] In America, every human has complete control over the direction of his or her spiritual passions. As we saw in Chapter 1, American spirituality flourishes under freedom of choice, and that's why freedom of choice is still the friend of the evangelical. Free choice, in aiding the triumph of Luther and Rick Warren's Saddleback Church alike, is the evolutionary arbiter.

Furthermore, Christians are free to express themselves and associate in ways that may seem offensive to others. Freedom of expression means that individuals should be free to express their faith in a manner they find most appropriate.

Skeptics and atheists may dislike this fact, but remember, no one else is to blame for the unpopularity of your views. In the words of the political theorist Robert Nozick, "[A] recalcitrant individual [may have] no alternative [except] to conform. Still, the others do not force to him conform, and his rights are not violated. He has no right that the others cooperate in making his nonconformity feasible."[256]

Not Another Brick in the Wall

Another essential social technology is education, and much like religion, its authentic content remains a highly controversial debate. Also much like religion, its cause has partisans who warn that the absence of government mandates will result in the continuing decline of society.

The controversy largely stems from the complexity of the issue, and that every politician seems to have his own ideas about how to run it all. The social technology of education is really a bundle of numerous pedagogical social technologies, with few (if any) established universal truths. Small class sizes may correlate to better education, but how small, and at what costs? Strict discipline and tolerance may each be effective teaching methods, but which works more often, and under what conditions? How should we evaluate performance? Test scores in math, science and history? How about

Name:_____   Date:_____

U.S. DEPARTMENT OF EDUCATION
Test of Academic Aptitude

Directions: Answer the following 100 questions based on the rote memorization that you have been taught over your public school career. No critical thinking is required. The questions, just like all things we teach you, have little or no bearing on real problems in real life.

Your score on this test will be used to determine whether your school gets a new soccer field next year, or maybe whether your teacher has her job next year, depending on the decision of the Test Administrator. Good luck!

---

1. In the war of 1812, the commander of the British navy was a decorated and admired military veteran. He also had a dog, and his dog's name was:

   a) Sparkey
   b) Limey
   c) Flash
   d) Bruce

No child left behind

improvement? Average or universal?

The difficulties in selecting the "perfect" educational social technology counsels experimentation and free choice. Unfortunately, instead of encouraging differentiation, public school education fosters one-size-fits-all approaches. Teachers get paid no matter how well they do. Curricula are set by state bureaucrats, and increasingly, federal bureaucrats.[257]

As we've emphasized, effective selection of social technologies takes place at the individual level. Parents, teachers and students are the best sources to discover the effectiveness of educational provisions, and new approaches should be encouraged.

A great example of such innovation is the Harlem Children's Zone, a semi-private institute in New York's most infamous ghetto. The HCZ was founded by Geoff Canada, who realized that a traditional public school would be insufficient to achieve the kind of changes necessary to improve the lives of at-risk children. Instead, the HCZ combines health, education and social services and delivers them from kindergarten through college in a variety of innovative programs. Currently, 6,500 children live in the Zone, 88% of children under 18 in the HCZ's 24-block core neighborhood are already served by at least one program, and the HCZ has now extended its outreach into the larger 60-block zone.[258]

70% of the Harlem Children Zone's funding is private, and the private support has allowed a level of experimentation in programs that no public school can match. Its new charter school, The Promise Academy, is housed in a $42 million building, with a teacher-student ratio of 1 to 6, state-of-the-art science labs, a first-class gym and a restaurant-quality cafeteria serving only healthy food.

Differentiation in the education market recognizes that different approaches should all have a chance to succeed. Sometimes comprehensive approaches like the Harlem Children's Zone work well. Sometimes home-schooling works well. Sometimes charter schools work well. Sometimes montessori schools work well. Sometimes public schools work well. The point of these examples is not to propose panaceas, but rather to articulate a system that encourages beneficial innovation for the benefit of America's future.

There is no incompatibility between providing K12 education free of charge (a legitimate goal of government) and giving parents choice regarding educational options. Toward this end, government-funded school vouchers can give lower income parents the ability to choose the school that educates their children best.

Free education doesn't need to be provided in just one way. State boards should instead develop schemes of accreditation that are flexible but establish minimum levels of educational quality; this would leave the development of new social-technological innovations to schools and teachers, respectively.

Distinct from America's one-size-fits-all K12 public school system, our universities are a wonderful example of the benefits of differentiation. A panoply of higher education options gives prospective students hundreds of choices to experience higher education. As a result, it's not surprising to see American universities dominating the world in nearly every conceivable measure.

However, all is not perfect in the ivory tower. A questionable system of tenure that makes it virtually impossible to remove professors from their jobs, plus an overreliance on government research grants that reduces the real-world relevance of university research, has made American colleges increasingly homogenous and out of touch.

All the news that fits your views?

Another area where misguided idealists persist in imaginary visions of One Best Way is journalism. For some reason, despite all evidence to the contrary, American media has persevered in a delusional worship of "objectivity" in news reporting. What is objective? Well, it's a perspective that everyone would agree with.

But hold on. In a world of 6 billion people and only a limited amount of time and space for the media to tell you what has happened in a single day, something's obviously going to miss the final cut. The decision of what's Newsworthy varies greatly according to the personal opinions of the audience. If you're liberal, you want to hear about starving Darfuri children and Hugo Chavez' latest economic proposal. If you're conservative, you want to hear about the latest terrorist raid in Pakistan and global market trends.

What most mainstream Americans think of the political center is considered conservative by European standards, socialist by Lew Rockwell standards, and fascist by Ralph Nader standards. This is why serious writers have written books called *Weapons of Mass Distortion: The Coming Meltdown of the Liberal Media* and *What Liberal Media? The Truth About Bias and the News.* This is also why some people think media reporting on Iraq is treasonous disrespect to our troops, and other people think it's an oil-driven corporate conspiracy to silence popular dissent. The uncomfortable fact is that true media objectivity—especially on contentious political issues—is simply an illusion.

The well-meaning effort to provide "equal access" to opposing views assumes a uniformity (or precise duality) of opinion that truly does not exist. There aren't two sides to a story any more than there is only one viewpoint. To recognize reality is to recognize the inevitability of bias in individual journalists; we are, after all, talking about human beings.

It just so happens that those who work in the mass media, like journalists, actors and writers, tend to have opinions more liberal than the average American. It's also the case that people want to listen to them more than economists, preachers or talk radio pundits, who tend to be more conservative than the average American. This doesn't mean that the media is a failure—it just means different people think differently. It's the average American's job to evaluate these different perspectives.

> **The well-meaning effort to provide "equal access" to opposing views assumes a uniformity (or precise duality) of opinion that truly does not exist.**

Objectivity isn't one correct viewpoint. It's the expression of every viewpoint. As *The Economist* observed, bias in news reporting is more often indicative of a healthy society.[259]

Everyone knows that informed consumers shop around and consider all of their options. So why would consumers of news behave any different? The response to media bias is the same response to low product quality in any other industry: Shop around. Ask your friends and coworkers for their opinions on an issue. Go online and research the issue. Go to a newsstand and read different views on the issue. Those who assume the bias of the media is something to worry about assume that people aren't capable of making decisions for themselves. And anyone ignorant enough to be politically duped by media bias is ignorant enough to be duped by a spouse, a pastor or a boss as well.

Perhaps media bias was a problem in 1954 when the average household had three TV channels, but in the modern internet age, it's nothing more than an imaginary crisis. Want a fair and balanced perspective? Go visit wsj. com, nyt.com, ft.com, bbc.com, nationalreview.com, huffingtonpost.com, and aljazeera.com. Then decide for yourself what you believe.

The principle of intellectual self-reliance was aptly summed up by Beatle George Harrison, in the song "Think For Yourself":

Do what you want to do
And go where you're going to
Think for yourself
'Cause I won't be there with you

Is technology a threat?

Depending on who you ask, the growth of the internet can either be a boon for the spread of information, communication and commerce; or it can be an apocalyptic invasion of cultural decay, social fragmentation and ignorance. Like most arguments over the ultimate social impact of a new technology, the answer depends on the choices of the people using it.

On the decay side, and perhaps as a cyber affirmation of Sturgeon's Law, gossip sites like PerezHilton.com are among the most popular in the world. In fact, the number one use of the internet is the acquisition of pornography. Most people clearly aren't using their freedom for socially positive purposes. But, some have used it to achieve unprecedented feats of human knowledge. So what should we do?

My view of technology is that of Robert M. Pirsig in *Zen and the Art of Motorcycle Maintenance*, in that technology's value is created by the people who use it, and that it harbors great potential or harmful risk depending on the choices of its human users.

Or as Denis de Rougemont put it in the context of the telephone years earlier, "If you run to answer, irritated by the noise, it is you who expected something which you wanted not to miss. So you are only your own slave."[260]

The solution is to effectively differentiate the internet in order to allow people to embrace its positive information-enhancing and communication-enhancing aspects. Most would agree with this, but the content of that goal is widely disputed.

The blog, for example, is heralded by many as a superior form of information dissemination. The question is, can this complex network eventually self-regulate? Philosopher Cass Sunstein thinks not. Sunstein argues that the blog network cannot evolve the spontaneous order that Friedrich

Hayek is famous for promoting. Hayek contended that the price system in the marketplace helps disseminate information. And because blogs lack a pricing system, Sunstein strangely concludes that information cannot be effectively disseminated in the blogosphere.

Now, Hayek certainly argued that the price system serves as an informational mechanism; in fact, the argument won him the Nobel Prize. But Hayek never claimed that the price system was the *exclusive* method of spreading information; quite the contrary, he argued that tradition, imitation and the spontaneous behavior of crowds, to name a few, yielded similar effects. Hayek's insights about informational dissemination were not limited to the price system any more than Darwin's evolutionary discoveries were limited to the flora and fauna of the Galapagos islands.

As Hayek would agree, free choice and the wisdom of crowds serve the same evaluative purpose that the price system does in the marketplace. Thanks to the growing development of blog tracking technology and other tools, web surfers can find and filter the information they desire. As the system develops, web traffic levels become an increasingly accurate indicator of relevance. In this sense, the internet is best thought of as the Wild West in 19th century America: anarchic, dangerous and unpredictable, but also worth the experiment.[261]

> *...the internet is best thought of as the Wild West in 19th century America: anarchic, dangerous and unpredictable, but also worth the experiment.*

One heartening trend is the government's general reluctance to regulate internet content with the same moral fervor with which the FCC regulates television and radio broadcast content. The FCC's approach to the latter is easily denounced by evolutionary choice theory in its ill-advised assumption that there is one level of "decency" to enforce nationwide.

Most Americans are not children, and most of those who are do not require government censorship to aid in their moral upbringing. Parents who are incapable of screening their child's entertainment are the last people who should ask the government to play Mommy for them, leaving millions of independent adults bereft of entertainment in the process. The desire to avoid watching certain television shows, in a free society, is achieved by changing the channel—not by the government fining the TV station.

Besides, a child's exposure to the modern indecent world is hardly fatal. When I was in fifth grade, my friends and I used to surreptitiously listen to Dexter Holland of the band The Offspring call a fellow driver a "stupid dumbshit goddam motherfucker" and we thought it was the greatest thing ever. Like the fictionalized third-grade children of *South Park* and most of my real-life peers in the Modern Era of NWA and Eminem, we were undoubtedly attracted to profanity and other forms of adult entertainment.

Yet, we somehow found a way to retain our ethical mores and avoid spiraling into devil-worship. Proof: Despite my voluntary exposure to pro-fanity, a phenomenon called Good Parenting allowed me to later graduate college in three years, go on to law school, and write the book that you are reading now. Really, I'm not sure if the FCC would view me as an aberration or the Antichrist.

Amazingly, even the Tube Czar, FCC Chairman Kevin Martin, argued that choice might solve the problem of indecency over the airwaves. Martin cited that subscription television services can give customers the option of blocking channels they find offensive. "Permitting parents to have more choice in the channels they receive may prove to be the best solution to content concerns," he observed in an unexpected moment of enlightenment.

In other words, free choice can solve this contentious issue. One presumes that this is the unstated Federal policy on internet decency as well. Too bad it will also put Mr. Martin—and his fellow thought police at the FCC—out of a job.

That music is garbage!

Cultural historians must be greatly amused by the hilarious regularity with which fans of "old-fashioned" or "classic" art forms berate the prolifera-tion of new music that they deem "trashy," "awful" or "uncultured."

I am not a professional music critic, so I won't pain the reader long with my layman musings. But I believe it is necessary to stand up to the curmudgeonly cultural Luddites who believe that nothing of lasting value was created in the past half-century of popular music.

Fans of Bach may tout his skill, but one must recognize that true classic art is extremely rare. The fact is that only a handful of such great composers over a period of several centuries are remembered as classics.

The beauty of the evolutionary process is that it eventually finds the proverbial diamonds in the rough. For example, Mozart wrote what are considered his three greatest symphonies at the end of his career, when he was ill, in debt and rejected by his patrons.

As Albert Einstein noted in his biography of the great composer, the innovation was typical of artistic progress, in all of its spontaneous idiosyncrasies. "We know nothing about the occasion for writing these [symphonies]," Einstein wrote, "but [they are] perhaps symbolic of human endeavor, representing no occasion, [or] no immediate purpose."

Through the choice-driven verdict of music history, brilliance is extracted while the pedestrian (or even atrocious) majority become long-forgotten. As music historian Leonard B. Meyer notes, even if one rejects evolutionary explanations, the history of musical art is still the result of the succession of choices made by individuals.[262]

The filtration of quality over time—in essence, the creation of music tradition—is a complex adaptive process. Like other adaptive processes, music follows the law of the vital few, Sturgeon's Law and the laws of the black swan, among others. Therefore, I sympathize with my elders' revulsion regarding the state of top 40 radio; my personal list of rubbish on today's charts includes Jo Jo, Soulja Boy and Britney Spears, and I agree that in the long tail age of music, there is a lot more garbage these days. I don't even watch MTV anymore. As a fan of classical and jazz music, I intimately understand the criticisms of the elder generations.

But I also believe there are elements in modern culture that will be destined for classic remembrance, and that history teaches us this. For example, despite being crowned as "awful", "appallingly dogmatic," "kings of antimusic" and subject to staged boycotts, the Beatles are increasingly recognized as some of the greatest musical composers and innovators of all time. The Beatles wrote classic tunes that have been covered thousands if not millions of times by everyone from jazz musicians to professional symphonies. Similarly, I believe 21st century art can and will render such timeless production.

The pessimism of such old school music critics, in my view, is strikingly akin to Malthusian pessimism, convincing itself that the presence of inferior options means that superior options will never arise. These critics are evidently incapable of learning lessons from the fact that both jazz music and the Beatles were once derided—in remarkably similar terms to which today's critics denounce today's music—as unmusical, cacophonous and/or immoral. The following section is necessary to disabuse America's modern culture warriors of such misconceptions, and inform them as to the lesson that musical evolution is even smarter than they are.

Those looking for a talented and classically brilliant musician alive today should give a listen to Portland, Oregon's Matt Ward, who goes by the stage name M. Ward. Each of Ward's albums achieves an unparalleled level of thematic creativity. Ward produces original songs that draw on styles from Dylanesque folk rock to advanced synthesized productions, as well as covers that range from a classical guitar adaptation of Bach's "The Well Tempered Clavier" to a warmly acoustic version of David Bowie's "Let's Dance."

Ward's third album, *Transistor Radio*, hearkens back to the 1930s and 1940s, with brilliant low-fi acoustic recordings. His magnificent fourth album *Post-War* is a diverse collection of tunes intended to aid the healing process of a nation after warfare, and has gained effusive praise from outlets ranging from *Rolling Stone* to National Public Radio. M. Ward is, in my opinion, among the greatest living songwriters today.

Perhaps even greater innovation, in my view, is demonstrated in the genre of modern hip-hop. Despite many admitted examples of Sturgeon's Law, the genre features highly intelligent rappers with unmatched rhetorical skills, who combine lucid social commentary, self-help inspiration and engaging biographies. I am a huge fan of hip-hop, even as I can recognize its often low quality. I am also keenly aware of its unpopularity in the grumpy critics of contemporary culture who only see that low quality and dismiss the genre outright.

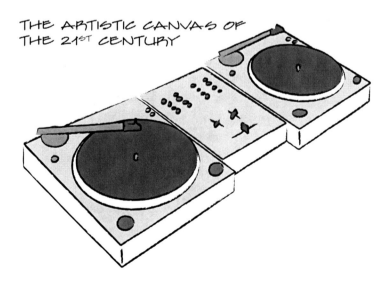

THE ARTISTIC CANVAS OF THE 21ST CENTURY

I would be remiss if I were not to defend this innovative and brilliant art form as an evolved musical technology like any other; one with its shortcomings and drawbacks, but also its unconventional production of social value.

Perhaps the greatest social-technological advantage of hip-hop music is its inspiring entrepreneurial ambitions. The goal to which many songs are dedicated is nothing less than the rescue of millions of at-risk, low-income young Americans. If there is one aspect where rappers can be role models, it is unquestionably through the example of self-improvement, entrepreneurship and hard work.

In this regard, few rappers can compare to Brooklyn's Sean Carter, who goes by the stage name Jay-Z. Rising from poverty in the Marcy housing projects of Brooklyn, Carter, CEO of his own record company and clothing line, is now worth an estimated $300 million. Carter's raps are filled with the type of passionate ambition that makes J.P. Morgan look like a lazy slob; Jay-Z represents a message to dream big, work hard and never give up.

Musically, hip-hop merges modernized lyrical poetry with beats inspired from nearly every genre of modern music. The beats, at their best, can help resurrect classic artists for modern audiences, as well as break new barriers in electronic music production.

In addition to the production, the rapper performs two distinct duties. First, his or her spoken words must function as a musical instrument. Rather than a melodic effect as in traditional music, the voice acquires a rhythmic quality, becoming part of the beat of the song. Second, the words afford the rapper creativity. Constrained within few rules of poetry beyond rhyming requirements, rappers can discuss a greater array of topics within a musical framework. The most talented rappers use multiple entendres combined with inflections and pronunciations to enhance the rhythmic value.

I feel compelled to give examples of such poetry, convinced that the skeptical reader needs additional evidence to believe what I just wrote. Given that this book is about evolution generally and not about the evolution of hip-hop, I can only give a few.

I hope these examples can give the reader a better appreciation of the ways that rappers, despite the popular view otherwise, can actually produce social technological evolution. In an effort to bridge the linguistic gap between standard English and the vernacular of the hip-hop culture, I have tried to include translations of relevant terms or subjects in footnotes, in order to help all readers appreciate the poetic value of hip-hop.

I'll begin with Jay-Z, and his impassioned defense of the social value of his music, in the song "Renegade":

> Say that I'm foolish, that I only talk about jewels
> Do you fools listen to music, or do you just skim through it?
> See, I'm influenced by the ghetto you ruined
> That same dude you gave nothin', I made somethin' doin'
> What I do through and through and
> I give you the news with a twist, it's just his ghetto point-of-view
> The renegade; you've been afraid
> I penetrate pop culture, bring 'em a lot closer to the block where they
> Pop toasters[263], and they live with their moms
> Got dropped roadsters[264], from botched robberies niggaz crotched over[265]
> Mommy's knocked up[266] 'cause she wasn't watched over
> Knocked down by some clown, when child support knocked
> No, he's not around;
> Now how that sound to ya? Jot it down
> I bring it through the ghetto without ridin' 'round,
> Hidin' down, duckin' strays from frustrated youths stuck in their ways
> Just read a magazine that fucked up my day
> How you rate music that thugs with nothin' relate to it?
> I help them see their way through it - not you
> Can't step in my pants, can't walk in my shoes
> Bet everything you worth; you lose your tie and your shirt
> ...
> No lie, just know I chose my own fate
> I drove by the fork in the road and went straight

In the song "Seasons," the creatively-titled rap group Cunninlynguists constructs a masterful narrative of hip-hop's history. In the song, the group laments much of the poor quality in contemporary hip-hop, poetically framing the evolution of the genre within the four seasons.

The irony is not only that the song denounces the state of hip-hop in a way that America's pundits would appreciate, if they only knew about it, but also that its indictment is so much more creative, eloquent and effective than any of those anti-rap culture warriors could have done themselves. Even more profoundly distinct from the grumpy pessimism of the gerontocracy, "Seasons" ends with an impassioned defense of optimism, with the hope that in the impending thaw of spring, substance and quality will finally return to the genre.

Here are some relevant excerpts from the song, footnotes included:

As we spring back to the past, it was all happening fast
When b-boys danced to the latest jam[267]
You could say this man was the greatest fan
Songs started to drop[268] - Ain't nobody start at the top
This is way before SPs and MPCs[269]
And long before CDs and MP3s
The game started to bloom and blossom[270]
And Masta's ready for the ceremony, like a groom in costume[271]
Growth from the rain of the previous years
I took notes from what I heard through these devious ears

As Summer's heat waves ascended in a splendid manner
Green was flooding our scene,[272] although the skin was tanner
Talent pools were full and fresh for swimming
Backstrokin' through Dark Sides and Illmatic beginnings[273]
Free speech pollination kept bees colonizing in hives
And stung Delores Tucker right in her pride[274]
The Tribe's ocean splash was rising the tide[275]
Strictly for my niggaz that were ready to die in the ride[276]
I wish the summer's vibe could've lasted forever
Too bad we had to have a change in that weather...

As the East vs. West winds blew
Causing two legends to fall like maple leaves from escalated beef[277]
Assumed that the worst was over
Til these cats started wearing shiny costumes like the 31st of October[278]
The weather's colder, but the word jacket
Is what they did to people's styles, not what they covered they backs with[279]
Tactics of the skill impaired
No limit to what they'll do when the green is scarce
No respect for the pilgrims who paved the way
So you could rock that pop crap and Plymouth Rock-Rap[280]
Born to roll, so I'm taking you back to school days of autumn

Before the bottom dropped out in 2K...

By the dawn of the new millennium, we saw bright chains
Winter brought along platinum, causing the ice age[281]
In winter it's snowed in, like the temperature's below ten
Citizens open up shows for more snowmen[282]
Scrawny boys rock bubblegooses to pose like grown men[283]
And you can catch freezer burn from women when they show skin
Jolly, fat, white men get paid when rap hits the shelves
And artists themselves get treated like elves
Matter of fact, Santa's gotten so greedy that when a rapper sells
You even need clearance to sample Jingle Bells! What the hell?
Even at the beaches of Daytona it's gotten colder
But it's about time for the cycle to start over...How we gonna start it?

Waiting for the spring

How *are* we going to start it? As readers of this book know, the spontaneous order of musical evolution is aided by free choice because progress will almost certainly arrive in unconventional ways.

The history of art is testament to the necessity of rebellion. For centuries, artists around the world mindlessly copied the Egyptian method of depicting human feet sideways, in the manipulated stance that would yield the Bangles a Billboard single in the 1980s as well as produce various dance maneuvers of varying entertainment value. But for centuries, artists were forcing every human they painted to Walk Like an Egyptian.

As art historian E.H. Gombrich put it, "It was a tremendous moment in the history of art, when, perhaps a little before 500 BC, artists dared for the first time...to paint a foot, as seen from the front."[284]

The evolutionary wars of expression rage today. Is hip-hop's vivid realism of inner city life a similar artistic advancement to forward facing feet? Cultural conservatives would answer with a resounding "no," but so did their intellectual ancestors answer to the impressionist works of Claude Monet.[285]

Who is right, the radicals or the conservatives? In all such questions, we can only guarantee that, in Prometheus' words, "Time, in his aging course, teaches all things."[286]

Recognizing these facts, we should embrace the evolutionary growth toward music choice, in order to leave the culture warriors to their Bach and leave the Bachs of the coming century to their keyboards, guitars, computers, turntables and microphones.

We should embrace the evolutionary growth toward music choice, in order to leave the culture warriors to their Bach and leave the Bachs of the coming century to their keyboards, guitars, computers, turntables and microphones.

The hazards of mandating goodness

In the complex network of human society, individuals make lifestyle choices for a near infinite variety of reasons. This complexity explains why attempts by governments to mandate good behavior so often backfire.

Take safety legislation, such as the recently enacted California law to require all drivers to use "hands-free" units for cell phones while on the road. A typical example of "one-size-fits-all" legislative solutions to complex problems, the law does nothing to address the fundamental issue of dangerously inattentive drivers; there are a variety of causes, a few of which include mental distraction, fatigue, personal distractions (e.g., children in the back), non-driving behavior (e.g. putting on makeup), and the plain old fallibility of *homo sapiens*.

But California politicians, deftly hurdling such inconvenient facts, decided they knew how to solve the problem and required the use of hands-free units. Unfortunately, hands-free devices are not the panacea, and until California decides to ban car radios, makeup or the presence of children in any vehicle, the law will do virtually nothing to actually improve road safety. (Of course, such vigorous authoritarian pursuit of safety at all costs would be intolerable, and would only serve to further demonstrate the hazards of mandating a preferred social technology—viz. safety—over all else.)

In the end, California's social politburo might succeed in making the state a few dollars by fleecing a few honest citizens who have the misfortune of putting a phone to their ear in front of a police officer. But meanwhile, the risk-inclined multitaskers who have obediently complied with a hands-free unit in their ear now have an extra hand for playing with their navigation system. Is that success?

The defect of paternalistic social programs isn't in their motives or ambitions, but in their initial assumptions that humans are choice-less automatons who cannot or will not adapt to new circumstances. Much like Walrasian economics, it assumes a level of staticity that does not exist in reality.

> *"The defect of paternalistic social programs isn't in their motives or ambitions, but in their initial assumptions that humans are choice-less automatons who cannot or will not adapt to new circumstances."*

Break on through to the other side

The evolutionary paradox undermines much of the rigid absolutism that comprises the current cultural debates. It is helpful to rely on our old friend Hegel, who is one of the few thinkers throughout history to understand that while conceptual opposites are necessary for the development of human understanding, they are not unchanging or absolute.

Before you think this discussion is only the concern of abstract philosophers, you should know about some recent discoveries in quantum mechanics. Until quantum mechanics, physicists had long believed that the distinction between waves and particles was fundamental: given their defintions, all matter could only be one or the other. But Albert Einstein was crucial in establishing the so-called wave/particle duality, that light is both a wave and a particle, and exhibits features of both depending on the environment. Later experiments by Louis-Victor de Broglie and others showed that *all matter* exhibited wave and particle features.[287]

In light of these discoveries (no pun intended), the inadequacies of our conceptual descriptions is apparent. As Heisenberg pointed out, the use of static words for changing conceptions means that "Every word or concept, clear as it may seem to be, has only a limited range of applicability."[288] But as all of us know, this insight didn't stop Heisenberg from expressing himself through words and concepts.

With all of this knowledge, we come full circle from our discussion in Chapter 3 of the paradox of structure and individualism in the evolutionary system. We need both sides, whether it means the classical and quantum, static and dynamic, objective and subjective, structure and independence, or conformity and rebellion, as essential means toward the end of greater knowledge.

Will to power

Even though we humans face a difficult, uncertain and chaotic environment, it doesn't mean we are helpless in the process. In fact, it is the difficulty of this process that justifies our freedom. Dobzhansky argued that human evolution is unique in having what he calls a "plasticity of personality traits", or the ability of individuals to learn and to adapt creatively to new environments.[289]

Similarly, Bergson believed that conscious choice is the liberation of human evolution. He believed that this freedom trumped all forms of reason, logic, and experiential thought, and that through the force of willpower, humans could create progressive evolution. In an enlightening passage, Bergson explains the concept as applied to swimming:

> "If we had never seen a man swim, we might say that swimming is an impossible thing...reasoning always nails us down to the solid ground. But if, quite simply, I throw myself into the water without fear; I may keep myself up well enough at first by merely struggling, and gradually adapt myself to the new environment: I shall thus have learnt to swim. Swimming is an extension of walking, but walking would never have pushed you on to swimming. So you may speculate as intelligently as you will on the mechanism of intelligence; you will never, by this method, succeed in going beyond it. You must take things by storm: you must thrust intelligence outside itself by an act of will."[290]

It's helpful at this point to mention the work of Jean-Baptise de Lamarck, an early evolutionary theorist. Lamarck thought that through the process of "striving", organisms could somehow acquire useful traits that they could pass down to descendents. While Lamarckian evolution has been dismissed in the natural world, many scientists including Stephen Jay Gould

HOW TO EVOLVE

JUST DO IT

argue that human cultural evolution indeed takes a Lamarckian form, allowing humans to quickly adopt new technologies during the course of their own lives.[291]

Evolutionary biologist Julian Huxley famously stipulated a "morality of evolutionary direction", namely that "anything which permits or promotes open development is right, [and] anything which restricts or frustrates development is wrong." According to this perspective, Huxley believed the highest duty of man was to empower the "untapped resources of human beings."[292]

Almost all writers who talk about interdependence or "feedback loops" rightly point out that individuals are influenced by their social environment. But they miss the additional fact, that we mentioned in Chapter 2, that social environments are also influenced by individuals. Thus, any hope of social evolution requires the internal evolution of the people themselves, through the type of striving that Lamarck talked about.

In Ancient Greece, the Oracle of Delphi taught the principle *gnothi seauton:* know thyself. Thinkers from Socrates onward taught that the pursuit of truth and justice arises through self-examination, and evolutionary science confirms the ancient oracle's lesson.

By following the light within and striving to better ourselves, we can create positive change in this world. The willpower of humans represents the ultimate trump card in the evolutionary process.

From this insight, we can circle back to Beinhocker's original conclusion that "wealth is knowledge", with the realization that our own experiential learning thus enriches out own lives. While we benefit from the knowledge of others, we also need to seek the knowledge from within.

So far, this chapter has demonstrated much about what rigid rules cannot do for the benefit of society. In the next chapter, we'll be discussing what they *can* do.

7

THE H.M.S. LEGAL[293]
The evolutionary genius of the American legal system

*I*F THERE'S A POINT on which historians, economists and policy analysts all agree, it's the importance of the rule of law. A fair and equitable legal system provides the necessary foundation for peaceful interpersonal interaction, community development and economic growth.[294]

Despite the law's apparent rigidity, however, it is actually an adaptive social technology that has evolved significantly over time. Arthur Linton Corbin, former Yale Law School professor and respected legal scholar, argued that the "growth of the law is an evolutionary process."[295]

"However 'well-settled' the rules may be," Corbin argued, "their application to life is always uncertain. A rule lives only in its application; apart from that, it is a dead, inert thing. A new and different application of the rule is the creation of a new rule."[296]

The result of this continual rule-adaptation, in constantly evaluating legal rules for their fitness, creates legal evolution. As one scholar put it, this process creates an inevitable "tendency to change, a continuing adjustment to environment, and a process of survival of the fittest, in the course of which the rules of human conduct less fitted to a particular milieu are squeezed out of existence and give way to rules best fitted to that milieu."[297]

But such an idea sounds dangerous to many. Some wonder, how does such legal "evolution" occur without destroying the structural foundation on which society rests?

The answer lies in the emergent property of consensus, through which new legal doctrines are established as binding and ineffective ones are discarded.

We began this book with the concept that America's success was thanks to a system that encouraged political, economic, and social evolution. This chapter is dedicated to finishing that argument, and demonstrating that the American legal structure has built a brilliantly effective framework for the progressive adaptation of social technologies.

The brooding omniscience

The original Anglo-Saxon evolutionary legal innovation is a dynamic system called the common law. The common law is simply a system of judge-made laws. It is distinct from "civil law" systems, such as those in place in Western Europe, where legislators put every law into a volume of laws, and the judges merely apply the written laws directly. In the common law, by contrast, legal rules are derived from the past decisions of common law judges (called "precedent").

Common law has created and modified some of the most essential legal doctrines in American society, from contract law and tort law to property law and corporate law. In all of these areas, rules were created by judges, modified by judges and eliminated by judges.[298]

The great American justice Oliver Wendell Holmes, Jr. believed that the common law was an evolutionary process, through which the "struggle for life among competing ideas" helped yield an "ultimate victory and survival of the strongest."[299]

Holmes believed that the power of choice was essential to evaluate the usefulness of the common law's doctrines according to the "felt necessities of the time." "Whenever a doubtful case arises," Holmes wrote, "what really is before us is a conflict between two social desires which cannot both have their way...[t]the simple tool of logic does not suffice, and even if it is disguised and unconscious, the judges are called on to exercise the sovereign prerogative of *choice*."[300]

Legal theorist Ronald Dworkin argues that the process of common law adjudication is similar to a "chain novel," through which each judge writes a new chapter after each new case. While the judge has the creative freedom to write essentially whatever he or she wants, Dworkin argues, the judge is constrained by the fact that the story must preserve some level of continuity with previous chapters; otherwise, the chapter may be eliminated or at worst, the entire literary project can lose its meaning.[301]

Thus, it is the competitive interplay between ideas on an aggregate level that creates evolutionary growth. As one evolutionary legal theorist writes, "Conscious choice operates at the level of individual decisions; evolution describes the patterns of those decisions at the level of a system."[302]

Much of this concept remains offensive to many legal conservatives, who view the prospect of judges exercising free choice as a recipe for jurisprudential anarchy at best, and societal devolution at worst. How, they charge, can we expect the aggregated decisions of unelected judges to be anything but a disaster?

Thus, it is the competitive interplay between ideas on an aggregate level that creates evolutionary growth.

Similar to the skeptics who doubt the ability of the marketplace to create a spontaneous order, such critics might have logic on their side, but experience belies their skepticism. The common law has been a great success in supporting society and enhancing well-being. Not only has its presence been shown to correlate with higher rates of per capita GDP growth, but legal scholars have consistently found a tendency toward efficient resolution in the common law, even though such a resolution was not the direct result of any single decision.[303]

Recall the point in Chapter 2 that it is not any single choice that represents evolutionary selection, but rather the verdict over time. The common law operates the same way. As philosopher David Hume argues:

> [A single act of justice] is even frequently contrary to the public interest; and were it to stand by itself, without being followed by other acts, may in itself, be very prejudicial to society...Nor is every single act of justice, considered apart, more conducive to private interest than to public...But, however single acts of justice may be contrary...it is certain that the whole plan or scheme is highly conducive, or indeed absolutely requisite, both to support of society and the wellbeing of every individual.[304]

The common law effectively uses the wisdom of crowds to guide American case law; efficient compromises have been shown to spontaneously arise from the experimental processes of the common law.[305] Through the litigation decisions of citizens, outdated legal doctrines may be challenged and new ones created. "The life of the law," Oliver Wendell Holmes wrote, "has not been logic; it has been experience."

Economist Paul Rubin, while arguing that the law was shaped by an "evolutionary mechanism," argued that the choices of litigants were just as essential to legal evolution as the decisions of judges.[306] The litigation decisions of citizens (and their lawyers) create differentiation in the form of cases, arguments and legal doctrines, making efficiency emerge from the chaotic common law selection process.

An evolutionary legal system is essential due to the inevitability of change. Robert C. Clark contends that external technological or social changes continuously create inefficiency in legal rules, which then creates opportunity for new legal rules to adapt to the new circumstances.[307]

The American common law is thus a powerful confirmation of evolutionary choice theory. It maximizes differentiation: each state has its own common law tradition, with its own doctrines, interpretive rules and court structure. It preserves selection: litigants freely choose cases to pursue and judges freely choose doctrines to apply. Finally, it respects amplification: the most popular rulings gain the force of law through *stare decisis*.

Because of the inevitability of change and the uncertainty regarding its evolution, the common law is always necessary to guide society through uncharted legal territory. In the words of Holmes:

"The law is always approaching, and never reaching, consistency. It is forever adopting new principles from life at one end, and it always retains old ones from history at the other...it will become entirely consistent only when it ceases to grow."[308]

The Constitutional Conventions

The genius of American law is our Constitution, which creates a government blueprint that brilliantly combines the open-source legal innovation of the common law with an efficient federal structure.

The Constitution provides a strict separation of powers among the three branches of American government. Congress, for example, retains the exclusive authority to regulate "commerce among the several states" and "declare War," while the President has the authority as "commander-in-chief" to prosecute such wars.

While many of these divisions are clear-cut, others are less so. There are various limitations on government power that have uncertain content. The Fourteenth Amendment, for instance, warns that no state can pass a law abridging the "privileges and immunities of citizens of the United States," but defines none of those privileges.

The genius of American law is our Constitution, which creates a government blueprint that brilliantly combines the open-source legal innovation of the common law with an efficient federal structure.

Other provisions can be subject to various interpretations, especially as times change. Congress has the power to "coin money," but does that mean the power to establish paper currency by legal tender, or can it only make currency backed by a commodity such as gold? Congress also has the power to provide for a "navy," but does that mean it can also provide for an Air Force? Congress may pass no law abridging "freedom of speech," but does "speech" mean audible utterances, any creative expression, or something in between?

Such issues limn the difficulty of interpreting the Constitution with scientific exactitude. Nevertheless, there are those, such as Supreme Court Justice Antonin Scalia, who believe that the only appropriate interpretive method for the Constitution is to define its terms in a way that was commonly understood at the time of the Constitution's adoption in 1787.

Such an approach, despite its romantic appeal, runs into several practical difficulties.

First, technological and social changes create realities—such as an Air Force, for one example—which are wholly alien to an eighteenth century mindset. As Arthur Corbin notes, even the most rigid rules can be interpreted differently in changed circumstances; thus, any attempt to use 1787 vocabulary to evaluate the necessity of a modern technology is futile.

Scalia's originalism ascribes to the founding generation a level of foresight that is simply unattainable by humans. The most brilliant generals alive today cannot begin to predict the precise defense policies we'll need in the year 2200, nor can today's most brilliant economists model the regulatory structure that will exist then. It is contrary to everything we know about human reason to believe that those living in 1787 could have foreseen a resolution to every problem that modern America faces.

Second, many of the most important Constitutional provisions had no agreed-upon meaning, even to those who agreed on them at the Constitutional drafting convention. Early drafts of the First Amendment contained a protection of the people's freedom of "conscience," but that right was eventually dropped without explanation, and only "free exercise" of religion was retained. What should we conclude? Does that mean the drafters thought that "free exercise" of religion encompassed "freedom of conscience" and thus the latter was redundant, or were they simply unwilling to extend the right so far? No one knows.

This is not to say, as many of Scalia's ideological opponents do, that such interpretive difficulties mean the Constitution's text—or its early understanding—should simply be disregarded as a historical artifact with no modern relevance. In fact, the Constitution's structure and interpretive guides are essential to our ability to meet the challenges of the 21st century. Just because we cannot accurately define a Constitutional provision without reference to our circumstances does not mean we should abandon the pursuit of such definitions.

Effective Constitutional adjudication requires a fusion of historical analysis, linguistic interpretation, practical reasoning and jurisprudential innovation. Much like the common law itself, the Constitution is a law with an evolving meaning, but not without structure. The duty of the judiciary is to give Constitutional provisions actual content.

For example, take Congress' power to "regulate commerce...among the several States." While such a power might seem specific, its actual meaning has been quite contentious. On one side, there is the original 1787 understanding of "commerce," which was so narrow as to not even encompass agriculture at all. On the other side, there is the federal government's modern understanding of "commerce," which even includes the growing of wheat on one's farm for *personal* use. Over time, the legal definition has evolved from a body of rules for merchants in the late eighteenth century to the proactive creation of regulatory institutions in the present day.[309]

Insisting on an original understanding would have ensnared our nation in the economic realities of the 18th century, rendering the regulatory structure ill-equipped to foster growth in the modern age. But the temptation to disregard the commercial nature of the clause has had the opposite effect: Congress squandering billions on pursuits that have nothing to do with commerce whatsoever.

With our founding document, we have yet another example of the dual importance of structure and change. The genius of the Constitution is not only due to its evolving content, but also to its brilliant structure.[310] To shed light on the Constitution's innovations, and especially how they can encourage beneficial evolution in the future, we will analyze a few of its most important doctrines.

The workshop of liberty

The 10th Amendment states, "The powers not delegated to the United States by the Constitution, nor prohibited by it to the states, are reserved to the states respectively, or to the people."

This amendment secures the Constitutional principle of federalism, by which states can adopt unique policies to meet their special needs and requirements. Federalism is the source of Madison's "workshop of liberty;" Madison believed the 10th Amendment was the only explicit limitation on federal power and created "a residual and inviolable sovereignty" of states.[311]

Due to its explicit inclusion in the 10th Amendment, federalism has long been respected and defended in the Supreme Court. In the words of former Supreme Court Justice Sandra Day O'Connor, American federalism helps encourage policy evolution by allowing "sensitivity to the diverse needs of a heterogenous society," encouraging more "innovation and experimentation in government," and creating responsiveness by "putting the states in competition for a mobile citizenry."[312]

As Justice Anthony Kennedy put it:

> Federalism was our Nation's own discovery. The Framers split the atom of sovereignty. It was the genius of their idea that our citizens would have two political capacities, one state and one federal, each protected from incursion by the other. The resulting Constitution created a legal system unprecedented in form and design, establishing two orders of government, each with its own direct relationship, its own privity, its own set of mutual rights and obligations to the people who sustain it and are governed by it.[313]

Constitutional law scholars agree that federalism is the "clearest example of American exceptionalism," and is "exceptional not only in its inception, inventiveness and derivation...[but] also in its emergent qualities, its ability to maintain itself, and to transform and recreate itself as a system both legally and in fact."[314]

Thus, federalism is a dynamic evolutionary order, capable of rising to the new challenges of the ages. The system is widely admired for its adaptive features, generation of new policy ideas and its permission of "unity without uniformity," in the words of another legal scholar.[315]

However, one need not be a legal scholar to appreciate the genius of federalism. As we mentioned in Chapter 1, federalism is an essential reservation of free choice for the people of the United States, allowing them the ability to choose novel approaches for their unique problems. The geographic, cultural and economic diversity of the United States is the source of its strength; differentiation allows policy choice to benefit all people.

As the "workshop of liberty," American federalism has distinct advantages over other countries' systems. As a triumph of differentiation, we enjoy 50 distinct experimental policy environments (and over 87,000 total jurisdictions), in which voters can create, test and evaluate new policies to satisfy their needs.[316] Rather than foisting one-size-fits-all federal approaches on our diverse nation, federalism allows the people to choose the policy approaches that work best.

...federalism is a dynamic evolutionary order, capable of rising to the new challenges of the ages.

A branch of economics that helps to understand the importance of federalism is *public choice theory*. Public choice theory applies economic reasoning to political decision-making and recognizes government policies not as the abstract ideal, but rather as the actual results of the behavior of individual politicians.[317]

One important insight of public choice theory regarding federalism is the importance of competition to help ensure quality. After all, one does not expect every corporation to create a perfect product; that's why we shop around, in order to utilize the power of choice to maximize our satisfaction.

Public choice theory explains why such logic applies as much, if not more so, to the politicians clamoring to offer beneficial government services. Why would you trust a power-hungry politician more than a money-hungry businessman?

This theory agrees that freedom of choice in local policy making is essential in order to innovate, experiment and develop distinctive policies.

The Marketplace of Federalism

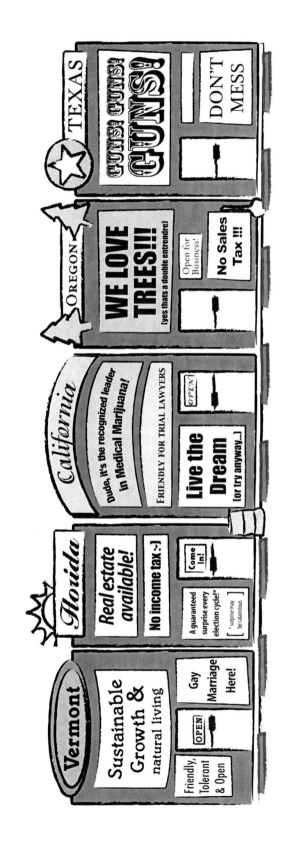

Differentiation and freedom of choice are essential in order to ensure quality in the diversity of contemporary American society. Public choice theorists argue that local competition is most effective as a "discovery procedure" that generates new services and innovative methods of service delivery.[318]

The principle underlying federalism is a concept Albert Hirschmann termed exit,[319] the simple process of voting with one's feet to reject a social system. As another public choice scholar argued, "The act of moving or failing to move is crucial....[replacing] the usual market test of willingness to buy a good and [revealing] the consumer voter's demand for public goods."[320]

It is not surprising, then, that Friedrich Hayek expressed admiration for American federalism, recognizing its dynamic ability to create spontaneous evolution.[321]

The discussion of network theory in Chapter 3 also explains why federalism works so well. Network systems can function with a lot of structure when there is a uniformity of behavior among nodes. Similarly, American states and localities can experiment with structures that might work at the state or local level, but would become a bureaucratic nightmare if pursued by the federal government.

Even as local communities preserve policy autonomy, public choice theorists also recognize the importance of "equality of opportunity," in terms of funding grants from the state and federal authorities, in order to be efficient.[322] This perfect balance, like all that must be struck in the law, is not easily articulable in an *a priori* fashion for all circumstances. It must be derived on the basis of experience, as the emergent property of numerous judicial decisions, and with the Constitution's structure as a guide.

Today, our federal government squanders billions of dollars through accounting inefficiencies while it funnels billions more back to the states. This leakage is part and parcel of the one-size-fits all system created by our Washington politicians, and it is wholly backward.

Rather, existing revenues should gradually be directed to the state governments, allowing them to capture the lion's share of tax revenues, simply because they are better placed to experiment with most of the social programs that our federal government insists on designing.

Privileges, immunities, and other phantasmagoria

The second level of the 10th Amendment speaks to the rights of the people. As the rights of the states encourage policy freedom, the residual rights of the people encourage personal freedom.

The rights of the people are alluded to several times in the Constitution. Many of those rights are specifically enumerated, such as "freedom of speech" in the First Amendment. However, the 9th Amendment warns that the enumerated rights are not exclusive: "The enumeration...of certain rights, shall not be construed to deny...others held by the people."

While the 9th Amendment does not constitute an independent source of rights, it is an interpretive guide to general protections of rights[323] such as the 10th Amendment's rights of the people, the 14th Amendment's protection of the "privileges or immunities of citizens of the United States," and Article IV's protection of "all privileges and immunities of citizens in the several states."

Despite the Constitution's text clearly confirming the presence of unenumerated rights, many conservative judges have argued that efforts to define and protect such rights are futile. Robert Bork, for example, famously argued that the 9th Amendment might as well be an "inkblot" on the Constitution's parchment, for that's how little it actually means.[324] Bork believed such vagueness rendered judges incapable of discerning the true nature of such "unenumerated" rights. But the Constitution provides plenty of vague phraseology, such as "unreasonable searches and seizures" or "just compensation." Does Bork view those amendments as inkblots as well?

Moreover, such a critique might as well be leveled against the entire common law, which for centuries evolved without any textual or legislative oversight, simply developing by the experimental decisions of activist judges. For example, take the tort of negligence. The legal definition of negligence, generally, is a harmful act or omission that was performed with an absence of "reasonable care" on the part of the tort-feasor.[325] Now, such a standard of "reasonableness" might seem as content-less as a claim about abstract privileges or immunities of citizens. But both, through the process of historical analysis, adversarial litigation, appellate review and reasoned argumentation, can be given substantial content. In the case of negligence, the impressive corpus of case law on the subject speaks for itself.

As for the case of unenumerated rights, history speaks as well. Over time, the Supreme Court has occasionally recognized a number of unenumerated rights.[326] Much like the development of the common law, some discoveries were clearly false and poorly reasoned, while others have stood the test of time.

In 1973, Justice William Douglas gave one of the most comprehensive analyses of such unenumerated rights, relying on over two centuries of Supreme Court case law:

> Customary, traditional, and time-honored rights, amenities, privileges, and immunities that come within the sweep of 'the Blessings of Liberty' mentioned in the preamble to the Constitution [are protected]....First is the autonomous control over the development and expression of one's intellect, interests, tastes, and personality...Second is freedom of choice in the basic decisions of one's life respecting marriage, divorce, procreation, contraception, and the education and upbringing of children.... Third is the freedom to care for one's health and person, freedom from bodily restraint or compulsion, freedom to walk, stroll, or loaf.[327]

These rights were gleaned from such Court decisions as the 1905 announcement that "there is...a sphere within which the individual may assert the supremacy of his own will and rightfully dispute the authority of any human government, especially of any free government existing under a written constitution, to interfere with the exercise of that will;"[328] in 1923, "Without doubt, [liberty] denotes not merely freedom from bodily restraint but also the right of the individual to contract, to engage in any of the common occupations of life, to acquire useful knowledge, to marry, establish a home and bring up children, to worship God according to the dictates of his own conscience, and generally to enjoy those privileges long recognized at common law as essential to the orderly pursuit of happiness by free men;"[329] and in 1958, "'Outside areas of plainly harmful conduct, every American is left to shape his own life as he thinks best, do what he pleases, go where he pleases.'"[330]

Other unenumerated rights include the right of association;[331] the right to privacy;[332] the right to the presumption of innocence;[333] mandating a standard of proof beyond a reasonable doubt;[334] the right to interstate travel;[335] the right of public access to criminal trials;[336] the right to marry a person of one's own choosing;[337] and the liberty to direct the education of one's own children.[338] None of those rights can be found in the Constitution's text, yet each has been upheld by Constitutional judges.

These decisions, much like the decisions of the common law, create an independent body of law subject to continual evaluation, reconsideration and testing. Scalia and Bork's reluctance to articulate these rights is understandable; neither has the individual knowledge to accurately enumerate them. However, the point of the common law is that they don't have to: it is the legal *system*, comprised of thousands of judicial decisions, that encapsulates such wisdom. The wisdom of crowds is smarter than the most learned philosopher-king wannabe.

The question facing modern America is how to navigate these difficult issues and ensure that our Constitutional structure can lead our nation into the new age. The answer is the same as it has always been: active debate and litigation over our Constitution. The Supreme Court has been wrong a lot, but it also recognizes that fact; and for that reason, it repeatedly overrules itself. Rulings that create confusion and excessive litigation in the lower-level courts are considered ripe for review by the Supreme Court. As a result, much innovation occurs through the common law-like process of judicial innovation and reconsideration.

Intellectual property

Intellectual property protections are legal technologies that are essential to encourage technological innovation in the broader economy. Patents, copyrights and other legal technologies help give innovators the incentive to produce and develop evolutionary advancements.

The protection of intellectual property is prescribed by the Constitution, which recommends the use of patents for "promoting the progress of science and the useful arts."[339] Not surprisingly, with such a vague mandate, but such an important purpose, intellectual property can be a contentious area of the law.

In the 21st century age of technological innovation, the patent office finds itself overwhelmed by the level and complexity of patent applications. 2,830 patent lawsuits were filed in U.S. district courts in 2006, which was up from 1,840 in 1996 and 1,129 in 1986. Currently, there is an estimated backlog of over 761,000 applications.[340]

The Department of Commerce, which runs the patent office, makes decisions on the usefulness or originality of the patents, but their judgment has been so questionable that the Supreme Court recently had to intervene in the process.[341]

But, there has arisen cause for hope. The patent office recently implemented an innovative system of patent review that harnesses the evolutionary wisdom of crowds. As CNN reported:

> The concept behind the program, called Peer-to-Patent, is straightforward: Publish patent applications on the Web for all to see and let anyone with relevant expertise -- academics, colleagues, even potential rivals -- offer input to be passed along to the Patent Office. By using the power of the Internet to tap the wisdom of the masses, Peer-to-Patent aims to dig up hard-to-find "prior art" -- evidence that an invention already exists or is obvious and therefore doesn't deserve a patent. The goal is to locate prior art that Patent Office examiners might not find on their own -- and to produce better patents by reducing ones granted on applications that aren't novel. The hope is that this will drive innovation by improving the patent process and reducing the patent infringement lawsuits clogging the courts.[342]

The innovative idea was taken from NYU law professor Beth Noveck, who introduced the concept of "open review" for patents in a widely respected paper. "Unlike ordinary peer review," professor Noveck wrote, "which is closed and therefore subject to manipulation, open review adopts a broader vision of collaborative expertise. It is both more expert and more participatory. Unlike other proposals for ex post patent reform, open review addresses the core problem of information deficit that cannot be solved by the courts. It requires no statutory change to try and [has] minimal [costs] to implement."[343]

Equal protection

What is the evolutionary interpretation of the Constitution's famous equal protection clause?[344] Well, I'd have to fully answer that question in another book. But I do believe evolutionary choice theory offers a helpful antidote to the paternalism of our current leaders, and also provides a fresh approach to aiding the inner city communities that the equal protection clause was originally designed to benefit.

Among policies impacting urban communities, there is great potential to encourage differentiation, in order to create opportunity for social-technological evolution.

Last chapter, we mentioned the case of education, where one-size-fits-all education approaches stifle creativity, foster resentment among youth, and fail to educate. By diverting education funds to empower the principle of diversity and choice for all citizens, we can better encourage the creation of innovative programs like Geoff Canada's Harlem Children's Zone, which are essential in the formation of young leaders. All children and parents should have the equal opportunity to find education suitable for their needs.

We also mentioned a number of other growth-oriented policies, such as personal accounts, allowing people to build wealth even if they haven't found permanent employment, and open trade, allowing consumers to save money on basic goods. All will benefit urban areas as much, if not more, than middle class areas, giving all individuals and families equal opportunity to improve their own situation.

Now, we can also highlight some legal obstacles that violate equal protection as well as the principles of evolutionary progress.

First, under current law, ex-felons are banned from voting for life, even after they have paid their debt to society. This punishment is vindictive and unnecessary. A system that permanently excludes individuals from the democratic process violates the most basic principles of fairness, as well as the evolutionary principle of differentiating between deeds and people themselves. Ex-felons should be enfranchised upon release from prison.

Second, the draconian drug laws are perhaps the greatest obstacle for progress in the inner city. While it is undoubtedly true that hard drugs ruin lives, it is also true that prison ruins lives, by tearing apart families, encouraging gang behavior, and hardening the moral sensitivities of individuals.

To avoid this social stagnation, differentiation is again essential. Protecting children from dangerous drugs doesn't mean criminalizing everyone who touches them.

Not only is the current war on drugs unwise, but it is also counter-productive for society, incarcerating the very people whose entrepreneurial talents are most needed to create economic and social growth.

Some drug dealers, such as Jay-Z before his rapping days, are among the most entrepreneurial and creative individuals in the urban areas. As

Jay-Z himself explains, the decision to deal is often made not to harm others, but rather to simply eke a living off of one of the few profitable commodities in such areas. To permanently exclude these entrepreneurs from civil society is perhaps the worst of all possible "solutions" to a very real problem. Jay-Z is a $300 million+ testimony to the fact that *some* of these entrepreneurs - *if* their passions were redirected to more positive ends - can become some of the most successful innovators that their communities have ever seen.

Now, I don't claim that any these reforms will be a panacea. But neither do such panaceas exist. No government program could have created snowboarding any more than one could have molded Sean Carter into Jay-Z. *C'est la vie.*

The right of choice

An unenumerated right that, if respected in Constitutional jurisprudence, would immensely aid the evolution of innovative technologies is the *right to pursue a lawful calling*. The right dates back to the Magna Carta[345] and was recognized by English historian William Blackstone as a cornerstone of the early common law.[346]

The right was also respected by the American founders. James Madison wrote that it is an injustice when "arbitrary restrictions, exemptions, and monopolies deny to part of its citizens that free use of their faculties, and free choice of their occupations."[347]

Furthermore, some scholars believe that the Declaration's defense of "life, liberty and the pursuit of happiness", as structurally similar to philosopher John Locke's defense of "life, liberty and property," was a defense of the right to freely trade and acquire property as the pursuit of happiness.[348] From the beginning of the nation, this right was recognized in the American common law,[349] and was famously defended in the Supreme Court by Justice Bradley (in dissent) in the 19th century:

"The individual citizen, as a necessity, must be left free to adopt such calling, profession, or trade as may seem to him most conducive to that end. Without this right he cannot be a freeman. This right to choose one's calling is an essential part of that liberty which it is the object of government to protect; and a calling, when chosen, is a man's property and right."

The right to pursue a lawful calling should be respected as one of the privileges and immunities of citizens of the United States; in fact, Representative John Bingham, one of the authors of the privileges and immunities clause, said that it included "the liberty . . . to work in an honest calling and contribute by your own toil in some sort to the support of yourself, to the support of your fellowmen and to be secure in the enjoyment of the fruits of your toil."[350]

In evolutionary choice theory, this right secures the ability of all citizens to fairly attempt to provide a new social technology to others. It respects the state's legitimate efforts to regulate for the public welfare, such as safety standards and worker's compensation.[351] However, it also recognizes the fact that the freedom of choice to pursue a calling is essential to create new and innovative social technologies.

> *...the freedom of choice to pursue a calling is essential to create new and innovative social technologies.*

In practice, the right to pursue a calling affords a method to challenge substantially unjust laws or regulations as excessively burdensome. When a law has the effect of inhibiting the right to pursue a lawful calling, the state should be required to show that the law is narrowly tailored to pursue a legitimate government end. In this way, policymakers will be forced to choose the most effective and least choice-restrictive means of economic regulation; a force that few deny would be helpful in trimming the worst excesses of red tape.

As we recognized in Chapter 3, government-imposed structure is essential to encourage the evolutionary process, but the fundamental source of innovation arises from new creative ideas. Again, the perfect balance between these two principles is not capable of being stated *a priori*. Rather, it must be evaluated by judges within the context of history, tradition and legal doctrine, through the application of the sovereign prerogative of choice.

Recognizing the right to pursue a lawful calling would immensely aid the American evolution in the 21st century. In these challenging times, we need American ingenuity more than ever. The right would help encourage the entrepreneurial initiative that is the source of the innovative advancements we desperately need.

Yet another evolutionary case study

For an example of the type of American Dream-crushing regulations that the right to pursue a calling would help to combat, take the story of Erroll Tyler. Mr Tyler is an entrepreneur based in Boston, Massachusetts, and the owner of Nautical Tours, an amphibious vehicle sightseeing tour that travels around the city. Nautical Tours utilizes the only Coast Guard-approved amphibious vehicle for transportation, and takes travelers on land and water to experience the sights of Boston.[352]

But the city of Boston forbids Mr. Tyler the right to cross the Longfellow bridge, one of the main bridges over the Charles River and essential to his tour project. Why? Because Nautical Tours doesn't have a sightseeing license. The city stopped issuing permits in 1995, ostensibly because of a public works project called the Big Dig. But the Big Dig ended in 2003, and yet the city still refuses to issue permits. Currently, a seven-company cartel is the only group that has sightseeing permits, holding an unjustified monopoly on the right to operate a lawful tour business.

Even though there is no rational basis for the refusal to issue the permit, Mr. Tyler is left unable to pursue his American Dream, while other established (and politically connected) companies profit from his difficulties. Were the right to pursue a lawful calling respected and enforced, a court would enjoin the city to allow Mr. Tyler fair access to the marketplace.

Examples like Mr. Tyler's abound as creative entrepreneurs are unjustly denied the ability to introduce new social technologies. These stories are difficult to discover and quantify in the aggregate, but the experience of entrepreneurs like Mr. Tyler demonstrates that they are far more numerous than anyone would like to admit.

By enforcing the right to pursue a lawful calling, we can better root out these injustices and empower the innovative growth that underpins the American system.

Closing arguments

With these perspectives, we arrive at a novel understanding of the law's importance. The American legal system has provided the necessary structure to enable sustained value-added political, economic, and social evolution.

By maximizing these essential evolutionary features, we can better empower growth in the new century. Federalism can empower effective resolution to difficult political issues. Unenumerated liberty can preserve the ability of the people to solve their own problems. The right to pursue a calling can maximize the ability of individuals to introduce innovative new social technologies. These and other constitutional innovations have led us through difficult times before, and we disregard them at our peril.

In the next chapter, we'll move on the question of what to do when people interfere with that peaceful growth. How can we protect our constitutional order in a complex and dangerous world?

8

NATIONAL SELECTION
An evolutionary approach to foreign policy

"We have entered the age of the faceless, agile enemy...stateless terrorist groups have emerged to score blow after blow against us. Driven by cultural fragmentation, schooled in the most sophisticated technologies, and fueled by transnational crime...terrorists have developed the ability to fight nation-states strategically - without weapons of mass destruction. This new method is called systems disruption, a simple way of attacking the critical networks (electricity, oil, gas, water, communications, and transportation) that underpin modern life." **-- John Robb, Brave New War (2004)**

"The dogmas of the quiet past are inadequate to the stormy present. The occasion is piled high with difficulty, and we must rise with the occasion. As our case is new, so must we think anew and act anew. We must disenthrall ourselves, and then we shall save our country." **-- Abraham Lincoln (1862)**

*T*ODAY, THE MAJOR THREAT to the safety and security of the American people comes from terrorism. Terrorism is a broadly defined phenomenon; our own government offers several different definitions, and a recent book on terrorism outlined over 100.[353] Terrorism in some form dates from the 19th century or even earlier, but few dispute that the threat has taken on new dimensions in the 21st century.[354]

In several important ways, the current threat of terrorism is materially different from any other threat the United States has faced.[355] First, unlike the nation-state wars of yesteryear, terrorists groups are *stateless and transnational*. Rather than operating as organs of governments, terrorist groups operate independently in small, decentralized networks, ranging from one member (e.g., the Unabomber, Cho Seung Hui and Timothy McVeigh) to thousands of members (al-Qaida, Hezbollah, Tamil Tigers and Mara Salvatrucha).

As terrorist networks have grown in complexity, they have become notoriously difficult to track, infiltrate and extinguish. Terrorist networks are decentralized and adaptive, which renders them supremely capable of reorganizing even when senior leaders are captured and killed.

Also, terrorists utilize asymmetrical warfare. As John Robb notes, one of the most alarming features about 9/11 was that despite hundreds of billions of dollars in defense spending, the American military was rendered wholly impotent—i.e., it wasn't even in the terrorists' plans—at the time that we needed it most. By using the tools of modernity (cell phones, airplanes, even box cutters) to strike civilian targets, terrorists are masterful at exploiting the networks of that undergird modern society.

But before one feels too pessimistic, respect for the American military is in order. The continual evolution of our defensive social technologies has been manifest throughout American history, from the creation of innovative guerilla warfare tactics in the Revolutionary War, through the development of cutting-edge military technology in the 21st century.

As President Lincoln noted, such new cases call for new strategies. So today we face the question, how can our nation's defensive technologies adapt to the new threat?

Different strokes

The first lesson of defense policy should be the embrace of differentiation, allowing states, localities and individual communities the autonomy to implement innovative defensive policies. This prescription is probably not surprising to anyone reading this book so far. But the position has been empirically verified, as terrorism experts and federalism scholars agree that federalist innovation is essential to develop dynamic policies to face the new terrorist threat. State and local authorities have a unique advantage as "first responders" during a terrorist attack; it is they who are most capable and knowledgeable regarding the unique needs of their communities in order to protect essential assets.[356]

Unfortunately, the Department of Homeland Security has markedly interfered with federalist innovation, dictating one-size-fits-all approaches to defense through the extensive usage of conditional funding (that is, grants with strings attached to their receipt, often having nothing do with the use of the funds) and heavy-handed regulation. One jarring example of this approach is the policy regarding America's ports, arbitrarily dictating which ports should receive what security measures.

...federalist innovation is essential to develop dynamic policies to face the new terrorist threat.

A 2005 Homeland Security audit found gross errors in the way that federal grants have been allocated, concluding that "the program has not yet achieved its intended results in the form of actual improvement in port security," and that there was "no assurance that the program is protecting the nation's most critical and vulnerable port infrastructure and assets." The Department's method of allocating grants was questioned as well. According to a Congressional report, Wyoming received four times as much antiterrorism money per capita as New York did in 2005. Furthermore, the report found widespread waste, corruption and redundant spending in grant allocation.

The audit mentioned a laundry list of questionable projects that were financed, including $130,000 for a closed-circuit television system, even after the department ranked the project 27th out of 29 applications and admitted in its internal review documents that the system would be "redundant to what the port authority has in place;" $180,000 for security lights at a port that the department noted is a "small, remote facility that receives less than 20 ships per year;" $10,000 to one port for encrypted radios that were perhaps not even compatible with federal and state radios; and so much more.

At one port—next to a luxury entertainment pavilion that included restaurants, a hotel and spa—$25,000 was given to install video surveillance equipment and alarms, a project that department staff members had ranked last among the applications, and that auditors concluced "appears to support the normal course of business" and was unrelated to terrorism. Another $935,000 grant was given for general security improvements to a port where an industrial park was being built, leading department staff members to question if the money was in fact an economic development grant, instead of antiterrorism financing. Many of the other grants also "appeared to be for a

"The DHS (Department of Homeland Security) Chairman decends from Mount Sinai with the security directives for the war on terror !!!"

purpose other than security against an act of terrorism."[357]

Such anecdotes exemplify the inefficiency of bureaucratic approaches to extremely complex issues.

To increase the effectiveness of our defenses, novel approaches should be encouraged. For example, in certain situations, private military companies (PMCs) could be used to provide additional defensive capabilities.

These companies have had a tarnished reputation ever since the experience of Blackwater in Iraq. However, the Blackwater experience demonstrates the precise opposite of the way PMCs should be used. In Iraq, Blackwater was granted legal immunity and monopoly status by the American government; with such an absence of choice, it's not surprising that the experiment turned awry.

To be effective, PMCs must be subject to the rule of law, competition, and ideally, should operate for strictly local and community level clients.

The art of war

"If you know the enemy and know yourself, you need not fear the result of a hundred battles. If you know yourself but not the enemy, for every victory gained you will also suffer a defeat."[358] **-- Sun Tzu**

In order to honor Sun Tzu's lesson, differentiation in military and foreign policy is essential. The essence of knowing the enemy—*especially* those aspects of the enemy that make it unique from other threats—is of unquestionable importance.

Given the stateless and transnational nature of the terrorist threat, strategies exclusively designed for the 20th century are doomed to fail. Our greatest threat in the 21st century does not come from an expanding imperial nation; it comes from an expanding underground network.

The problem with nation-state thinking is that it blurs the true target. In the age of a transnational enemy, there is no workable universal distinction between nation-states that harbor terrorists and ones that do not. Though al-Qaida leader Osama bin Laden is Saudi, as were a majority of the 9/11 hijackers, America considers Saudi Arabia an ally. Al-Qaida operates from myriad locations around the world, including Sudan, Pakistan, Afghanistan and Germany, yet many of those nations are also considered allies.

Modern terrorists operate in a shadowy underworld, but also pursue separate lives in plain sight. As William F. Buckley, Jr. noted, "Individual terrorists were only yesterday engaged in ordinary occupations, shocking friends and family when they struck as terrorists."[359] This observation is essential to understanding the new difficulty of fighting terrorism: identifying terrorists from non-terrorists.

Despite the claims of many neoconservatives, the United States is not at war with "Islamic extremists;" rather, we are at war with Islamic extremists who seek to kill or harm American citizens. Islamic extremists represent solid majorities and pluralities throughout the Muslim world, preferring to live under *sharia* law, but pose absolutely no violent threat to American citizens.

> *Our greatest threat in the 21st century does not come from an expanding imperial nation; it comes from an expanding underground network.*

The Muslim extremists who translate their religion into violent aggression against the United States are our enemies. This war will not be won against nations; it will not be won by invasion, occupation or regime change. It can only be won by intelligent differentiation, and the recognition that our enemies no longer lie within geographical borders.

In the war on terrorism, our enemy is not as clear-cut as a litmus test of religious fervor. The neoconservative approach manifests a severe ignorance of our enemy; the approach spits in the face of the great teacher, Sun Tzu.

The essential approach in the war on terrorism is not of "shock-and-awe" but of outwit and surprise; not of plodding alliance-building but dynamic action; and not of invasion but of intelligence. Granted, it is not easy to admit changes in strategy in the face of new realities. But that difficulty is precisely the reason why empires have not long endured; that same difficulty, if we can embrace it, will hold the key to our success.

Harold and Kumar go to Guantanamo Bay

The writ of *habeas corpus* is an iconic feature of Anglo-Saxon jurisprudence. The writ is a legal tool to challenge the legality of one's imprisonment, allowing any person to dispute the justice of any detention. In the words of the great Justice Oliver Wendell Holmes, *habeas* is not "a static, narrow, formalistic remedy; its scope has grown to achieve its grand purpose." It "cuts through all forms and goes to the very tissue of the structure. It comes in from the outside, not in subordination to the proceedings, and although every form may have been preserved, opens the inquiry whether they have been more than an empty shell."

The writ of *habeas* is essential to the effective and fair prosecution of the war on terrorism, given the exceptional difficulty in distinguishing enemy combatants. Again, the Arab world is filled with radical Islamists. But we're not supposed to be killing and detaining all of them—only the ones that try to kill Americans. The determination of murderous intent is essential to the effective prosecution of the war on terrorism. But because we want to severely punish terrorists, and rightly so, the high human cost makes the potential for injustice that much greater.

The new battlefield is not static, its soldiers are not uniformed, and as I'm sure we'd all concede, neither Congress nor the president is omniscient.

Those are the reasons why *habeas* rightly applies to detainees in the war on terrorism.[360]

Why not a Marshall plan?

Without passing judgment on the question of the effectiveness of the Cold War-era foreign policy in the past century, the unique features of the terrorist threats render it wholly otiose in the modern age. Pretending that the war of the 2000s is the same as the wars from 1940-1991 might tickle the nostalgia of grizzled military vets, but it ignores Sun Tzu's lesson and leaves the United States gravely at risk.

Despite all the evidence to the contrary, many conservatives and liberals alike persist in the belief that the United States can or should somehow lavishly bestow the peaceful social technology of democracy on the people of the Middle East. These neocolonialists somehow think we can persuade terrorist radicals to drop their Kalashnikovs in order to pick up a ballet, and aver that the solution to America's security is to rebuild the Middle East in our own image.

These well-intentioned and well-read individuals inevitably compare such an effort to the Marshall Plan—America's post-World War II effort to rebuild the nations of Germany and Japan. But these individuals fail to recognize that nothing of relevance is similar to our situation in 1945 and the current terrorist threat today.

As former CIA analyst Michael Scheuer put it:

> The Marshall Plan analogy...provides a road map to disaster. Europe in 1945 was economically devastated and convinced that fascism was untenable; the enemy states and their militaries were annihilated; and the continent as a whole was, after witnessing the Red Army rape eastern Germany, afraid to death of the USSR. Perhaps more important, the United States shared a common heritage with Europe; both sides of the Atlantic were grounded in the Classical experience, Christianity, the Renaissance, the Reformation, the several Enlightenments, and the Industrial Revolution....in the Pacific, the annihilation of Imperial Japan's armed forces and the Japanese will-to-war were complemented by a culture willing to submit to the U.S.

conqueror...None of the conditions that allowed the Marshall Plan and its Pacific counterpart to succeed are present in the Muslim world. [W]ith this lack of positive culture, historical and religious commonalities, a Marshall Plan for the Muslim world would be as successful as pouring water on sand and hoping for a bumper crop of wheat.[361]

Germany and Japan had declared war on the world as part of an imperial conquest and lost at the hands of the American military. Under such unique circumstances, nation building was appropriate and necessary. But in the 21st century war on terrorism, the aggression is counterproductive.

A democratic government is a social technology of the utmost complexity, one that cannot be simply imposed on a country by external forces. Governments derive their power from the consent of the governed, and their constitution is a matter of public choice for the people of a given nation, according to their unique history and traditions. It is not capable of being willed by an outside power. Even back in the nineteenth century, Hegel pointed out that one cannot coerce another into freedom as long as the people aren't ready for it, observing that "Napoleon could not coerce Spain into freedom any more than Philip II could force Holland into slavery."[362]

There is a reason why the American Revolution was organic and came from within, not bestowed upon us by some benevolent imperialist. Scheuer highlights the uniqueness of the American experience, noting that our Revolution was not simply some whimsical decision by the Founding Fathers, but the culmination of centuries of social and political evolution:

A plausible starting point for the political evolution that would lead to the American polity lies eight centuries back at the time of the drafting and signing of the Magna Carta in 1215, which circumscribed the arbitrary powers of England's King John. Then Americans, as Americans, had 150 years of self-governing experience and reliable political stablility in North America before the signing of the Declaration of Independence.[363]

The success of democracy lies in the will of the people, not the specific structural institutions thrust on a citizenry. As historian J.B. Bury wrote, "A long time was needed to arrive at the conclusion that coercion of opinion is a mistake, and only part of the world is yet convinced."[364] Guns and tanks, no matter how skilled the soldier manning them, do not aid this persuasive process.

In America and other Western countries, the social technology of democracy indeed aided our social, economic and political growth. But that doesn't mean the exact same institutions will aid social, economic and political growth elsewhere. The crucial fallacy of the neo-Marshall Plan enthusiasts is the typically arrogant imperialist assumption that one's native social technology is a) immediately necessary for growth in other nations, and b) capable of being imposed through the use of military force.

There is a reason why the American Revolution was organic and came from within, not bestowed upon us by some benevolent imperialist.

The social-technological history of the Arab world is so foreign and antithetical to the growth of American-style democracy that our attempts to bring "democracy" to the people of the Middle East will forever backfire. Many people in that region firmly believe that any government other than a theocracy is completely sacrilegious. We may earnestly desire for this social-technological consensus to be changed; we may justifiably believe that it is harming the growth prospects of the region. But none of that means that we are capable of changing any of it ourselves.

We Americans should understand better than anyone else the futility of mandating democracy at the barrel of a gun. Our own experience is a clear demonstration that a nation will always rise to expel a foreign ruler—no matter how benevolent the imperialist motives. The evolution of democracy is driven organically by the choice of the people, and no military effort, foreign aid expenditure or muscular presidential rhetoric can change that.

The Iraq question

Given the discussion thus far, the reader likely has a keen sense of why America's effort to bring democracy to Iraq is so misguided.

Of course, many readers also vehemently object to that statement. As I write this book, Iraq war supporters are convinced that a sustained military effort can succeed in bringing democracy to Mesopotamia. Such optimism is understandable, but it rests on an unfortunate ignorance of the distinction between the social technology of democracy and the social technology of a military.

Militaries kill people and break things; this is the fundamental rule of warfare. The successful "surge" of American troops indeed succeeded in quelling violence, because it was a raw demonstration of the absolute superiority of the American military. The best military in the world can always use a sustained and conspicuous use of force to coerce an opponent into submission. The United States military, thanks to the brave and talented young men and women who serve in it, will always succeed in this regard.

"Good news kids, we come bearing gifts!"

What a military can't do is give people a democracy. Democracy is a social technology of legitimate governance, based on a solemn social contract between a people and their government. It rests on a principle of *legitimacy* that cannot be mandated by any general, but can only be consented to by the free will of the people. The surge ensures law and order, but it does nothing to help achieve democracy.

Unfortunately, the imperialist effort is forever flawed. As Michael Scheuer noted:

> [America] failed to replace Saddam's regime with a functioning, durable government precisely because we tried to export our

political model to Iraq....the Iraqis had no appreciable experience with a democratic system, are deeply torn by sectarian differences, and are divided among three major ethnic groups, none of which had more than a modicum of interest in sharing power with the others, each fearing it would become the target of Saddam-like abuse if one group finagled a way to come out on top. Moreover, a great majority of Iraqis saw secular democracy as anathema to their Islamic faith. To a people whose religion rejects as apostasy the concept of deliberately separating church and state, American advice suggesting that the Iraqis govern themselves on the basis of such a separation is tantamount to telling the advisees to turn their backs on God.[365]

The Afghanistan question

Unfortunately, the same difficulties are hobbling our progress in the second front of the War on Terrorism: Afghanistan. There arguably could be no country more ill-suited for the institution of democracy than Afghanistan—the country is deeply divided on ethnic, religious and tribal lines. Only the most iron-fisted regimes have succeeded in retaining power; many regions of the country remain completely anarchic.

To make it even worse, the Afghans are notoriously hostile to outsiders. As Michael Scheuer explains with eloquent detail in *Imperial Hubris: Why The West is Losing the War on Terror,* Afghanistan is irredeemably divided, xenophobic, and socially conservative in the first century sense. Despite all this, we decided it was a good idea to bring liberal democracy—complete with schools and free elections—to a society that could care less for it.

British historian Sir John Keegan argued shortly after 9/11 that Afghanistan is "unstable, fractious, and ultimately ungovernable," and urged America to avoid "general war and of policies designed to change the society or government in Afghanistan." Sir Keegan warned:

Efforts to occupy and rule [Afghanistan] usually ended in disaster. But straightforward punitive expeditions...were successful on more than one occasion. It should be remembered that, in 1878, the British did indeed succeed in bringing the Afghans to heel. The Russians, moreover, foolishly did not try to punish rogue Afghans, as [Britain] did, but to rule the country. Since Afghanistan is ungovernable, the failure of their effort was predictable...America should not seek to change the regime, but simply to find and kill the terrorists. It should do so without pity.[366]

But instead of heeding Sir Keegan's advice, America went ahead to try to do the impossible: bring democracy to Afghanistan. Our failure to differentiate the essential task (viz., killing terrorists) from the inessential task (viz., building roads, schools and democracy), has deprived our effort of success.

There is a fundamental distinction between al-Qaida, the justified target of America's war on terrorism, and the nation of Afghanistan, an underdeveloped, sectarian and tribal land whose political decisions are their own business. Afghan voters won't bring us any closer to finding Osama bin Laden.

Afghan voters won't bring us any closer to finding Osama bin Laden.

The true American empire

The purpose of these discussions is not to propose a one-size-fits-all solution or to predict the greatest threats of the future. Rather, the effort is to highlight the fact that these threats can come from anywhere, and that our defense policy should maximize adaptation in this environment.

Most of all, I hope that we Americans can recognize the uniqueness of our own experience in this process, and realize that healthy democracies are not decreed from outside, but rather grow organically from within.

A truly American foreign policy aggressively responds to direct threats, but refrains from building other people's societies. With these concepts in mind, we can close our chapter with wisdom from another president, John Quincy Adams:

And now, friends and countrymen, if the wise and learned philosophers of the older world... should find their hearts disposed to inquire, what has America done for the benefit of mankind? Let our answer be this – America, with the same voice which spoke herself into existence as a nation, proclaimed to mankind the inextinguishable rights of human nature, and the only lawful foundations of government. America, in the assembly of nations, since her admission among them, has invariably, though often fruitlessly, held forth to them the hand of honest friendship, of equal freedom, of generous reciprocity. ...Wherever the standard of freedom and independence has been or shall be unfurled, there will her heart, her benedictions and her prayers be. But she goes not abroad in search of monsters to destroy. She is the well-wisher to the freedom and independence of all. She is the champion and vindicator only of her own. She will recommend the general cause, by the countenance of her voice, and the benignant sympathy of her example. She well knows that by once enlisting under other banners than her own, were they even the banners of foreign independence, she would involve herself, beyond the power of extrication, in all the wars of interest and intrigue, of individual avarice, envy, and ambition, which assume the colors and usurp the standard of freedom.

9

A More Perfect Union
The past, present, and future evolution of American democracy

AS SOCIAL AND PHYSICAL TECHNOLOGIES continue to evolve in the 21st century, our political leaders keep us stuck with a 1960s-era political debate, 1950s-era social policy, 1940s-era defense policy, 1930s-era social welfare legislation, and a Roman Empire-era pile of unsustainable entanglements.

How is politics so behind the times?

The choice that isn't

"Democracy is supposed to give you the feeling of choice, like Pain-killer X and Painkiller Y. But they're both just aspirin." **-- Gore Vidal**

"Democracy must be something more than two wolves and a sheep voting on what to have for dinner." **-- James Bovard**[367]

A lot of Americans are probably wondering why our democracy isn't more evolved. After all, voters have a choice, and millions of people exercise it, supposedly as an evaluation of our politicians and the social technologies they're providing. So why haven't more effective political institutions arisen? Why, instead, are we saddled with a bumbling leviathan foisting a burning platform of unsustainable policies on the people? Or, put another way, why does the wisdom of crowds seem to never assert itself in the voting booth?

The answer lies in the nature of political choice, which lacks the necessary elements to effectively differentiate, select and amplify the social technologies provided by our government.

Voters get to cast a single vote to evaluate a politician's performance, even though said politician makes hundreds (if not thousands) of votes on various issues throughout the course of his term, not even including his auxiliary appointments of hundreds more unelected regulators, judges and bureaucrats who make hundreds of thousands of additional decisions regarding our welfare. The Federal Register, the chronicle of American regulation, adds about 75,000 pages *every year*, in addition to the 5,000 plus laws passed directly by Congress every term.[368] What do American voters get to say about all of that? Alas, only a single decision.

The political choice today

In the hyperpartisanship of 21st century Washington, choice is inhibited even further. If you happen to oppose the war in Iraq but support free trade or school selection, your choice is between candidates who both disagree with you, and who are equally likely to interpret your vote as an affirmation of a policy you actually find repugnant. Up to half of American voters define themselves as "fiscally conservative and socially liberal," yet such voters have no

Political choice lacks the necessary elements to effectively differentiate, select and amplify the social technologies provided by our government.

outlet for their views. Instead, their independent viewpoints are cast into one of two catch-all bins: R or D.

Hyperpartisanship further obscures the relevant political issues. Important policy questions such as whether a political institution like the filibuster has any public value, have only been answered by those who use it as a convenient tool to strengthen the power of one's political party. Sadly, the lust of political power is so great that the contemporary punditry evaluates issues with regard to the impact on Team Blue or Team Red, rather than the true implications for each issue.

Faced with two parties seemingly incapable of evolving, democracy becomes a Zugzwang. (Zugzwang. n. A chess term meaning a choice among inferior options. Great word for politics, huh?)

To weaken the selection process even further, many political decisions don't have major impacts until years after their original adoption. As our burning platform of unsustainable policies demonstrates, politicians specialize in sacrificing the future for short-term gain and pursue feel-good policies that end up saddling future generations with massive economic and political burdens.

As David Walker, the former comptroller general who warned Congress of the aforementioned burning platform of unsustainable policies, explained:

> [P]oliticians have increased spending, expanded government entitlement programs, and agreed to tax cuts without considering their long-term costs.... Our fiscal policies have created a disconnect between today's citizens and future taxpayers. Today's taxpayers benefit from high government spending and

low taxes, while future generations are expected to pay the bill.[369]

In this way, the people who are impacted by these political decisions (America's youth, or more accurately, America's unborn future children) have no input in their selection.

It's the worst form of choice regulation known to an American: taxation without representation. The entire principle of the Lockean social contract—consent of the governed—is violated. This pernicious trend in contemporary American politics is a nationally-self-destructive policy if there ever was one, threatening to stifle America's future development and tarnish the principles of this great nation.

So, what do we do about it?

Plugging the leaks

Certainly, as we've seen, the responsiveness of government is limited by its very nature. In the winner-takes-all game of politics, 49% of voters can prefer a given perspective and still have their desires unsatisfied.

In the long tail era of the marketplace, minority perspectives constitute lucrative niche markets and everyone can find what they want. But in politics, you have to get half the country to agree with you. Given the majority-rules approach, political evolution is painfully slow, and the range of choices for the voter will always pale in comparison to the choices for the consumer.[370]

However, despite these intrinsic difficulties, there are several areas for improvement in order to help our political institutions to better evolve. The United States was the first nation to conduct regular elections involving large numbers of voters;[371] and so the maximization of choice in the political sphere is part of our national mission. With luck, we can continue to lead

---

In the long tail era of the marketplace, minority perspectives constitute lucrative niche markets and everyone can find what they want. But in politics, you have to get half the country to agree with you.

---

the world in democratic expression.

The following are important reforms that can help choice become more powerful and effective in evaluating our democratic technologies.

Solution 1: Federalism

The first option, as mentioned in Chapter 7 and throughout this book, is to increase state and local governments' power to devise their own policies. The ability for citizens to influence policies at the local level is much more conducive to civic activism and yields additional opportunities for citizens to experiment with desired policies.

Imagine that instead of a Red/Blue presidential slugfest every four years in order to determine so many essential issues, we had continuous local elections. Individual communities could be offering their own diverse solutions for health care, security, economic growth and social issues, rather than letting one person (or one political party) choose them for three hundred million people. Madison certainly would be proud.

As we mentioned, public choice theorists agree that competition among policies at the state and local level can help enhance responsiveness and innovation in policy.[372] This aspect of the United States system, world-renowned for its dynamism, should be permitted to seek positive solutions to our pressing national issues.

Federalism has the additional advantage of encouraging greater citizen activism. As states and localities enjoy autonomy and independence, individuals within those jurisdictions enjoy a larger menu of political choices.

Solution 2: Campaign finance reform

Another worthwhile option would be to reform the antiquated campaign finance legislation that interferes with effective political choice.

Under current laws, your donations to a political party (called "soft money") are unlimited, but your donations to a specific candidate (called "hard money") are limited to about $2,000. As a result of this asinine distinction, the easiest way for candidates to raise lots of money is not to persuade individual voters to support them, but rather defer to the flush-with-cash party orthodoxy.

To encourage the success of new ideas and independent candidates, the rules should be reformed to allow unlimited "hard money" donations. This way, upstart candidates would have an easier time finding the necessary funding to compete with the major party candidates. Furthermore, party mavericks would be able to secure substantial financial resources without having to kowtow to the party orthodoxy.

Now, some might argue for the opposite approach. Why not, some argue, limit *all* campaign finance contributions—hard money and soft money—and simply require equality of money, media time and other helpful resources among all candidates?

The reason we shouldn't is because we don't need equipoise among our existing politicians; we need new politicians. We need new ideas and fresh approaches, not more of the same failed approach from the gerontocracy that currently runs our government. The principle of differentiation explains this fact, and the reality of complex evolution means that such new ideas will likely come from unforeseen places.

Another objection is that the open funding of candidates might create corrupt candidates. Such fears are similar to arguments about the market's common provision of undesirable options; it's true but irrelevant. While free funding might field a few oleaginous corporate shills, it is also likely to encourage more robust political entry. We *already* have corrupt candidates; what we need most are *new* ones.

Solution 3: Fair Redistricting

As a result of population change, voting districts must be periodically modified to make sure districts have roughly equal numbers of people. This process is prescribed by the Constitution and helps ensure that each Representative in the House is representing roughly about the same amount of people.

Unfortunately, politics always gets in the way. Back in the day, Southern politicians used to redraw Congressional district boundaries to confine minority voters to specific districts, limiting the amount of political clout they could wield, and entrenching segregation in this country. Now, the political heirs to these manipulative "representatives," ostensibly no longer interested in white supremacy, redraw the districts to keep other modern undesirables, such as Republicans, similarly confined to politically homogenous districts.

Because the redistricting process is largely controlled by the party in power, there is an incentive to redraw districts in a way that includes more people of that same party.

This manipulative practice, awkwardly known as "gerrymandering" in political science terms, is terribly anti-democratic. The system is that of politicians classifying you and defining your voting authority, by the party they think you'll vote for. Evolution usually involves scrapping the old for something new. Differentiation is essential to this process, and the choice-restriction of gerrymandering takes its toll.

The result is entirely predictable: competition is reduced, and we're stuck with the same windbags year-in, and year-out. As *The Economist* wryly put it, the level of predictability in Congressional elections was approaching "North Korean levels:" in 2004, only 30-40 Congressional seats were deemed truly competitive—a quarter of the number in the 1990s. Since 1964, the share of House incumbents re-elected with over 60% of the vote has risen from 58% to 77%.[373] Compare that turnover rate to the experience of the Fortune 50 companies mentioned in Chapter 1, experiencing a winning rate of only 20%.

The very essence of federalist democracy is differentiation, and it is sabotaged by the shameful practice of gerrymandering. Both parties redraw these districts with impunity, and thus neither one really wants the practice to stop.

Instead, Congress should slowly reverse the partisan consolidation of voting districts. They should do so with the goal of *increasing* ideological diversity, making every district the statistical equivalent of a swing state. In politics as elsewhere, competition is good.

Solution 4: Open primaries

Another policy limiting political choice is various states' "closed primary" laws, which restrict the voting in a given party's primary to members of that party. The trouble with that policy is that it squelches the power of party mavericks to gain support for their party's nomination.

For example, in 2008, Congressman Ron Paul—whose views on foreign policy, government power and many other issues differ sharply from his Republican colleagues—ran for the Republican nomination.

Not surprisingly, Paul's support came substantially from independent voters, many of whom had little or no affinity with the Republican Party. Yet thanks to closed primary laws, one had to be a registered Republican in order to vote in the primary. Not surprisingly, Mr. Paul garnered over twice as many votes in open primary states than closed primary states.[374]

Scholars have found that open primaries can help reduce polarization among politicians, thanks to the increased competition.[375] States should take this lesson to heart and empower the choices of the people by eliminating the antiquated and unnecessary closed primary laws.

Solution 5: Term limits

Finally, a crude but effective method of increasing choice in the political sphere is the use of term limits. Term limits, such as those for President of the United States, limit a politician to a given number of terms in office. Limits are a crude method in the sense that they dispose of politicians without regard to their achievements, but they are effective in the sense that they increase badly-needed opportunity for new faces and new candidates.

Term limits can be thought of as mandated differentiation in politics, and they deliver increased opportunity for new political entry. Were term limits universally implemented at the federal level, it is likely that more political competition would arise.

Term limits are fighting for the people, more than any politician ever could. They vote the wheedlers out, with convenient regularity.

The conscience of an evolutionary

A recent political bestseller is Paul Krugman's *Conscience of a Liberal*, intended to be a sort of center-left manifesto for the 21st century. The book also represents some of the most anti-evolutionary perspectives available from a major economist today. Given its popular status, and the fact that the author has recently been awarded some of the most impressive intellectual recognition available, including the Nobel Prize, I feel obliged to explain its major deficiencies.

First, Krugman suffers from a peculiarly acute case of hyperpartisanship that skews his reasoning on every political issue. Krugman is so partisan that he views seemingly everything in shades of Red or Blue, as if he were literally walking around wearing the duochromatic paper goggles that they give out in movie theaters. But real-world policy is multidimensional, and Krugman's partisanship painfully obfuscates his understanding of the real issues.

Krugman's major obsession is the alleviation of economic inequality. He wistfully longs for his childhood days of the 1950s, where there was a more narrow distribution of income than today. He apparently believes that the quality of life improves once the aggregate spread of income resembles a bell curve. But given that we've shown that evolutionary systems tend to follow power laws, with exponentially skewed distributions, Krugman appears to be hoping against hope.

Now, I'm the first to admit that the inequality of the marketplace is intuitively bothersome, and it's never friendly or kind. Most sensitive people, myself and Krugman included, find it personally distasteful.

But the evolutionary process does not conform to our idealistic preferences. We made that point back in Chapter 4, when we said that it's easy to see job losses, industry evaporation and widespread outsourcing, and angrily curse Adam Smith and everything he stood for. It's not nice to be a telephone operator losing your job any more than it's nice to be a wagon wheel repairman losing your job.

But as we talked about in Chapter 3, we also recognized why this destruction was essential to evolutionary growth. That was the point of the rambling philosophic dialogue from Epicurus through Hegel and Darwin: negativity can create positivity, assuming the right mindset. That's also why the fundamental lesson of evolutionary economics is the necessity of failure, learning and adaptation. Again, we put up with the messy and uncomfortable evolutionary process not because it's messy and uncomfortable, but because it has gotten us as far as it has.

But Krugman doesn't buy the evolutionary argument at all. In fact, he pretty much declares war on evolutionary economics with his triumphant thesis:

"Middle class societies don't emerge spontaneously as an economy matures, they have to be created through political action. Nothing in the data we have for the early twentieth century suggest that America was evolving spontaneously into the relatively equal society I grew up in."[376]

So here we have Krugman's rallying cry for the war on biobabble. There is no such thing as spontaneous market progress, he insists. If you have a comfortable middle class life, it's only because FDR and his ideological progeny started taking money from rich people.

Well, let's unpack that whopper and see what there is to it.

As an initial matter, Krugman's methodology is wholly unsuited for the thesis he hopes to prove. Nothing in the data suggest spontaneous emergence? Well, yeah. How, exactly, *could* economic data prove spontaneous emergence? Krugman never says, but his shoddy logic compromises his whole project.

The data analysis Krugman employs is, by his own admission, mere speculation. Some politician passed Law X on some day, hoping to create Effect Y. At some point, Effect Y occurred, and the question is whether Effect Y would have occurred absent Law X, or whether it occurred "spontaneously".

Let me share with you the dirty little secret. We'll never know. Regression analysis will never give you the answer, because it relies on counterfactual reasoning that is sheer speculation. The data are incapable of adjudicating between the two claims.

To find out the truth of the matter, you'd have to actually get on the ground and into the lives of individual human beings. Krugman is never willing to travel there, though, so he just sits and plays with numbers in his ivory tower.

However, class-based quantitative reasoning is the most suspect form of social science. Now, as this book has shown, I'm not a Thatcherite who denies the existence of society; the collective aspects of evolution have been a main theme throughout these chapters. But studying social groups without reference to the individuals who comprise them is an act of scientific negligence, on the level of a biologist who denies the phenotypic nature of selection. Society influences individual action, but only individuals act.

The evolutionary rules of complex networks that we covered in Chapter 3 perfectly explain the distributional oscillations in income that we've seen in the past century. The middle class societies of the 1950s perfectly exemplify the structured phase of network growth, when changes from growth phases become consolidated and widely spread. But what Krugman ignores is that the structured phase must follow the random and growth phases, and the latter tend to exacerbate differences, feedback loops, and other chaotic occurrences.

Network phases explain how cars, air conditioners and automatic kitchen equipment were toys of the rich in the 1920s, but were widely available to the American

> *American institutions have empowered a level of social-technological evolution that is unprecedented in any country.*

family in the 1950s. (*Hint:* There was no Affordable and Efficient Technology Act in Congress that did any of that.) Evolutionary systems continually shift between chance and structure, entrepreneurship and corporate mass-production, and change and stability. The widespread distribution of new technology undoubtedly empowered the growth of the Middle Class in the 1950s, but they were undeniably the result of the innovations of the 1920s.

Krugman recognizes the argument that innovative new technologies create Schumpeterian gales of creative destruction, and that the marketplace excels in mass producing these innovations to distribute them throughout society. But for some odd reason that can only be explained by an economist, Krugman believes this process has some terminal point at which disruptive growth ceases.

But as network theory explains, the structured phase can't last forever, and the system must eventually adapt to the next wave of changes. The essential point is that these cycles are continual, and that left to its own self-organizing devices, there will be no point that the modern economy will be permanently stuck in any phase.[377]

Evolution, on the other hand, perfectly explains the exceptional economic experience of this great nation. American institutions have empowered a level of social-technological evolution that is unprecedented in any country. This creates rapid growth, along with the network effects that accompany it, such as booms and busts.

Even Krugman, in his nostalgic yen for the 1950s, ignores the disadvantages of the closed, stagnant systems that comprised the period.

Racism was rampant, excluding blacks and immigrants from the promise of American prosperity. The rest of the world was largely war-ravaged and impoverished, allowing for an unsustainable period of American monopoly in global economic production. Social restrictions abounded; economic success required the adherance to conservative and mainstream lifestyles. Yes, we were stable, but as the 1960s showed, that stablity came at a severe social cost.

Krugman, an academic, clearly prefers old fashioned homogeneity. As a result, it's not surprising that he lionizes the Company Man days where one was permanently mired in a boring and unfulfilling job. But millions of my fellow Americans, learning from the insights of Abraham Maslow, realize that the good life requires a far more subjective set of economic values.

Today, professional athletes can make a prosperous living; they could not, at least certainly not to today's standards, in the 1940s and 1950s. Same for professional musicians. Unlike the 1950s, the ranks of today's multimillionaires includes kids from the Marcy Projects area of Brooklyn, like Jay-Z. Does Krugman really wish to return to the Good Ol' Days lacking racial equality, globalization and computer technology? Does he really find it disturbing that in the 21st century, kids can grow up to make millions as computer programmers, internet entrepreneurs, rappers, or professional snowboarders?

Perhaps so. Krugman generally views great wealth as some sort of blight on human society; he cites the number of billionaires as a bad thing, and notes that in the happy days of the Great Depression there were none. One thus presumes that Krugman believes the government was derelict in allowing Bill Gates to create Microsoft.

Indeed, Krugman actually compares the modern economy to Bill Gates simply walking into a bar: the "average" income of the bar (and thus our economy) goes up, Krugman argues, but none of the other individual bar patrons (or citizens) are actually any better off. The whole idea of techno-logical evolution making us all better off, Krugman provocatively concludes, is a delusion.

It is an amusing argument, given Krugman's inability to see through its implications. Even if it were true that Bill Gates' self-enriching creation of Microsoft had zero effect on anyone else's wages - a proposition dubious at best - Krugman still proves nothing. Because in Krugman's thought experi-ment, even if the bar patrons' incomes stay the same, they now magically have personal computers that allow them to be more productive, more easily communicate with friends and family, and learn more than they ever could before. They also can check their email at the bar with their mobile phones running on the very operating system Bill Gates designed. So much for being no better off.

The beauty of the marketplace isn't just told by the dollars people make at the end of the day, but the way that market-based innovations improve our lives.

Krugman's macro focus on income distributions renders him legally blind to these qualitative shifts that represent true evolution. Evolutionary economics is about far more than supply, demand, or aggregate income. There is evolution in the fact that I have near-instant access to nearly any book in the world through Amazon.com, nearly any album on the iTunes music store, and nearly every *thing* on Ebay, whether or not I can trace an increase in income to any of those companies. When I cited examples of the marketplace evolving in Chapter 1, I picked the iPhone for its empowerment of my lifestyle, not because I'm making money off of it.

Krugman's obsession with aggregate income - and his crucial starting assumption that it should be normally distributed - damns his entire project. Differentiation empowers evolution, and evolution causes cycles of skewed distributions. That's the major thesis of this book, and I believe that it is time for the public policy profession to finally recognize it as fact. Concentrating on income distributions, *ipso facto*, tells you little about how people are living.

A social science based on real science nowadays must recognize the reality of spontaneous growth.

A social science based on real science nowadays must recognize the reality of spontaneous growth. The shared lessons of complex systems, evolution, and quantum mechanics, as we mentioned in Chapter 3, is that they describe systems that are capable of emergent self-organization.

It is always in vain to stand athwart evolution, yelling Stop. If I may be bold, Krugman - Nobel Prize and all - is on the wrong side of scientific history.

Hoping for change

So, how do we help American politics get on the *correct* side of scientific history?

As Thucydides preciently stated, "For as in every other technical skill, so in the art of politics the new must always prevail over the old."[378]

With the election of President Obama, this is an extraordinary opportunity to repudiate the stale and discredited policies of the past and embark on a new journey of progress and freedom. I, with my fellow countrymen, are excited at the prospect of a leader willing to embrace a rupture with the failed policies of the past.

Unfortunately, despite much rhetoric to the contrary, Mr. Obama's policy has shown little in the way of new ideas or breaks with the past. Running up huge deficits by spending future generations' money was the *modus operandi* of President Bush. Mr. Obama's spending plans might equal a few trillion dollars of more debt than his predecessor, but it is certainly not much change in the main approach.

One-size-fits-all spending isn't anything new. Well-intentioned political leaders have tried for millennia to spend lots of money in order to placate their populations or avoid economic downturns. Such an approach has failed repeatedly. The brilliance of the American system, on the other hand, is its freedom-maximizing structure, unlike any in the world, that is wholly reliant on the ingenuity of the people for its dynamism.

If we really desire a fresh new approach, why not learn from evolution and empower freedom of choice? Why not maximize the adaptive capabilities of the American people? Why not recognize the complexity of self-organizing systems, and stop with a futile and discredited belief that rigid rules can create this progress?

The seven essential principles of evolutionary choice theory

Even the most radical structural changes will be insufficient if the governing *philosophy* of America's leaders does not adapt. Politicians' use of outdated policies to combat our modern challenges is the equivalent of fighting the Gulf War with Civil War muskets.

I hope this book so far has helped highlight the unique perspectives that evolutionary choice theory can bring to our modern challenges. Of course, there are more issues than could ever be discussed here, so in the end I hope this writing can provide a useful framework for evaluating policies and institutions in the future.

Beyond establishing elements of differentiation, selection and amplification, there are several aspects of evolutionary choice theory that are particularly relevant for policy makers. As a guide for aspiring policy makers, here are seven relevant fundamental principles of evolutionary choice theory, as applied to the pressing problems that our nation faces.

1) Maximize selection

Scientists and historians alike are nearly unanimous in recognizing Darwin's principle of natural selection as among the greatest ideas in the history of human thought. The purpose of this book is to help expand the principle to the development of ideas and technology.

In the same way that the survival of organisms over time represents the verdict of natural selection, the adoption of ideas over time represents the verdict of social-technological selection. It is a simple concept, although it is so routinely ignored by our political leaders that this book is necessary.

One can go on a fascinating journey analyzing the most corrupt, inefficient, and pathetic institutions of government and business alike, and one will find a shockingly perfect correlation between such failures and an absence of selection through free choice. The entitlements crisis spending other people's money. The Iraq fiasco making other people's political choices. The continuing economic difficulties after the ill-advised bailout.

However, we can also see how the expansion of selection has defined our greatest successes, helping us get better institutions and live better lives. The Founders knew that letting the people control their own lives was the greatest way to create a prosperous society. The leaders of the Civil Rights Movement realized that the cooperative venture required equal freedom for all. Will we, the citizens of the 21st century, continue this legacy?

2) Maximize differentiation

We dedicated an entire chapter on the value of differentiation, so the point should not be belabored. But this concept is central to the understanding of evolution, in the way that evolution produces a "differentiated unity", in Hegel's words. This paradoxical concept means that while we seek to maximize freedom and diversity, we recognize the interdependence of society at the same time.

Differentiation is the method by which the force of chance can create positive change; it is the method by which the impossible becomes possible.

Put simply, all ideas are not created equal, and all ideas must face the evolutionary selection process. There is a qualitative difference between GM's and Fisker's ideas for running a car company, Apple and Microsoft's ideas of how to build an operating system, or Geoff Canada and the New York State Board of Education's ideas of how to educate a child.

In this, we concur wholly with Justice Brandeis in Chapter 1, that in "differentiation, not uniformity, lies the path of progress."

3) We have nothing to fear except the fear of failure

One of the important philosophical lessons in evolution is the evolutionary paradox, specifically the essentiality of failure in order to have progress. Just as natural selection works by letting some organisms die, so human selection works by letting some ideas similarly perish. Through this negative force, the evolutionary system can produce positive results.

Applied to the real world, this concept was enshrined by Eric Beinhocker that businesses are the "grist for the evolutionary mill." This selection process should not be taken personally. Those that fail in business are not necessarily failures in life, as Herbert Spencer believed. The evolution is of social technologies, which are simply ideas. Governments must protect people, but we must leave ideas to their natural fate.

Failure is necessary in order to discover what works successfully. Growth - whether as a people or individually - stems from the overcoming of some negative force, and internalizing the lessons that the challenge teaches. As Heraclitus, the great philosopher of change, aphoristically reminds us, "the way up and the way down is one and the same."[379]

It's up to all of us to decide which of those ideas works best. It's time that politicians stop rigging the game, put every idea on a level playing field, and let the best ones win.

4) Change is constant

"The political system of a highly differentiated society...can no longer be regulated by rigid external guidance...or base its stability on fixed foundations, practices, or values. It can become stable only by creating possibilities for change."[380] -- **Niklas Luhmann**

One of the most fundamental lessons of evolutionary choice theory is the constancy of change. Ideas, technologies and environmental factors operate not in a state of static rigidity, but of dynamic flux. This fact is fatal for grand plans to manipulate human behavior, simply because people are always changing and adapting to new situations.[381]

By the time the neoclassical economists design their model or the sociologists construct their ideal society, the facts on which they've based their assumptions have changed. Everything from the nature of the problem addressed to its severity or relative significance is in constant flux. This fact cautions against the construction of laws according to some arbitrary pattern of personal preference.

Disorder increases over time,[382] and innovation is necessary to cope with the increasing chaos. Even the most deeply-rooted traditions must change and adapt at some point, just like the new Lutheran interpretation of the Bible or the new Air Force-oriented interpretation of the Constitution.

Evolutionary science recognizes that in a system of uncertainty, differentiation is essential.[383]

5) Technology (physical and social) is complex

"The nature of man is intricate; the objects of society are of the greatest possible complexity; and therefore no simple disposition or direction of power can be suitable either to man's nature, or to the quality of his affairs."[384] -- **Edmund Burke**

"Governing a great nation is like cooking a small fish. Too much handling will spoil it." -- **Lao Tsu**

The complexity of modern society dictates the inevitability of uncertainty and interconnectedness. In such an environment, Procrustean policies are worthless. It is time that policy makers finally recognize the wisdom contained in Lao Tsu and Edmund Burke's aphorisms and abandon the pursuit of perfecting society themselves.

While evolutionary forces operate with cause and effect, the specific linkages in the complex network of social technologies are impossible to discern by the individual human. In the interconnected interactions that define contemporary society, the phrase "there is more than meets the eye" is quite appropriate.

We must also realize that such complexity, even as it crushes the dreams of America's social planners and politicians, is beneficial to our nation in its own right.

James Madison has given the most explicit defense of political and social complexity in his views on American government. Madison realized that the dynamic tensions of American federalism create a social benefit and argued that differentiation is essential to social harmony.[385]

6) The wisdom of crowds is a discovery procedure

Rather than promising to solve all of the nation's problems, politicians should seek to design institutions that maximize the people's ability to do so themselves. The focus should not be attempting to design perfect solutions, but instead empowering the choices of the people.

Freedom of choice, as an evolutionary selection mechanism, is the only tool capable of discovering the black swan innovations in a complex and changing environment. Through the creation of multiple options and the exercise of free choice, the evolutionary process functions best.[386]

Freedom of choice answers the questions that no politician or policy expert can answer, questions like how Shabnam Moshref or Glenna Fouberg can live most happily, how ski resorts can avoid future economic calamities, how one can best pursue an environmentally friendly shopping style, how to best create jobs, or how Christianity can embrace modernity.

America is a nation that thrives on the wisdom of crowds. William F. Buckley, Jr., encapsulating this quintessential American spirit, said that he'd rather be governed by the first two thousand names in the Boston telephone directory than the entire faculty of Harvard University.

Our freedom of choice is a better guide to living than any idea produced in an ivory tower. Choice is the means toward the value-added innovation, the emergent property and the Hegelian synthesis. Most of all, it fuels the evolutionary process that is smarter than you are.

7) Evolution is a cooperative venture

Differentiation and selection require the acts of individuals, but the emergence of evolutionary progress always requires a larger group.

Thus, the clear command of public policy is to help people participate in the cooperative venture of the evolutionary process. It is the survival of everyone that helps find the fittest social technologies. This principle dictates that the verdict of the marketplace should not be politically manipulated, but that government must find ways to protect people *outside* of the marketplace.

This perfect balance, as G.W.F. Hegel noted, is painfully difficult to strike. Excessive welfare protections, by discouraging productive effort, interfere with evolution. However, inadequate welfare protections, by creating an angry and disaffected "rabble" in Hegel's words, creates instability and threatens the very public legitimacy of the market system. The balance is easy to articulate—a "hand up," not a "hand out"—but nearly impossible to design in practice.

The philosopher John Rawls attempted to solve this difficulty with his "difference principle," which states that inequalities in society should be arranged so they are to the greatest advantage of the least well-off.[387] Rawls recommends that such arrangements should take place in the design of society, in an effort to design institutions conducive for justice and fairness.

The problem remains in determining permissible levels of inequality. Surely the unemployed wagon wheel manufacturer believes his economic inequality is unjust, but few would argue that the technological transfer to motor vehicles benefits everyone, and thus satisfies the Rawlsian difference principle.

But retrospect is a luxury in which real-world societies cannot easily indulge. Is the Iowa farmer in a similar situation? How about the West Virginia coal miner?

At any rate, the inability of any politician to accurately answer these questions is manifest. Instead, American society should recognize our own bounded rationality and embrace the fact that an accurate Rawlsian economic distribution can never occur in the complex and changing real world in which we live.

In the meantime, the effort should be to help people enter into the cooperative venture as best as we can. Provisions of education, of welfare support, of unemployment insurance, and of emergency health coverage are necessary but cannot be unlimited. No matter how wealthy a society becomes, Orgel's Second Rule does not disappear.

What we can do

Unfortunately, the idea of politicians reading this book and conforming their platforms according to evolutionary choice theory is a delusion. It is incumbent on we the people to lead the movement toward progress-oriented policies.

Evolutionary theory recognizes the importance of "political entrepreneurs" creating innovative change in society similar to the way that traditional entrepreneurs create innovative change in the marketplace.[388] Political entrepreneurs can take the form of agitators, preachers, prophets or philosophers, but all have in common the desire to bring new and innovative political technologies to the public.

It is incumbent upon all of us to become political entrepreneurs, whether through activism at the local level, technological innovation, or simply helping our fellow citizens understand how progress works.

I hope it is clear how distinct this pursuit is from the current pastime of America's most popular pundits, which seems to be a cacophonous medley of *ad hominem* ridicule, conflation of complex issues into glittering generalities, mischievous wordplay, and political gossip generally. I have no clue as to why such a dismal state of affairs has gripped America's pundits, or why their rhetoric should traduce the legacies of William F. Buckley, J.K. Galbraith, and the rest of the brilliant minds to whom our modern pundits owe their jobs. Nor does it matter, for we the people enjoy the eternal prerogative to correct it.

Toward that end, here are some ways that we can become the change that we can believe in.

Jam out on Gideon's Trumpet

The adaptability of the American system requires the active engagement of its citizens. As we mentioned in Chapter 7, our Constitutional provisions cannot evolve except through active litigation. Thus, one of the most effective actions we the people can take is to challenge the laws of our nation as unconstitutional. In the book *Gideon's Trumpet*, author Anthony Lewis chronicles the story of Clarence Earl Gideon, who was arrested on theft charges and denied a defense attorney even though he couldn't afford one. In prison, Gideon immersed himself in constitutional law, concluded that such denial was unconstitutional, represented himself on appeal, and took the case all the way to the Supreme Court. The Court agreed, and in *Gideon v. Wainright*, held for the first time that all criminal defendants have the right to an attorney, even if they can't afford one.

The story of Gideon's trumpet should inspire us today; no matter how great our challenges are, the United States Constitution can deliver justice in the face of seemingly insurmountable injustice.

Whether it's small businesses challenging regulations as violating the right to pursue a lawful calling, citizens challenging social regulations as interfering with the right of privacy, or states challenging federal mandates as violating the 10th Amendment, active adjudication of our fundamental Constitutional principles is essential. Nothing is more American.

One, Two, Three, Four, Please Don't Protest Anymore

One method of activism that is currently *en vogue* politically is that of the mass protest. However, the method is wholly incompatible with the goals it seeks to achieve. Put simply, reform will never arise from a demand that one group of citizens see a contentious issue a certain way simply because the group demanding it has signs, banners and pithy chants in the form of rhyming couplets.

Granted, a conceivable benefit of public demonstration is that protests can raise public awareness of issues. This is almost always a positive development, obviously, and is thus cited as one of the civic advantages of a protest-happy citizenry.

In the modern age, however, mass protest is hardly the best method of achieving civic awareness. Today's methods of publically expressing political displeasure without sacrificing reason and rationality involve the civilized media of the 21st century. These include the use of televised debate, advertisement, newspaper column writing and/or letter writing, internet blogging and publication, magazine publication, legal challenges, organized boycott and many more. There is no excuse for protesting as the only option for activism.

Consider the absurdity of a citizen somehow being persuaded by a protest. "Gee, I was really on the fence about this issue," says the hypothetical persuaded passer-by, "but now that I've seen all of these people I've never met on my local street, holding signs, wearing T-shirts emblazoned with bald

partisan assertions, and generally shouting various angry refrains about the alleged motives of our elected leaders, I am definitely convinced that the legislature should attempt to pursue alternative action, per the requests of these fine protesters."

Of course, it never works that way, simply because a) political persuasion is not facilitated by a 50 mph drive-by of community activists, and more importantly, b) the protest makes no attempt whatsoever at forming a reasoned, principled political argument.

Despite being right about the faulty intelligence of the Iraq War, liberals failed to get public support for their views because they cast them in shrill dissent, personal attacks, conspiracy theories and other futile 1960s political tactics.

On the fifth anniversary of the war, as American tanks continued to shell Baghdad without a pause, San Francisco protesters were found marching down the same parade route they had been using since their first Iraq protest, complete with the charming refrain, "One, two, three, four, we don't want this racist war; five, six, seven, eight, U.S. is a terror state."[389] How's that working out for you?

Not well, in fact. "It doesn't seem like our voices are being heard," glumly observed Jamie Jones, a protester donning a "Not My President" T-shirt with Bush's lips covered by the word "liar" in red. "We need to take it to another level."[390] Good luck with that, Jamie. You of all people should know how well escalation works to win hearts and minds.

Engage the fellow citizen

The best method of political engagement is the time-honored method of calm, rational and friendly conversation. Persuasion might require passionate debate, but it never requires hostility or hatred.

The best all of us can do is to engage our friends, colleagues and acquaintances, as appropriate, and articulate our views and the reasons for holding them. The common methods of "debate" so popular today—guilt by association, *argumentum ad absurdum,* or *ad hominem* attacks—are counterproductive.

In the effort to persuade one's fellow citizen, it is advisable to avoid questioning the motives or ethics of one's political opponent. Odds are, the person with whom you strongly disagree wants to make the world better as much as you do.

It's easy to point out what's wrong in the world, or with someone else's view. It is far more difficult, and far more worthy of praise, to find common ground.

The principle of political cooperation is beautifully illustrated in *The Voice of the People: The Transpartisan Imperative in American Life,* written by A. Lawrence Chickering and James S. Turner.[391] Chickering and Turner highlight a conception of political thought that embraces cooperation, understanding and the recognition of eternal unity. Most interestingly, the authors even recognize that this fusion, similar to the discussion of network theory in Chapter 3, represents a dynamic combination of structure and independence.

If we want to progress as a society, it is time to reject the stale old prejudices and biases of the last century. A house divided against itself cannot evolve.

Concluding thoughts

The subject of evolution always humbles the writer. For the subject, properly understood, is a system of the utmost complexity, dynamism and fluidity. The complex features of this study makes one question the validity of one's own perspective. Given the law of the vital few and others like it, I am supremely confident in predicting that much of this book will be deemed wrong or irrelevant by most readers.

Charles Darwin recognized such limitations in his own evolutionary perspective. In a letter to a friend after *The Origin of Species* was published, Darwin confided, "I look at it as absolutely certain that very much in the *Origin* will be proved rubbish; but I expect and hope that the framework will stand."[392] On the sesquicentennial of the publication of his book, we can be assured in saying that Darwin's framework has stood the test of time as an axiom of the biological sciences.

In a similar sense, I hope that the framework of this book will be deemed useful to the political, economic and social sciences. I hope it can serve as a helpful guide to analyzing unprecedented challenges.

I hope it inspires my fellow countrymen to recognize the inalienable value in their fellow Americans—even with all of the diversity and conflict—as partners in the cooperative evolutionary venture we call American history. I hope it inspires them, in turn, to express their support for a political order conducive to our future progress, one where the uniqueness of individual human ingenuity is unleashed to solve the greatest problems in our day.

In this political debate, it is time for a new level of discourse. We all want to make society better; right, left, anarchists and socialists alike.

Our enemy is not malice, but misunderstanding. The fundamental political question is not of motive but of execution; not of effort but of impact. The only relevant difference in political viewpoints is in the specific understanding of how to make society better; all sides have the general ambition to do so.

If there's one lesson this book can impart, I hope it is that each of us has the inability to design the improvement that we all desire. Neither desire nor good intentions suffice to design the evolutionary order. If such a process can fool the brilliant minds of Thomas Malthus, Joseph Schumpeter and William Buckley, then you can understand the ignorance that your average politician or pundit possesses.

Centuries ago, the great philosopher Socrates set about to disprove an admirer's contention that he was the wisest human alive. But after seeking greater wisdom from politicians, poets and artisans in order to find someone wiser, Socrates realized all of them were quite ignorant, despite their estimations of their own wisdom. In the end, Socrates concluded that he was wiser than the others, but only through his awareness of his own ignorance.[393]

As Friedrich Hayek pointed out, much more recently, in his Nobel Prize acceptance speech:

> The recognition of the insuperable limits to [human] knowledge ought indeed to teach the student of society a lesson of humility which should guard him against becoming an accomplice in men's fatal striving to control society... a striving which makes him not only a tyrant over his fellows, but which may well make him the destroyer of a civilization which no brain has designed but which has grown from the free efforts of millions of individuals.[394]

The message is thus of our bounded rationalities as free individuals, but yet of our eternal wisdom as a *collection of free individuals*. The message is one of hope, deriving from history a clear affirmation of reasoned optimism, perpetual growth, positivity and a Hegelian view of continuous expansion.

Finally, I hope that the message of this book strikes my countrymen as nothing new, despite all of the fancy trappings of network theory and evolutionary thought. I hope they view the message at its core, as an affirmation of the ideals fundamentally rooted in our nation's history and traditions.

I hope then, this distinction of national purpose renders an ultimate message that the United States of America will not simply fall, as other weaker nations have. We stand for something more, something not rooted in the ephemeral spheres of ethnicity or religion, but rather in a creed of fundamental truth; a truth now confirmed with the most modern of sciences. This value, freedom of choice, is our greatest asset.

In these challenging times, it is reliance on this unique aspect of our national character that will lead us through. Our nation must realize its own greatness, and seize the opportunity. If we can do so, one thing we will know is that the 2000s will again be the American century.

About the Author

MATT HARRISON is founder and executive director of the Prometheus Institute, a nonprofit public policy institute. Matt graduated from the University of Miami with a Bachelor of Business Administration in Political Science and is currently a joint law degree and Master of Public Policy candidate at the University of Southern California. He has authored over 200 articles, publications and other features for Prometheus, has been a guest on several talk radio shows and has been quoted in the *Chicago Tribune*.

About The Prometheus Institute

THE PROMETHEUS INSTITUTE is a public policy organization dedicated to discovering independent policy solutions to reduce the burden of government on the people, and creatively marketing these ideas to the lay public of the United States, in order to create the political demand for positive change.

We encourage you to visit our website to learn more about our work. Thanks for reading.

www.ThePrometheusInstitute.org

NOTES

[1] Presentation by the Honorable David M. Walker, Comptroller General of the United States, *Transforming Government to Meet the Demands of the 21st Century,* The Federal Midwest Human Resources Council and the Chicago Federal Executive Board, August 7, 2007, Chicago, IL

[2] Statement of Douglas Holtz-Eakin, CBO Director, *Medicare's Long-Term Financial Condition,* before the Joint Economic Committee Congress of the United States, April 10, 2003

[3] Carmen DeNavas-Walt, Bernadette D. Proctor, and Jessica Smith, "U.S. Census Bureau, Current Population Reports," *Income, Poverty, and Health Insurance Coverage in the United States,* 2006, 60-233

[4] "Public educational system" refers to the K-12 system.

[5] For views pro and con on the "knowledge economy," see Stephanie Flanders, "Survey of World Economy and Finance – Industry," *Financial Times,* September 30, 1994, and "Through the Looking Glass," *Crossfire,* CNN, January 2, 1995

[6] Steven Ohlemacher, "Number of Illegal Immigrants Hits 12M," *Associated Press,* March 7, 2006

[7] Lexington, "American Idiocracy," *The Economist,* March 22, 2007

[8] Theodocious Dobzhansky, *The Biological Basis of Human Freedom*, Columbia 1956 at 134

[9] François Jacob, *The Possible and the Actual,* University of Washington 1992, at 61, relying on ideas expressed by Ernst Mayr regarding "open" biological systems. See E. Mayr, "The Evolution of Living Systems," in *Evolution and the Diversity of Life,* Harvard, 1976, at 23.

[10] "American Voices: Across U.S., people say what freedom means," *Knight Ridder/Tribune,* July 4, 2002

[11] Ibid.

[12] Ibid.

[13] Christy Nicholson, "Freedom and Choice, Culture and Class," *Observer,* Association for Psychological Science, August 2006, Volume 19, Number 8

[14] Ibid.

[15] Address of Louis D. Brandeis at Faneuil Hall, Boston, July 5, 1915

[16] Ben Harper, "Burn One Down," *Fight for Your Mind,* © 1995 Virgin Records America

[17] Akhil Reed Amar, *America's Constitution: A Biography*, Random House, New York, 2006, 5

[18] Quoted in Eric Foner, *The Story of American Freedom* at 55

[19] Ibid.

[20] "Zundel turned over to German authorities," *CBC News*, March 1, 2005

[21] Arthur H. Schaffer, *To be an American: David Ramsay and the Making of the American Consciousness,* Columbia, SC, 1991, 107-12

[22] Tori DeAngelis, "Too many choices?: Today's abundance of consumer options can stall our decision-making and even wear away our well-being. But there are solutions," *Monitor on Psychology, American Psychological Association,* June 2005, at 56

[23] Chris Anderson, *The Long Tail*

[24] For an example, see William Niskanen, *Reflections by a Political Economist,* Cato Institute press, 2008, at 341, and the discussion in Chapter 6, infra

[25] The example here is the Arctic Monkeys, a UK band

[26] See www.pandora.com

[27] Jessica Mintz, "Starbucks Closing 600 Stores in the US," *Associated Press,* July 1, 2008

[28] Data taken from Fortune 50 1980 and Fortune 50 2000

[29] Information gathered from Fresh and Easy website, www.freshandeasy. com

[30] Jonathan Birchall, "Wal-Mart goes purple with Marketside," *Financial Times,* August 26, 2008

[31] Naomi Klein, *No Logo: Taking Aim at the Brand Bullies,* Picador Press, New York, 1999

[32] Nike Press Release, "Nike Responds to *No Logo,*" March 8, 2000, currently available at http://web.archive.org/web/20010618162615/http://nikebiz. com/labor/nologo_let.shtml

[33] Editorial, "Freedom of choice underlies USA's religious vibrancy," *USA Today,* February 27, 2008

[34] See Robert D. Putnam, Lewis M. Feldstein, Don Cohen, *Better Together: Restoring the American Community,* 2003, Chapter 6

[35] Alexis de Tocqueville, *Democracy in America*, Book II, Chapter 5

[36] James Brooke, "Snowboarders Ride to Ski Industry's Rescue; A Winter Sport's Image Has Changed From Bad Boy to King of the Mountain," *New York Times,* December 22, 1997

[37] Erin Gartner, "Once shunned, snowboarders now coveted by ski industry," *Associated Press,* December 6, 2004

[38] *Meet the Press,* NBC, May 22, 2005

[39] Barbara Boxer, "Voting for choice this election year," *The San Diego Union-*

Tribune, February 15, 2000

[40] Dick Armey, "Where We Went Wrong," *The Washington Post*, October 29, 2006

[41] Beth Fouhy, "Clinton health care plan built around universal coverage, federal subsidies," *The Associated Press*, September 17, 2007

[42] George F. Will, "Freedom vs. Equality," *The Washington Post*, February 1, 2004

[43] Samuel P. Huntington, "American Ideals versus American Institutions," *Political Science Quarterly*, Vol. 97, No. 1 (Spring, 1982), 1-37

[44] Thomas Hobbes, *Leviathan*, Oxford University Press, 1998, 84

[45] Thucydides, Crawly translation, I, 1, 2

[46] Ibid.

[47] Bjorn Lomborg, *The Skeptical Environmentalist*

[48] Eric Beinhocker, *The Origin of Wealth,* Harvard Press, 2006 at 11

[49] Thanks to Fred Frohock, my college professor and mentor in political theory at the University of Miami, for this perspicuous argument. As you can tell, it has profoundly affected my thought.

[50] Richard R. Nelson, "Physical and Social Technologies and their Evolution," Working Paper, quoted in Beinhocker at 15, also generally Nelson, "The Coevolution of Technologies and Institutions," in Richard W. England, ed, *Evolutionary Concepts in Contemporary Economics*, The University of Michigan Press, 1994, 139

[51] Beinhocker at 262

[52] Malthus, *An Essay on the Principle of Population*, Chapter 1

[53] Quoted in Nathaniel O. Keohane and Sheila M. Olmstead, *Markets and the Environment*

[54] Patrick J. Michaels, "What's Hot, and What's Not," *San Diego Union-Tribune*, March 11, 2007

[55] For more examples, see http://www.pocketgadget.org/2008/01/14/serendipity-10-accidental-inventions

[56] See, e.g., Oded Galor and Omer Moav, "Natural Selection and the Origin of Economic Growth", *The Quarterly Journal of Economics*, Vol. 117, No. 4, (Nov. 2002), 1133-1191

[57] See, e.g., G.M. Hodgson: "There is a core set of general Darwinian principles that, along with auxiliary explanations specific to each scientific domain, may apply to a wide range of phenomena." "Darwinism in economics: from analogy to ontology," *Journal of Evolutionary Economics,* 12, at 270

[58] Robert N. Bellah, "Religious Evolution," *American Sociological Review,*

Vol. 29, No. 3, (Jun. 1964), 358-374 (emphasis added)

[59] R.A. Fisher, "The measurement of selective intensity," *Proc. R. Soc. B.*, 121, (1936), 58

[60] For evolutionary theorists recognizing "blind chance" as a substantial force in evolution, see R.C. Lewontin, "Sociobiology: another biological determinism," *International Journal of Health Services*, 10, 347; M. Kimura, *The Neutral Theory of Molecular Evolution*, Cambridge, 1983; and J.S. Jones, "How much genetic variation?" *Nature*, 288, 10-11

[61] Adam Smith, *The Wealth of Nations*, Book I, Chapter 2, paragraph 2

[62] Ibid., Book I, Chapter 1, paragraph 1

[63] Thorstein Veblen, "Why Is Economics not an Evolutionary Science?" *Quarterly Journal of Economics*, 12, (1898), 390-1

[64] Joseph Schumpeter, *Capitalism, Socialism, and Democracy*. 5th ed. London: George Allen and Unwin., at 82

[65] See, e.g., Burton Klein, E*volutionary Economics: Applications of Schumpeter's Ideas*; and N. Luhmann, *The Differentiation of Society*, Columbia, 1982, at 192: "...the economy does not exist naturally, but instead is in every way an evolutionary achievement."

[66] See, e.g. Birner and van Zijp, *Hayek, Coordination and Evolution: His Legacy in Philosophy, Politics, Economics, and the History of Ideas*, Routledge, 1994

[67] Friedrich august von Hayek, *The Fatal Conceit: The Errors of Socialism*

[68] David Hume, *A Treatise of Human Nature*, Oxford University Press, 1978, ed. L. A. Selby-Bigge, 2nd ed., revised by P. H. Nidditch bk. III, pt. II, sec. II; also see G. Dietze, *In Defense of Property*, (1971) 93, for the argument that rules of property aided the evolution of Western civilization

[69] Carl Menger, *Principles of Economics*, trans. by J. Dingwall & B. F. Hoselitz. New York: New York University Press. [1871] (1981). Menger, *Problems of Economics and Sociology*, trans. by F. J. Nock. Urbana: University of Illinois Press, [1883] (1963) discussing the "organic origin of institutions," and Ferguson, A, "An Essay on the History of Civil Society," London: Millar and Caddel, (1767) p. 187, "Nations stumble upon establishments, which are indeed the result of human action, but not the execution of any human design"

[70] See, e.g., Michael Hunter, "Communication in Economic Evolution: The Case of Money," in Richard W. England, ed, *Evolutionary Concepts in Contemporary Economics*, The University of Michigan Press, 1994, 111

[71] See Chapter 8, infra

[72] See, e.g, Martin A. Nowak and David C. Krakauer, *The Evolution of Language, Proceedings of the National Academy of Sciences of the United States of America,* Vol. 96, No. 14, (July 16, 1999), 8028-8033

[73] See, e.g., Sir Francis Palgrave, *Truths and fictions of the Middle Ages. The merchant and the friar* (1844) "Our constitutional form of government has been produced by evolution.", at 138, and Norman Schofield, "Evolution of the Constitution", *British Journal of Political Science*, Vol. 32, No. 1, (Jan. 2002)

[74] See, e.g., Kent V. Flannery, "The Cultural Evolution of Civilizations," *Annual Review of Ecology and Systematics,* Vol. 3, (1972), 399-426, Alexander Alland, Jr, "Evolution and Human Behavior" (1967), and W. Penn Handwerker, "The Origins and Evolution of Culture," *American Anthropologist,* New Series, Vol. 91, No. 2, (Jun. 1989), 313-326

[75] Michael Allen Fox, *The Accessible Hegel*, Humanity Books, New York, 2005, 16

[76] Beinhocker at 11

[77] Richard R. Nelson and Sidney G. Winter, "Evolutionary Theorizing in Economics," *The Journal of Economic Perspectives*, Vol. 16, No. 2, (Spring, 2002), 23-46

[78] See generally, Beinhocker chapter X

[79] Veblen, *Essays on our changing order,* New York, Viking Press, at 8

[80] Veblen, "The place of science in modern civilization," at 165, emphasis added

[81] Hayek, "The Use of Knowledge in Society," *American Economic Review,* XXXV, No. 4, September, 1945, 519–30

[82] This argument can be impugned by supporters of punctuated *equilibrium* theory, a concept first developed by Stephen Jay Gould and Niles Eldridge in biological contexts, which argues that evolution occurs in short punctuated bursts followed by long periods of static (or semi-static) equilibrium. However, even Gould himself recognized that although the punctuated equilibrium model recognizes the inevitable presence of *stasis*, evolutionary processes still created rapid change, and the study of change justifiably remained the major focus of evolutionary theory. In my view, Gould's theory served primarily to undermine Darwinian assumptions that change was constant, but also undermines the neoclassical economic assumption that staticity is permanent. See Gould, *The Structure of Evolutionary Theory*, Harvard, 2002, at 957

[83] For the fact that scientific revolutions need not repudiate all of a prior

paradigm, see Thomas Kuhn, *The Structure of Scientific Revolutions,* Univ. of Chicago, 1962

[84] Fritz Rohrlich, "Facing Quantum Mechanical Reality", *Science* 23 1983, 1251-1255

[85] Elliott Sober, *The Nature of Selection,* MIT Press 1984 at 104

[86] Robert Brandon and Scott Carson, "The Indeterministic Character of Evolutionary Theory: No 'Hidden Variables' Proof by No Room for Indeterminism Either", *Philosophy of Science* 63 (1996): 320

[87] Jacques Monod, *Chance and Necessity: An essay on the natural philosophy of modern biology,* Harmondsworth, England: Penguin 1971, 112-113

[88] See Amit Goswami, *The Visionary Window* (Quest Books 2000), for the argument that free choice "collapses" the "waves of possibility" into actuality.

[89] In this sense, neoclassical economics is quite analogous to the Ptolemaic method of astronomy that had yielded (and still can yield) accurate predictions regarding the movements of stars and planets. The method was only disregarded when the superior Copernican system was created and shown to yield more accurate results regarding the procession of the equinoxes and other complex phenomena. See T. S. Kuhn, T*he Structure of Scientific Revolutions,* at 68

[90] Beinhocker at 318.

[91] This point fits well within the neoclassical framework, see Alfred Marshall, *Principles of Economics,* 8th edition, Macmillan, London (1920), 115: "Knowledge is our most powerful engine of production; it enables us to subdue Nature and force her to satisfy our wants. Organization aids knowledge."

[92] Ernst Mayr, *Animal Species and Evolution,* Harvard, 1963, at 586, arguing that evolution is due to "the accumulation of small genetic changes," which is "guided by natural selection," which is then followed by an "extrapolation and magnification" of the previous evolutionary events.

[93] Op cit.

[94] Charles Darwin called used the term variation for this concept, and evolutionary theorists today use both terms. I will use differentiation, because it more effectively conceptualizes the process of human decision-making as opposed to genetic modification. While the two terms are similar (and, in my view, effectively interchangeable), I believe differentiation is a better concept to use, if one must pick. To differentiate is "to recognize or ascertain what makes something different, or to make or become different in the process of growth." Variation is defined as a "change or slight difference...

typically within certain limits". (Source: OED) Because freedom allows a greater degree of divergence than implied by the term variation, and because differentiation encapsulates the concept of the recognition of difference, I use differentiation.

[95] Luhmann at 214, "The concept of differentiation refers to the construction of subsystems...system differentiation is a form of strengthening selectivity."

[96] Smith, *The Wealth of Nations*, Book 1, Chapter 1, and David Ricardo, *The Principles of Political Economy and Taxation*, Chapter 7, London: John Murray, 3rd ed, 1821, respectively.

[97] John Stuart Mill, *On Liberty*, 34-40, (Longmans, Green, Reader & Dyer, London, 1863) Original from Harvard University, digitized Nov 8, 2007

[98] Marina Chicurel, "Can Organisms Speed Their Own Evolution?",*Science*, New Series, Vol. 292, No. 5523, (Jun. 8, 2001); also see R.A. Fisher, *The Genetical Theory of Natural Selection*, (Oxford 1999 at 46) arguing that the rate of increase in fitness is equal to the genetic variance of a population

[99] See Sober, *The Nature of Selection* at 21-22, Gould, *Structure of Evolutionary Theory* at 13, or Robert N. Brandon, *Concepts and Methods in Evolutionary Biology*, Cambridge 1996 at 6

[100] Will Durant, *The Story of Philosophy*, Simon & Schuster New York (1926/2005) p 52

[101] Gould, *Structure of Evolutionary Theory*, at 139

[102] Therefore, evolutionary choice theory argues that volitional choice, regarding a social technology's achievement of a goal as *determined by the chooser*, is the force analogous to natural selection in Darwinian theory, and the essential feature of any evolutionary system. Thus, fitness is a subjective measure, although through amplification measures over time, the emergent property of objective progress arises. (See Chapter 3, *infra*.)

This discovery, to the best of my knowledge, has yet to be argued explicitly by evolutionary economists. (For an overview of the prevailing theories on economic selection theory, see Thorbjørn Knudsen, "Economic Selection Theory", *J Evol Econ* (2002) 12: 443). The closest I have seen yet to a volition-based selection theory is in an obscure article in the *Journal of Evolutionary Economics* by Hardy Hanappi: "What gave the human species the decisive advantage over the rest of the animal kingdom—at least this is the speculation—was the possibility to internalize mixed strategies in the brains of each single individual, a capacity that was experienced by the emerging consciousness as choice." (H. Hanappi, "The concept of choice: why and how innovative behaviour is not stochastic," *J. Evol Econ* (2008) 18: 285, emphasis added) Hanappi also argues that recent discoveries in evolutionary game theory - especially by John von Neumann - have confirmed this point, recognizing "choice as a creative process emerging in the interplay in between social entities as well as in between real processes and visions... [and part of an] innovative process that enables an entity to build an internal model to guide its actions." Stephen Jay Gould has also vaguely implied that humans' evolutionary advantage lies in their ability to mentally experiment. (S.J. Gould, *Ever Since Darwin*, p. 71) A similar point was made by François Jacob, discussed infra.

The profundity of evolutionary choice theory is in its giving a direct explanation of why political, economic and social evolution seems to be moving at such a fast pace *vis-a-vis* biological evolution, especially so in the modern world. Natural selection, by definition, can only evaluate a biological mutation upon death or biological reproduction; free choice, on the other hand, is continually and actively employed as an evaluation process. Choice allows humans to function as replicators as well as interactors. (See Knudsen for the biological relevance of those Darwinian concepts). The political, moral and institutional protections for free choice that arose in the mid-eighteenth century, in my view, are directly responsible for the radically accelerated path of social-technological and physical-technological evolution. As this book argues, such institutions can continue to accelerate this beneficial process into the 21st century.

[103] See Gould, *Structure of Evolutionary Theory*, at 595-644, explaining at length the concept of phenotypic selection and its incompatibility with Dawkins' "selfish gene" theory, among others

[104] World-record swimmer and decorated Olympic gold medalist Michael Phelps, for example, listens to hip-hop before his swim meets, as reported by NBC during the 2008 Olympic games in Beijing.

[105] J. S. Metcalfe, "Evolutionary Economics and Technology Policy," *The Economic Journal,* Vol. 104, No. 425 (Jul., 1994), 931-944

[106] See Hayek, *Studies in Philosophy, Politics and Economics*, University of Chicago, 1967, 233: "[R]emuneration, in accordance with the value of a man's services, inevitably is often very different from what we think of his moral merit." Arguably, the amorality of the market is a benefit: as Luhmann argues in *The Differentiation of Society,* supra at 203: "Economic communication becomes indifferent to circumstances, to biographical details, and to personal acquaintances. People do not need to know each other and to size up each other morally in order to come to an understanding."

[107] Oded Galor and Omer Moav, "Natural Selection and the Origin of Economic Growth," *The Quarterly Journal of Economics*, Vol. 117, No. 4 (Nov. 2002), 1133-1191

[108] Richard Dawkins, *The Selfish Gene*, (Oxford 1989), 1976, at 192; See also Susan Blackmore, *The Meme Machine*, (Okford 2000) at 52; Why do I not use the "meme" concept in this book? The answer is because it was derived directly from Dawkins' genotypic selection theories, which directly seek to counter phenotypic selection theories. Just as I believe that phenotypic concepts (i.e. the emergence of individual traits worth more than the sum of their genotypic parts) are essential to biological evolution, so I believe that social technologies represent emergent properties more than their memetic parts. Thus, even referring to social technologies as "memeplexes" dangerously ignores the emergent properties of technology, as well as the central role of human individuals in creating them. (More on the concept of emergence in Chapter 3.)

[109] Hayek, F.A. 1979. *Law, Legislation, and Liberty, Vol. 3: The Political Order of a Free People*, Chicago, University of Chicago Press, at 157 and Hayek, F.A. 1988. *The Fatal Conceit*, edited by W.W. Bartley III. Chicago: University of Chicago Press, arguing that rule adoption "simulates" Lamarckian evolution, at 25

[110] Hayek, *The Fatal Conceit*

[111] Herbert Spencer, the founder of Social Darwinism, harbors several views that collide violently with evolutionary choice theory; the first being the view that evolutionary cause and effect are strongly linked, justifying the conclusion that those who make poor decisions in the marketplace can be deemed "unfit." However, as we've discussed, the complexity and unpredictability of the evolutionary system renders such simplistic views dangerously inaccurate; brilliant and talented individuals have failed numerous times. Second, Mr. Spencer is a determinist known for his open hostility toward the principle of free choice, as he expressed bluntly, "That anyone could desire or not desire arbitrarily, which is the real proposition concealed in the dogma of free will, is refuted as much through the analysis of consciousness as through the content of [my preceding work]", in H. Spencer, *The Principles of Psychology* (1855). For these reasons, as well as to purge the evolutionary perspective from such hostile ideas, Mr. Spencer's work - and those of his Social Darwinist acolytes - will be conspicuously absent from this book. For more, see Hayek, F. A. (1973), *Law Legislation and Liberty, Vol. I*. London: Routledge, at 23, further denouncing the Social Darwinists from

an evolutionary perspective.

[112] See Luhmann at 200-201: "[Market differentiation] allows risky and improbable heightenings of abstraction and specification to arise, as well as a mobilization of possibilities that from the beginning are only economic ones, and not political, legal, technical, moral, or emotional ones as well....Actions that otherwise would have had to rely on wide-ranging considerations about all of society can thus be specialized for purely economic functions."

[113] Thanks to David Seymour for this construction

[114] Karl Popper, *All Life is Problem Solving*, trans. Patrick Camiller, Routledge, London and New York, 1999, at 39

[115] Ibid. at 10.

[116] Dobzhansky, at 78-79

[117] Hayek, *Constitution of Liberty*, Chapters 2-3

[118] *Laissez-faire* was never more than rule of thumb. It indeed expressed protest against abuses of governmental power, but never provided a criterion by which one could decide what were the proper functions of government' Hayek, F.A. (1973) *Law, Legislation and Liberty: A New Statement of the Liberal Principles of Justice and Political Economy, vol. 1: Rules and Order*, London and Henley: Routledge and Kegan Paul 61-2, and 'While the presumption must favor the free market, *laissez-faire* is not the ultimate and only conclusion.' Hayek, F.A. (1933b) 'The Trend of Economic Thinking', *Economica*, vol. 13, May: 134

[119] Hayek, *Studies in Philosophy, Politics and Economics*, University of Chicago, 1967, at 175: "There is of course no reason why a society which, thanks to the market, is as rich as modern society should not provide outside the market a minimum security for all who in the market fall below a certain standard...With regard to these functions, for the discharge of which the government is given money, we will here only say that government should be under the same rules as every private citizen, that is should possess no monopoly for a particular service of this kind, [and] that it should discharge these functions in such a manner as not to disturb the much more comprehensive spontaneously ordered efforts of society..."

[120] See S. J. Gould, *The Structure of Evolutionary Theory*, Harvard, 127-128, and C. Darwin, *The Origin of Species*, Sixth Edition London: Murray at 87: "In social animals, [natural selection] will adapt the structure of each individual for the benefit of the community; if each in consequence profits by the selected change."; and at 489, "As natural selection works solely by and for the good of each being, all corporeal and mental endowments will tend

to progress toward perfection."

[121] Aristotle, *Politics*, London: Oxford University Press (1972) (translated by E. Barker), at 123: when individuals "all come together . . . they may surpass—collectively and as a body, although not individually— the quality of the few best . . . . When there are many who contribute to the process of deliberation, each can bring his share of goodness and moral prudence . . . some appreciate one part, some another, and all together appreciate all."

[122] James Surowiecki, *The Wisdom of Crowds*, 10

[123] Surowiecki, especially 5, 36 and 58

[124] Percy Bysshe Shelley, "Love's Philosophy"

[125] Read, Leonard E., "I, Pencil," Foundation for Economic Education, Inc. 1999. *Library of Economics and Liberty*. 20 August 2008. http://www.econlib.org/LIBRARY/Essays/rdPncl1.html

[126] Niels Henrik Gregersen, *From Complexity to Life: On the Emergence of Life and Meaning;* Oxford University Press, 2003 Chapter 2

[127] Packard, N.H., "Adaptation Toward the Edge of Chaos," *Dynamics Patterns in Complex Systems,* J.A.S. Kelso, ed., et al, Singapore: World Scientific (1988) 293-301

[128] A new field in network theory has combined evolutionary theory, economics and computer simulation to further explain the fascinating emergence of complex social actions. Called agent-based computational economics, or ACE, this new field uses computers to simulate and understand the emergence of spontaneous value-added properties from a collection of individual actions. (Not surprisingly, ACE theorists have identified Friedrich Hayek as an intellectual forerunner of the field.)

[129] See A.E. Emerson, "The evolution of adaptation in population systems," in S. Tax, ed., *Evolution After Darwin*, Volume I, The Evolution of Life (U. Chicago 1960), at 307, and S.J. Gould, The Structure of Evolutionary Theory, 656-666

[130] Smolin, Lee. 1997. *The Life of the Cosmos*. New York: Oxford University Press., 194; also see "Our Relationship with the Universe." *In Many Worlds: The New Universe, Extraterrestial Life, and the Theological Implications*, edited by Steven J. Dick. Philadelphia: Templeton Foundations Press. 84–85)

[130.5] Prigogine, Ilya. *From Being to Becoming: Time and Complexity in the Physical Sciences*, W.H. Freeman 1980. at 100-115 and 128, and *Exploring Complexity* (W. H. Freeman 1989), 72 and 238-242. Prigogine is among the most profound theorists on the essentiality of choice in complex self-organizing systems. In the network theory context, see William A. Brock and

Cars H. Hommes, "A Rational Route to Randomness," *Econometrica*, Vol. 65, No. 5 (Sep., 1997), pp. 1059-1095, arguing that changes in "intensity of choice" can set off keystone changes and other nonlinear effects in complex systems.

[131] Peacocke, Arthur. 2001. *Paths from Science towards God: The End of All Exploring.* Oxford: Oneworld. 75-78.

Science philosopher Stuart Kauffman has argued that spontaneous self-organization may be a deeply embedded principle of the universe, expanding and completing Darwin's theory of natural selection. (See S. Kauffman, *At Home in the Universe,* Oxford 1995) In the human context, I simply argue that free choice is the force capable of unleashing this progressive self-organization, and I hope to analyze Kauffman's theories in depth in subsequent works.

[132] Surowiecki, 58

[133] Surowiecki, 60

[134] See, e.g., Armen A. Alchian, "Uncertainty, Evolution, and Economic Theory," *The Journal of Political Economy,* Vol. 58, No. 3 (Jun. 1950), 211-221, arguing that innovations in firm structure arise spontaneously in a competitive environment

[135] William J. Baumol, Robert E. Litan and Carl J. Schramm, *Good Capitalism, Bad Capitalism, and the Economics of Growth and Prosperity,* Yale University Press, 2007, 83, 92

[136] Amar V. Bhide, *The Origin and Evolution of New Businesses*, Oxford, 2000, 321

[137] Seth Godin, *Survival is Not Enough,* Simon and Schuster 2002 32

[138] Michael T. Ghiselin, "Perspective: Darwin, Progress, and Economic Principles," Evolution, Vol. 49, No. 6 (Dec. 1995), 1029-1037; see also, Gould, *The Structure of Evolutionary Theory,* at 127 and 595, arguing that Adam Smith's individualism underpins Darwin's evolutionary theory

[139] B.F. Skinner, *About Behaviorism*, New York: Knopf, 1974 189

[140] See Rudolf Steiner, *Philosophy of Freedom*, for a philosophical justification

[141] S. A. Barnett, *Biology and Freedom*, Cambridge, 1988, 54 (emphasis added)

[142] van den Berghe, P.L., "Bridging the paradigms: biology and the social sciences," *Sociobiology and Human Nature,* ed., M.S. Gregory, A. Silvers & D. Sutch. San Francisco: Jossey-Bass,1978, 52

[143] Will Durant, *The Story of Philosophy,* Simon & Schuster New York (1926/2005) p 52

[144] Ibid.

[145] See Lucretius, *De Rerum Natura (The Nature of Things)*, Book 2, 251-294

[146] Arato, Andrew, "A reconstruction of Hegel's theory of civil society," in D. Cornell, M. Rosenfeld and D.G. Carlson, ed., *Hegel and Legal Theory*, New York and London: Routledge, 1991, 301; see also, *Hegel, Philosophy of Right*, § 189, observing the "interesting spectacle" of the "mutual interlacing of activities...governed by individual whim...which initially displays to the eye only irregular movements but whose laws can nonetheless be ascertained."

[147] Hegel, *Lectures on the History of Philosophy*, Chapter I, Section D, stating that there was no proposition of Heraclitus that he had not adopted.

[148] Hegel, *Philosophy of Right*, § 31 (with comment)

[149] Quoted in Cristi, Renato, *Hegel on Freedom and Authority*, University of Wales Press, Cardiff, 2005, 64

[150] Fred R. Dallmayr, *G.W.F. Hegel: Modernity and Politics*, Rowman and Littlefield, Lanham, 140

[151] Hegel, *The Phenomenology of Spirit*, trans. A. V. Miller (Oxford, Clarendon Press, 1977), sect. 2, p.2 (emphasis added)

[152] Cristi at 56

[153] Hegel, *Philosophy of Right*, § 258

[154] Nietzsche, *The Gay Science*, tr. Kauffman 1974 357

[155] Quoted in Dallmayr, Fred R, *G.W.F. Hegel: Modernity and Politics*, Rowman and Littlefield, Lanham, 2002, 29

[156] Hegel, *Philosophy of Right*, § 182

[157] Hegel is widely regarded as one of the most abstruse and difficult philosophers to read, one whose arguments are so dense that there exists little consensus on the actual meaning of most of his writings. This uncertainty has actually spawned disparate ideological movements - known as "Left Hegelians" and "Right Hegelians" - each using Hegel's opaque language to justify their own respective views of radical socialism and conservative traditionalism, respectively. With the little understanding of Hegel that I possess, I humbly argue that evolutionary choice theory as a cooperative venture better fits his views than the historical misperceptions that have unfortunately plagued his reputation. I also believe this perspective explains the inadequacies of Karl Marx's "dialectical materialism" - his quasi-Hegelian philosophy - as Ideas act on material, not the other way around. I leave it to those more knowledgeable than I to continue the debate.

[158] Henri Bergson, *The Creative Mind*, Philosophical Library, New York 1946 at 20

[159] H. Bergson, *Creative Evolution*, Henry Holt, New York 1913 at 96

[160] Ibid at 255

[161] *The Creative Mind* at 123

[161.5] Robert M. Pirsig, *Lila: An Inquiry into Morals,* Bantam 1991 at 133, 139, 160, 166, and 255.

[162] De Tocqueville's comments about voluntary associations, supra, tracks the definition of social technologies

[163] Thanks to David Seymour for this formulation

[164] Holt Paperbacks, 2002

[165] S.J. Gould, *Ever Since Darwin*, 36-37

[166] Haldane, J. B. S., *The Causes of Evolution*, London: Longmans Green (1932) 152-153

[167] In reference to Pangloss, the character in Voltaire's Candide whose delusional optimism led him to believe that reality is the best of all possible worlds.

[168] Kauffman at 208, citing David M. Raup, *Extinction: Bad Genes or Bad Luck?* New York: Norton 1991

[169] Gould, *The Structure of Evolutionary Theory*, (note 13)

[170] Surowiecki at 5

[171] Hayek, *Constitution of Liberty*, 41

[172] Luhmann, *The Differentiation of Society*, xxii

[173] Cited in Beinhocker at 440

[174] Anderson at 126

[175] Taleb, *The Black Swan*

[176] Anderson at 132

[177] Nelson, "The Coevolution of Technologies and Institutions," in Richard W. England, ed, *Evolutionary Concepts in Contemporary Economics,* The University of Michigan Press, 1994, 154

[178]Hayek, F.A. 1991b (1946) "The Meaning of Competition." In *Austrian Economics*, edited by Richard M. Ebeling. Hillsdale, MI: Hillsdale College Press: 264-280

[179] Friedrich August von Hayek, "The Use of Knowledge in Society," 1945 Edition used: "The Use of Knowledge in Society," *American Economic Review*, XXXV, No. 4; September, 1945, pp. 519–30., Section I

[180] W. Heisenberg, *The Physical Principles of Quantum Theory* (Chicago: University of Chicago Press, 1930).

[181] See Roberto Cardarelli, et al, "The Changing Housing Cycle and the Implications for Monetary Policy," in *World Economic Outlook: Housing and*

Business Cycle, Ch 3, p 21

[182] *The Economist*, "Giving credit where it's due," November 8, 2008

[183] Francesco Guerrera and Saskia Scholtes, "JPMorgan and Wells Fargo beat forecasts," *Financial Times*, October 15, 2008

[184] Francesco Guerrera, "AIG in talks with Fed over new bail-out," *Financial Times,* November 8, 2008

[185] Aline van Duyn, "Credit markets hit by bank debt guarantee," *Financial Times,* October 26, 2008

[186] John Kay, "Taxpayers will fund another run on the casino," *Financial Times*, September 16, 2008

[187] *The Economist*, "Shifting the balance", October 9th, 2008

[188] See Schumpeter, *Capitalism, Socialism and Democracy*

[189] Wm. F. Buckley, "Internet...go with it?" April 30, 1996

[190] Adam Lashinsky, "100 Best Companies to Work For: Google is No. 1: Search and enjoy," *Fortune,* January 10, 2007

[191] See Nelson, "Incentives for Entrepreneurship and Supporting Institutions," *Weltwirtschaftliches Archiv* 120(4) (1984) p 646, defining entrepreneurs as those who create "the carrying out of innovation"

[192] Steven J. Davis, John Haltiwanger, and Ron Jarmin, "Turmoil and Growth: Young Businesses, Economic Churning, and Productivity Gains", U.S. Bureau of the Census, June 2008; and John Haltiwanger, Ron Jarmin, and Javier Miranda, "Business Dynamics Statistics Briefing: Jobs Created from Business Startups in the United States", U.S. Bureau of the Census, January 2009. Also see Gentry, William M. and R. Glenn Hubbard. 2000, "Tax Policy and Entrepreneurial Entry." *American Economic Review* 90(May): 283-287, finding that every one percentage point cut in tax rates generates 1.5 percentage points more in entrepreneurial activity and reduces by nearly 4 percentage points the likelihood that those who are already engaged in a start-up will exit the field.

[193] David Audretch and Roy Thurik, "Capitalism and Democracy in the 21st century: From he Managed to the Entrepreneurial Economy," *Journal of Evolutionary Economics,* Volume 10, Number 1

[194] The exceptions since Schumpeter include Ludwig von Mises, Israel Kirzner, William Baumol, and others. See David A. Harper, *Foundations of Entrepreneurship and Economic Development.* Routledge, New York, 2003 at 28, noting that entrepreneurship simply cannot fit into standard supply and demand models, simply because "it is not possible for [markets to] demand a service that is supposed to discover that very maladjustment [of which the

market is currently unaware.]"

[195] See PeopleForTheAmericanDream.org

[196] C.J. Schramm, *The Enterpreneurial Imperative*

[197] Jacob, *The Possible and the Actual*, Chapter 2

[197.5] Nassim Nicholas Taleb, "You Can't Predict Who Will Change The World," *Fortune*, May 24, 2007

[198] Andrew Cassel, "Why jobless numbers don't show total picture," *The Philadelphia Inquirer*, October 3, 2003

[199] Dylan Loeb McClain, "Job Forecast: Internet's Still Hot," *New York Times*, January 30, 2001

[200] Daniel Griswold, "Trading Up: How Expanding Trade Has Delivered Better Jobs and Higher Living Standards for American Workers," *Cato Institute*, 9 (source: U.S. Bureau of Labor Statistics)

[201] Timothy Ferris, *The Four Hour Workweek*, Crown 2007

[202] Klein, 236-244

[203] Hayek, *Studies in Philosophy, Politics and Economics*, 229

[204] A. H. Maslow, "A Theory of Human Motivation", *Psychological Review* 50 (1943) 370-96

[205] For the evidence that New Deal programs prolonged the economic downturn of the 1930s, see, e.g, Richard Vedder, Lowell E. Galloway, *Out of Work: Unemployment and Government in Twentieth-Century America*, NYU Press 1997, Chapter 7. By 1940, eight years into the New Deal, unemployment was still a staggering 17%, making the Great Depression by far the longest, deepest, and most severe recession in American history. Given that all of the nation's most severe recessions before the 1930s were followed by a swift recovery, the recession-fixing record of government spending is questionable at best.

[206] Debora L. Spar, *Ruling the Waves*, Harcourt New York 2001, 11-22

[207] 2005 Social Security Board of Trustees Report, Sections B and D

[208] For more information, see the Prometheus Institute's Upgrade Social Security initiative, upgradesocialsecurity.org

[209] Richard Brazenor, Di(versify) hard: with a vengeance, *Financial Adviser*, August 2, 2007

[210] Information gathered from Yahoo Finance - Dow Jones Industrial Average, which was just below 1,000 points in 1970, and still above 8,000 after the collapse in 2008.

[211] U.S. savings rate hits lowest level since 1933, MSNBC.com, January 30, 2006

[212] See Luhman, *The Differentiation of Society*, Columbia University Press, 1982, xxvii-xxviii

[213] Quoted in Anderson

[214] Information gathered from the Washington DC organization of Professional Organizers - dcorganizers.org

[215] Hayek, "The Sensory Order after 25 Years," in Weimer, W. and Palermo, D., *Cognitition and the Symbolic Process,* London; Lawrence Erlbaum (1982), 128

[216] U.S. Department of Labor, Bureau of Labor Statistics, Employment and Earnings, September and various issues, 1996

[217] Federal Communications Commission, Statistics of Communications Common Carriers, 1994-95 Washington, D.C.: U.S. Government Printing Office, 1995

[218] *Luhmann, Grundrechte als Institution.* Berlin, Dunker und Humblot. 1965, p. 131

[219] Argued by Beinhocker at 236, conceptualizing the range of prospects for social technologies (the Library of Babel, a theoretical collection of all the books that could ever be written in the English language, numbering approximately $100^{1,000,000}$; by contrast, the whole universe itself only has about 10^{80} atoms.) Also see Beinhocker at 193

[220] Jagdish Bagwati, *In Defense of Globalization*, 96

[221] Beinhocker at 11

[222] See Sidney Pollard, *The Idea of Progress*, Basic Books (New York 1968) at 15-17

[223] Data from the National Bureau of Economic Research, cited in Anderson 167

[224] Frederic Bastiat, *Economic Fallacies*, Simon Publications, 2001, 28, originally published in French under the title Sophismes Economiques by Frederic Bastiat (1801-1850)

[225] Michael Elliott, "Globalization Is Good for You," *Newsweek*, April 10, 2000, summarizing the messages of A Future Perfect by John Micklethwait and Adrian Wooldridge, and The Global Soul by Pico Iyer

[226] Vincent N. Parrillo, "Diversity in America: A Sociohistorical Analysis," *Sociological Forum,* Vol. 9, No. 4, Special Issue: Multiculturalism and Diversity (Dec., 1994), pp. 523-545

[227] Charles Hirschman, "Immigration and the American Century," *Demography*, Vol. 42, No. 4 (Nov., 2005), pp. 595-620

[228] Hirschmann at 600

[229] Robert D. Reischauer, "Immigration and the Underclass," *Annals of the American Academy of Political and Social Science*, Vol. 501, The Ghetto Underclass: Social Science Perspectives (Jan., 1989), pp. 120-131

[229.5] Wadhwa, Vivek, Rissing, Ben, Saxenian, AnnaLee and Gereffi, Gary, "Education, Entrepreneurship and Immigration: America's New Immigrant Entrepreneurs," Part II (June 11, 2007). p 2 Available at SSRN: ssrn.com

[230] Joanne C. Gerstner, "Liukin family realizes its American dream," *Detroit News*, August 16, 2008

[231] Daniel T. Griswold, "Howling at the Trade Deficit," cato.org, June 3, 1998, and "The Causes and Consequences of the U.S. Trade Deficit," Testimony before the Senate Finance Committee, Washington, D.C., June 11, 1998

[232] Organization for Economic Cooperation and Development (OECD), "Agricultural Policies in OECD Countries: Monitoring and Evaluation 2005," June 2005, 76

[233] P. Romer, "Two Strategies for Economic Development: Using ideas and producing ideas," World Bank, *Proceedings of the World Bank Annual Conference on Development Economics*, 1992 (Washington DC, World Bank 1993). One would note that this definition of ingenuity tracks the definition of social technologies nearly exactly.

[234] T. Homer-Dixon, *The Ingenuity Gap*, Knopf, New York/Toronto, 2000, 21

[235] Wm. F. Buckley, Jr., "Debate with James Wechsler," Hunter College, New York, April 9, 1959, published in Buckley, *Let Us Talk of Many Things: The Collected Speeches*

[236] Matthew L. Wald, "Faulty Design Led to Minnesota Bridge Collapse, Inquiry Finds," *New York Times*, Janunary 15, 2008

[237] See Downtown Business Improvement District website, http://www.downtownla.com/

[238] Jerry Garrett, "Fisker, a Little Company with Big Dreams", *New York Times*, January 15, 2008; and Chuck Squatriglia, "Gorgeous Convertible Improves Fisker's Plug-in Karma", *Wired.com*, January 12, 2009

[239] George F. Will, "Obama on energy: A fairy tale," *Sacramento Bee*, August 24, 2008

[240] Business Roundable, Released: 4.4.01, "Unleashing Innovation: The Right Approach to Global Climate Change" http://www.businessroundtable.org/pdf/524.pdf

[241] Ibid.

[242] Wm. F. Buckley, "God Bless The Rich," *Saturday Evening Post*, December 30, 1967

[243] Adam Smith, *The Wealth of Nations*, ed. Edwin Cannan, New York Modern Library, 1937, 81

[244] Tyler Cowen, "Creative destruction: The idea that globalization will produce a bland McWorld is a myth," *National Post* (Canada), November 2, 2002

[245] Shirley Leung, "Armchairs, TVs and Espresso - Is it McDonalds?" *The Wall Street Journal,* August 30, 2002

[246] Dobzhansky at 26

[247] Hayek, *The Fatal Conceit,* Routledge at 75 and Gray, *Hayek on Liberty,* Blackwell, New York, 1984, 51

[248] Quoted in Gray at 230

[249] Hayek, F. A. (1979) "The Political Order of a Free People." Vol. 3 of *Law, Legislation and Liberty.* Chicago: University of Chicago Press. 161

[250] R. Steiner, *Intuitive Thinking as a Spiritual Path*, 160

[251] K. Popper, *The Open Society and its Enemies,* London: Routledge 1966, 134-5

[252] Durkheim, *Rules of Sociological Method* (New York: Free Press, 1964), 140

[253] Charles A. Ellwood, "Social Evolution and Christianity," *The Journal of Religion,* Vol. 3, No. 2 (Mar., 1923), pp. 113-131

[254] Kathryn Jean Lopez, "An Unplanned Education: Sex and the loneliest number," *National Review,* August 11, 2008

[255] Wilbur Zelinsky, "The Uniqueness of the American Religious Landscape," *Geographical Review,* Vol. 91, No. 3 (Jul., 2001), pp. 565-585

[256] Nozick at 322

[257] See No Child Left Behind

[258] 60 Minutes, "The Harlem Children's Zone: How One Man's Vision To Revitalize Harlem Starts With Children," May 14, 2006

[259] *The Economist*, "A Biased Market", October 30th, 2008

[260] De rougemont, Man's Western Quest, tr. Montgomery Belgion, World Perspectives no 13, Harper and Bros New York 1956 at 145

[261] Debora L. Spar, *Ruling the Waves*, Harcourt New York 2001 p 2

[262] Leonard B. Meyer, "Innovation, Choice, and the History of Music," *Critical Inquiry*, Vol. 9, No. 3 (Mar., 1983), pp. 517

[263] Pop toasters, v. to brandish or discharge firearms

[264] Dropped roadsters, n., convertible sports cars

[265] Referring to the victims of gun violence

[266] Knocked up, n., impregnated, especially as part of a transient (nonperma-

nent) relationship

[267] B-boys, n. break dancers, dancers especially popular during the infancy of hip-hop music, in the eighties and nineties

[268] Drop: to release or publish (as an artistic work)

[269] SP, n.: Emu SP1200 drum machine/sampler. MPC: MIDI Production Center, a line of samplers/sequencers designed by the Japanese company AKAI. The MPC has become very closely associated with hip-hop and many producers claim to use an MPC.

[270] The game, n. referring to hip-hop as a genre, or generally any pursuit, such as a career, industry, etc., in which there is some level of competition.

[271] A double entendre, self-referencing Masta Ace, the rapper who wrote the first verse, being ready to "marry" the developed "game" of hip-hop. Also referencing "Masters of Ceremony" (MC), the acronym for rappers generally.

[272] Green, n., money

[273] Illmatic is the first album of Nas, considered one of the best rappers alive; the album was released in the mid 1990s

[274] C. Delores Tucker, activist and politician, known for her strong and vocal criticism of gangsta rap

[275] Tribe Called Quest, another highly regarded rap group popular during this period

[276] *Strictly 4 my Niggaz*, 1993 album by Tupac Shakur, who later was murdered, as well as *Ready 2 Die*, an album by Notorious B.I.G. (see note *infra*)

[277] Beef, n., sustained conflict or disagreement with another individual, i.e. "I have a beef with my landlord". Refers to the well-publicized conflict between rappers from the east coast (predominantly Chris Wallace, or Notorious B.I.G.) against those from the west coast (predominantly Tupac Shakur), considered two of the greatest rappers of all time, both of whom were killed from street violence. The line is also a doubt entendre on the title of the movie *Legends of the Fall*.

[278] Cats, n, individuals, Referring to P. Diddy and other rap moguls known for the flamboyant attitudes and appearance.

[279] "Jack", v., to steal, e.g. "he jacked my wallet"; the line refers to the increased (alleged) amount of copying and a lack of innovation in the market

[280] "Pop crap", referring to the aforementioned Top 40, and Plymouth Rock-Rap, referring to "crossover" rock/rap groups, such as Limp Bizkit, with little continuity from the original founders of the art form

[281] "Ice", n., diamond jewelry, especially when worn in an ostentatious fashion, also referring to bright chains and platinum.

[282] Shows referring to rap concerts, "snowmen," a group of mindless and homogenous people, referring to mindless supporters.

[283] Bubblegoose, n., an oversized jacket, popular wear in the hip-hop culture of the East Coast

[284] E.H. Gombrich, *The Story of Art*, London: Phaidon, 1966

[285] *Biology and Freedom*, 280

[286] David Greene, ed., *The Complete Greek Tragedies, Aeschylus II* (Chicago, 1956), 981

[287] Valerio Scarani, *Quantum Physics: A First Encounter,* Oxford 2006 at 95

[288] W. Heisenberg, *Physics and Philosophy*, New York: Harper Torchbooks 1958 at 125

[289] Dobzhansky at 52

[290] *Creative Evolution* at 192

[291] Gould, *Structure of Evolutionary Theory* at 722

[292] Quoted in Dobzhansky at 127

[293] H.M.S. (Her Majesty's Ship) Beagle was the vessel on which Charles Darwin was aboard when observing the phenomena that inspired his landmark work on evolutionary theory, *The Origin of Species*. "The H.M.S. Legal" thus is a play on the name on the ship, and the fact that subject matter of this chapter, namely the American common law legal system, also originated from Britain. But if you had to read this in order to get it, you probably aren't laughing. Sorry.

[294] G. Dietze, *In Defense of Property*, 1971, 93

[295] A. Corbin, "The Law and the Judges," 3 *Yale L. Rev.* 234 (1914)

[296] Ibid at 239

[297] W. Jethro Brown, "Law and Evolution," *The Yale Law Journal*, Vol. 29, No. 4 (Feb., 1920), pp. 394-400, 398

[298] Howe, Introduction to O. Holmes, *The Common Law* xiv (M. Howe ed. 1963)

[299] Holmes, *The Common Law*, 449

[300] Ibid at 460-1 (emphasis added)

[301] Ronald Dworkin, *Law's Empire*, 1986 229-232 and Ronald Dworkin, "Law as Interpretation," *Critical Inquiry*, Vol. 9, No. 1, The Politics of Interpretation (Sep., 1982), pp. 179-200 at 192

[302] E. Donald Elliott, "The Evolutionary Tradition in Jurisprudence," *Columbia Law Review*, Vol. 85, No. 1 (Jan., 1985), pp. 38, 54

[303] Paul G. Mahoney, "The Common Law and Economic Growth: Hayek Might Be Right," *The Journal of Legal Studies*, Vol. 30, No. 2 (Jun., 2001), pp.

503-525

[304] Quoted in T.H. Green and T.H. Gross, *Hume* (1890) at 269

[305] Douglas Glen Whitman, "Evolution of the Common Law and the Emergence of Compromise," *The Journal of Legal Studies*, Vol. 29, No. 2 (Jun., 2000), pp. 753-781

[306] P. Rubin, "Why is the Common Law Efficient?" 6 *J. Legal Stud.* 51 (1977)

[307] Robert C. Clark, "The Interdisciplinary Study of Legal Evolution," 90 *Yale L. J.* 1238 (1981)

[308] Holmes, *The Common Law*, 32

[309] Irvine Lairg, "The Law: An Engine for Trade," *The Modern Law Review*, Vol. 64, No. 3 (May, 2001), pp. 333-349

[310] J. Harvie Wilkinson III, "Our Structural Constitution," *Columbia Law Review*, Vol. 104, No. 6 (Oct., 2004), pp. 1687-1709

[311] Federalist No. 39

[312] *Gregory v. Ashcroft*, 501 U.S. 451 (1991)

[313] *U.S. Term Limits, Inc. v. Thornton*, 514 U.S. 779, 838,

[314] Samuel Krislov, "American Federalism as American Exceptionalism," *Publius*, Vol. 31, No. 1, (Winter, 2001), pp. 9-26

[315] See Charles S. McCoy, "Federalism: The Lost Tradition?" *Publius*, Vol. 31, No. 2, (Spring, 2001), pp. 1-14; and Ann Bowman, "American Federalism on the Horizon," *Publius*, Vol. 32, No. 2, The Global Review of Federalism (Spring, 2002), 12

[316] Dale A. Krane, "The State of American Federalism, 2001-2002: Resilience in Response to Crisis," *Publius: The Journal of Federalism* 32:4 (Fall 2002)

[317] James M. Buchanan, "Toward Analysis of Closed Behavioral Systems," in Buchanan and Tollison, *Theory of Public Choice: Political Applications of Economics*, Univ. of Michigan, Ann Arbor 1972, 12

[318] Vilhanto, M., "Competition between governments as a discovery procedure," *Journal of Institutional and Theoretical Economics*, 148, 1992, 411

[319] Albert O. Hirschmann, *Exit, Voice and Loyalty*, Cambridge: Harvard, 1970

[320] Tiebout, "A pure theory of local expenditure," *Journal of Political Economy*, 64, 1956, 420

[321] Hayek, *The Constitution of Liberty*, note 9, at 177–78 vol III, pp 146-7

[322] Buchanan, "Federalism and fiscal equity," *American Economic Review*, 40, 1950, 589

[323] *Doe v. Bolton*, 410 U.S. 179 at 210

[324] R. Bork, *The Tempting of America*, (1990) 166

[325] Kenneth S. Abraham, *The Forms and Functions of Tort Law*, Second Edi-

tion, Foundation Press, New York, 2002, 46

[326] During the first half of the 19th century, a number of legal scholars and state courts endorsed Washington's conclusion that the Clause protected only fundamental rights. See, e.g., *Campbell v. Morris*, 3 Harr. & M. 535, 554 (Md. 1797) (Chase, J.) (Clause protects property and personal rights); *Douglass v. Stephens*, 1 Del. Ch. 465, 470 (1821) (Clause protects the "absolute rights" that "all men by nature have"); 2 J. Kent, Commentaries on American Law 71-72 (1836) (Clause "confined to those [rights] which were, in their nature, fundamental"). See generally Antieau, "Paul's Perverted Privileges or the True Meaning of the Privileges and Immunities Clause of Article Four," 9 Wm. & Mary L. Rev. 1, 18-21 (1967)

[327] *Doe v. Bolton*, 410 U.S. 179 at 211-213

[328] *Jacobson v. Massachusetts*, 197 U.S. 11, 29

[329] *Kent v. Dulles*, 357 U.S. 116, 126

[330] *Meyer v. Nebraska*, 262 U.S. 390, 399

[331] 357 U.S. 449 (1958)

[332] 381 U.S. 479 (1965), 394 U.S. 557 (1969)

[333] 425 U.S. 501 (1976), 436 U.S. 478 (1978)

[334] 425 U.S. 501, 503 (1976)

[335] 394 U.S. 618 (1969)

[336] 448 U.S. 555 (1980)

[337] 388 U.S. 1 (1967)

[338] 268 U.S. 510 (1925)

[339] U.S. Const. art. I, § 8

[340] CNN, "Program brings Web's collective wisdom to patent process," online, September 15, 2008

[341] *KSR International Co. v. Teleflex Inc.*, 550 U.S. ___ (unpublished as of writing)

[342] CNN

[343] Beth Simone Noveck, "Peer to Patent: Collective Intelligence, Open Review and Patent Reform"

[344] Amendment XIV, § 1, U.S. Constitution

[345] "All merchants are to be safe and secure in leaving and entering England, and in staying and traveling in England ... to buy and sell free from all maletotes by the ancient and rightful customs" (qtd. in Holt, J. C. 1992. *Magna Carta*. 2d ed. Cambridge: Cambridge University Press., 448–73)

[346] Blackstone, William. [1765] 1979. *Commentaries on the Laws of England*. 4 vols. Facsimile ed. Chicago: University of Chicago Press, 1:415; also see

Parry v. Berry, 92 Eng. Rep 1066 [1718], and "[a] mans trade is accounted his life, because it maintaineth his life...no man ought to be put from his livelihood without answer" (Coke, Edward. [1797] 1986. Institutes of the *Laws of England.* 7 vols. Facsimile ed. Buffalo,N.Y.: William S. Hein., 3:181

[347] Rakove, Jack, ed. 1999, *Madison: Writings,* New York: Library of America, 516

[348] See Sandefur, Timothy, "The Common Law Right to Earn a Living," *The Independent Review,* v. VII, n.1, Summer 2002, 73

[349] It is undoubtedly the right of every citizen of the United States to follow any lawful calling, business or profession he may choose, subject only to such restrictions as are imposed upon all persons of like age, sex and condition. *Dent v. West Virginia* (129 U.S. 114 [1889], at 121) See also, *Corfield v. Coryell,* 6 F. Cas. 546 [1823], at 551–52; *Sewall v. Jones,* 26 Mass. 412 [1830], at 413; *City of Memphis v. Winfield* (27 Tenn. 707 [1848]); *Washington Electric Vehicle Transportation Co. v. District of Columbia,* 19 App. D.C. 462 [1902], and *Meyer v. Nebraska,* (262 U.S. 390 [1939], at 399–400: "['Liberty'] denotes not merely freedom from bodily restraint but also the right of the individual to contract, to engage in any of the common occupations of life, to acquire useful knowledge, to marry, establish a home and bring up children, to worship God according to the dictates of his own conscience, and generally to enjoy those privileges long recognized at common law as essential to the orderly pursuit of happiness by free men."

[350] *Congressional Globe,* 42d Cong. 1st sess., App. 86 [1871]

[351] Charles W. McCurdy, "Justice Field and the Jurisprudence of Government-Business Relations: Some Parameters of Laissez-Faire Constitutionalism, 1863-1897," *The Journal of American History,* Vol. 61, No. 4 (Mar., 1975) 979

[352] Gathered from the Institute for Justice

[353] Robi Chakravorti, "Terrorism: Past, Present and Future," *Economic and Political Weekly,* Vol. 29, No. 36 (Sep. 3, 1994), pp. 2340-2343

[354] Anthony Oberschall, "Explaining Terrorism: The Contribution of Collective Action Theory," *Sociological Theory,* Vol. 22, No. 1, Theories of Terrorism: A Symposium (Mar., 2004), pp. 26

[355] Thomas Homer-Dixon, "The Rise of Complex Terrorism," *Foreign Affairs,* No 128, Jan-Feb 2002, 58-60

[356] John Kincaid and Richard L. Cole, "Issues of Federalism in Response to Terrorism," *Public Administration Review,* Vol. 62, Special Issue: Democratic Governance in the Aftermath of September 11, 2001 (Sep., 2002), pp.

181-192

[357] Eric Lipton, "Audit Faults U.S. for its Spending on Port Defense," *The New York Times*, February 20, 2005

[358] Giles, Lionel, trans. *Sun Tzu on the Art of War,* Plain Label Books, p. 39

[359] William F. Buckley, Jr., "The Role of Casualties", *National Review*, August 5, 2005

[360] See Boumediene v. Bush, 553 U.S. ___ (2008)

[361] Scheuer, *Marching Toward Hell: America and Islam After Iraq*, 143-144

[362] Hegel, *Philosophy of History*, trans J. Sibree, 453, and Philosophy of Right, trans T.M. Knox, sect. 274

[363] Scheuer, *Marching Toward Hell*, 145

[364] J.B. Bury, *A History of Freedom of Thought,* New York: Holt 1913, p. 14

[365] Scheuer, *Marching Toward Hell,* 144

[366] Keegan, "How America Can Wreak Vengence," *Daily Telegraph*, September 14, 2001

[367] Thanks to Richard Weddle for this quote

[368] Clyde Wayne Crews, "Ten Thousand Commandments: An Annual Snapshot of the Federal Regulatory State," *Competitive Enterprise Institute*, June 30, 2005 and THOMAS

[369] David Walker, "Washington must heed fiscal alarm bell," *Financial Times*, September 22, 2008

[370] See Maurice Duverger, "Factors in a Two-Party and Multiparty System," *Party Politics and Pressure Groups* (New York: Thomas Y. Crowell, 1972), pp. 23-32.

[371] David B. Johnson, *Public Choice: An introduction to the new political economy,* Mayfield Mountain View, 1991, 128

[372] George A. Boyne, *Public Choice Theory and Local Government: A Comparative Analysis of the UK and the USA*, Macmillan, London, 1998, 6

[373] *The Economist*, "Politics as warfare," November 6, 2003

[374] Data gathered from CNN Elections - http://www.cnn.com/ELECTION/2008/primaries/

[375] Elizabeth R. Gerber and Rebecca B. Morton, "Primary Election Systems and Representation," 14 *J.L. Econ. & Org.* 304, 318-22 (1998)

[376] Paul Krugman, *The Conscience of a Liberal,* Norton, New York, 2007 (2009)

[377] This point is actually more rigorously proven with reference to the Second Law of Thermodynamics, which holds that entropy (i.e., disorder) always increases in closed systems. The inevitability of entropy, as many philoso-

phers of science argue, creates the necessity of value-added evolution. This value-added evolution arises through the creation of complex systems, which can self-organize in a way that defeats entropic forces.

[378] Thucydides, I, 71, 2

[379] Kahn, C. H., *The Art and Thought of Heraclitus*, Cambridge 1979, CI; Diels 60

[380] Luhmann, *The Differentiation of Society*, 158

[381] Ulrich Witt, "Economic policy making in evolutionary perspective," *Journal of Evolutionary Economics* (2003) 13: 84-86

[382] Derived from the Second Law of Thermodynamics

[383] Armen Alchian AA (1950) "Uncertainty, evolution, and economic theory," *Journal of Political Economy* 58: p.218

[384] Edmund Burke, *Reflections on the Revolution in France* (Garden City, NY; Doubleday-Dolphin 1961) 74-75

[385] See Federalist No 51: "The society itself will be broken into so many parts, interests and classes of citizens, that the rights of individuals, or of the minority, will be in little danger from interested combinations of the majority. In a free government the security for civil rights must be the same as that for religious rights. It consists in the one case in the multiplicity of interests, and in the other the mulitplicity of sects."

[386] Marcus Feldman, Luigi L. Cavalli-Sforza, and Lev. A. Zhivotsky, *Complexity, Metaphors, Models and Reality*, ed G. Cowan, et al., Addison-Wesley, 1994, 47

[387] John Rawls, *A Theory of Justice,* Harvard, Sect. 13

[388] Ulrich Witt, "Economic policy making in evolutionary perspective," *Journal of Evolutionary Economics* (2003) 13, 82

[389] John Simerman and Kristin Bender, "Day of anti-war rage," *Contra Costa Times*, March 20, 2008

[390] Ibid.

[391] A. Lawrence Chickering and James S. Turner, *Voice of the People: The Transpartisan Imperative in American Life*, Da Vinci Press, Goleta, 2008

[392] Charles Darwin, Letter to Hugh Falconer, Oct 1, 1862, quoted in Gould, *Structure of Evolutionary Theory*, 2

[393] Plato, *The Four Socratic Dialogues,* Oxford: Clarendon, 1903, 59-63

[394] Hayek, "The Pretense of Knowledge," Prize Lecture, Lecture to the memory of Alfred Nobel, December 11, 1974

Appendix A
Major concepts of evolutionary choice theory as discussed in The American Evolution

I. Social Technologies

Definition: Ideas or designs in pursuit of a goal or goals; methods to bring order out of chaos

Analogous to (scientific concepts):
- Memes (Richard Dawkins)
- Genetic programming (DNA)
- Network schemata (See below)

Examples (real world):
- Governments and laws
- Business strategies (Starbucks, Whole Foods, Nike, etc.)
- Cultural pastimes (music, snowboarding, religions, etc.)
- Information technology (Google, Wikipedia, Amazon, etc.)

II. Evolution

Generally: "Progressive adaptation"; Search process for beneficial adaptations

Human context: Search process for beneficial social technologies; discovers knowledge to live better and bring order out of a chaotic world

- Advanced evolutionary systems allow **openness, learning, and choice**
- **"Businesses are the grist for the evolutionary mill"**; social technologies compete so we can live better
- Evolution works best with **strong reciprocity**; we all benefit by encouraging entry and transitions in the "cooperative venture"

3-step Process: Differentiation, selection, and amplification

III. Differentiation (First step in evolutionary process)

Generally: Variation, diversification, experimentation, etc.

Purpose: Encourage discovery of beneficial advancements

Human purpose: Produce positive innovations in social technologies

Examples:
- Entrepreneurship (introducing new ideas into the market)
- Division of labor (different talents for different jobs)
- Free debate (a thriving marketplace of ideas)
- Open trade/immigration (comparative advantage)
- Open source/crowd-sourcing/long tail (opening up the pursuit of knowledge)
- Polymerase IV (mutation-creating enzyme)

IV. Selection (Second step in evolutionary process)

Generally: "Differential reproduction"; some variations survive and others don't

Human context: Differential adoption of the ideas that underpin social technologies, through freedom of choice

Purpose: Extract the best ideas from a sea of chaos and failure

- Phenotypic: Selection takes place at the individual level
- Superfecundity: More options are created than can be sustained by selection, thus the survival rate is extremely low (e.g. over 99% of species go extinct; over 80% of the Fortune 50 ended up off the list within a decade)
- "Time, in his aging course, teaches all things": Not every death is the verdict of natural selection; only the long-term result of differential reproduction creates evolution; all things are subject to change.
- Creative selection: Through the negative elimination of the "unfit", evolution can empower positive innovation (e.g. Market failure creates opportunity for market success for more evolved social technologies)

V. Amplification (Third step in evolutionary process)

- Emergent properties: A whole that is greater than the sum of its parts (see networked systems, below)
- Feedback effects: Network interference (either positive or negative) created endogenously within the system
- Exponential growth: Amplification processes tend to follow a power law, growing exponentially

VI. Networked systems

Generally: Collection of nodes and connectors, governed by schemata (or rules), and capable of adaptation

Human context: Connections of individuals according to the adoption of various schemata (social technologies); network adaptation creates social-technological evolution

- Networks are governed by choice (0 or 1), but emergent properties can form from these simple individual behaviors; systems are self-organizing
- Systems are highly interconnected; individual behaviors can have large effects on larger groups, and vice versa; feedback effects occur
- Systems are nonlinear, follow power laws, and can learn (i.e. adapt) to various situations
- Structure and randomness are both necessary for efficient network performance; successful networks balance features of both
- Adaptive networks tend to evolve on the edge of chaos
- Complex systems, upon reaching a critical level of disorder, adapt at a "bifurcation point" where the system can "choose" among new structures (Prigogine)

VII. Quantum mechanics

- Chance fuels evolutionary creativity: The universe is indeterministic on the most basic level; quantum indeterminacy can "percolate up" into the behavior of biological systems
- Uncertainty principle: One cannot predict two conjugate variables (e.g. position and momentum) with certainty; the more one knows about one,

the less one knows about the other
- The best we can ever do is give a probability of an event, while recognizing that even that observation impacts the universe in some way (a concept popularized by the Butterfly effect)
- Wave/particle duality: All matter exhibits both wave and particle features, demonstrating that even the most fundamental distinctions in the natural world are relative and nonpermanent
- Conscious choice creates the "collapse" of the wave function into a particle or real event (Goswami)

VIII. Other concepts

- *Evolition:* The choices made in pursuit of social progress (i.e. invention, creation, innovation); not necessarily everyone's choices

- *The evolutionary paradox:* Logical contradictions in how growth processes operate (e.g. death empowering life, the possible overcoming the impossible, and the dual necessity of structure and individualism) - see below

- *Hegelian dialectic:* Creation of synthesis that combines contradiction into a greater truth, embracing both sides

- *Bergsonian evolution:* Changes in universe are spurred by creative intuition

- *Law of the vital few:* Inequality is endogenous in large networks: 80% (or more) of quality comes from 20% (or less) of the population

- *Black swan:* A logically or statistically impossible event that only becomes possible upon a specific invention or discovery

Appendix B
Major policy proposals discussed throughout The American Evolution (and their significance in empowering evolutionary adaptation)

1. Let businesses be the grist for the evolutionary mill

How: End all corporate bailouts in favor of bankruptcy protection or government-orchestrated private buyouts. Companies should be allowed to fail freely, while depositors should be insured against loss through the FDIC.

Evolutionary purpose:
- Empowers selection of innovative new banking technologies
- Maximizes differentiation by ensuring that profitable ideas remain
- Maximizes differentiation by maintaining opportunity for new entry
- Maximizes differentiation by protecting depositors' livelihoods from banks' failures

2. Empower federalism

How: Allow states to experiment with innovative policies to solve pressing issues, such as education, social services, and more

Evolutionary purpose:
- Maximizes differentiation in pursuit of innovative government programs
- Empowers selection, allowing voters a greater ability to satisfy their unique preferences

3. Reduce trade barriers

How: Gradually remove all tariffs and other restrictions on foreign goods, as well as subsidies intended to support domestic industry

Evolutionary purpose:
- Maximizes differentiation of social technologies, giving Americans access to the best ideas from around the world
- Empowers selection by allowing Americans to choose what works best for them
- Encourages amplification of beneficial technologies, spurring positive economic feedback throughout the domestic economy

4. Universal health care accounts

How: Divert existing employer health care contributions, tax free, into a plan selected by each individual worker. Workers can choose among various insurance plans or can select to simply pay for health care on a case-to-case basis with the funds in the account. Accounts would be accepted as payment at any licensed medical facility in the United States, and ideally, facilities abroad as well.

Evolutionary purpose:
- Maximizes differentiation in pursuit of innovative health care technologies
- Empowers selection regarding health care programs, as determined by what works for patients and doctors - not bureaucrats and politicians
- Empowers selection regarding various jobs, by breaking the restrictive link between employers and health care
- Ensures equal opportunity (maximum participation in in the evolutionary process) by supplementing accounts when necessary
- Empowers selection by not spending future generations' money

5. Universal retirement accounts

How: Divert existing Social Security taxes and 401(k)s (if desired) into personal accounts controlled by each worker. Funds should include a number of low-risk default options. Governments should continue to support existing retirees and can supplement accounts if necessary.

Evolutionary purpose:
- Allows differentiation and selection regarding various retirement

planning systems
- Empowers selection regarding various jobs, by breaking the restrictive link between employers and retirement
- Empowers selection regarding investment by allowing all Americans to build their own wealth, regardless of income or socio-economic background
- Ensures equal opportunity (maximum participation in in the evolutionary process) by supplementing accounts when necessary

6. Choice-enhancing regulation

How: Gradually inject free choice into government regulations, preserving the rights of affected individuals to select alternative methods of pursuing government goals

Evolutionary purpose:
- Maximizes differentiation among social technologies
- Empowers selection among social technologies

7. School Choice

How: Give low-income parents a government-funded voucher redeemable for tuition at the K-12 school of the parents' choice

Evolutionary purpose:
- Maximizes differentiation in pursuit of innovative education technologies
- Maximizes selection regarding education programs, as determined by what works for parents and teachers - not bureaucrats and politicians
- Ensures equal opportunity by providing education free of charge
- Encourages the evolutionary process by sharpening minds and inculcating social values necessary for social participation

8. Job-based immigration reform

How: Facilitate swift entry of all immigrants with a secure offer of employment from a documented American business, while securing the border regions with any and all technologies available

Evolutionary purpose:
- Maximizes cultural and economic differentiation in pursuit of innovative new social technologies

9. Permit competing currencies

How: Allow alternative currencies as legal tender in the United States.

Evolutionary purpose:
- Maximizes differentiation regarding monetary policy

10. Create a derivatives clearing house

Evolutionary purpose:
- Empowers selection by providing transparency

11. Government spending within one generation only

How: Pay for government programs with the tax dollars of current citizens

Evolutionary purpose:
- Empowers selection over the use of finances

12. Enshrine the right to pursue a lawful calling

How: Pass a constitutional amendment protecting the right to pursue a lawful calling

Evolutionary purpose:
- Maximizes differentiation in pursuit of innovative social technologies, by guarding against arbitrary restrictions

13. Reduce barriers to entrepreneurship, generally

How: Reduce individual and small business taxes, and eliminate regulations intended to decree a given technological preference in the marketplace

Evolutionary purpose:
- Maximize differentiation in pursuit of innovative social technologies
- Encourages amplification of beneficial technologies, spurring positive economic feedback throughout the domestic economy

14. Keep the internet free

How: Keep the internet free of social regulation and taxation

Evolutionary purpose:
- Maximize differentiation among social ideas
- Maximize differentiation among internet technologies

15. Criminal justice reform

How: End the War on Drugs in favor of rehabilitation, prevention and transition programs; enfranchise ex-felons

Evolutionary purpose:
- Maximize differentiation among lifestyle choices

16. Increase feedback for government programs

How: Give beneficiaries a choice of provisions, publicly disclose all activities and expenditures, subject individual programs to voter referenda, and other methods

Evolutionary purpose:
- Empowers selection of government provisions

17. End Redistricting abuse

How: Remove redistricting power from politicians, and redraw districts in order to increase political competition

Evolutionary purpose:
> - Maximize differentiation and empower selection among candidates

18. Campaign finance reform

How: Remove restrictions on soft money contributions

Evolutionary purpose:
> - Maximize differentiation among political candidates

19. Term limits

How: Limit all politicians to a specific number of terms

Evolutionary purpose:
> - Maximize differentiation among political candidates

20. Open primaries

How: Allow all citizens to vote in any political party's primary elections

Evolutionary purpose:
> - Maximize differentiation, encouraging candidates outside of the party orthodoxy
> - Maximize selection regarding a candidate's platform, as determined by the citizens at large

Appendix C
Further Reading on Evolution and Related Ideas

Anderson, Chris. *The Long Tail: Why the Future of Business is Selling Less of More*, Hyperion 2006

Barnett, S.A., *Biology and Freedom*, Cambridge 1988

Beinhocker, Eric. *The Origin of Wealth: The Radical Remaking of Economics and What it Means for Business and Society*, Harvard 2006

Bergson, Henri. *Creative Evolution,* Holt 1913

Boulding, Kenneth. *Evolutionary Economics*, Sage 1981

Capra, Fritjof. *The Tao of Physics*, Shambhala 1983

Chickering, A. Lawrence, and Turner, James S., *Voice of the People: The Transpartisan Imperative in American Life*, da Vinci Press, 2008

Dobzhansky, Theodocious. *The Biological Basis of Human Freedom*, Columbia 1956

England, Richard, ed. *Evolutionary Concepts in Contemporary Economics,* University of Michigan 1994

Gordon, Wendell, and Adams, John, *Economics as Social Science: An Evolutionary Approach*, Riverdale 1989

Goswami, Amit. *The Visionary Window: A Quantum Physicist's Guide to Enlightenment,* Quest 2000

Gould, Stephen Jay. *The Structure of Evolutionary Theory,* Harvard 2002

Hayek, Friedrich. *The Fatal Conceit: The Errors of Socialism* (W.W. Bartley, ed.), University of Chicago 1991

Hayek, Friedrich. *Studies in Philosophy, Politics, and Economics,* University of Chicago 1967

Hayek, Friedrich. *The Constitution of Liberty,* University of Chicago, 1960

Homer-Dixon, Thomas. *The Ingenuity Gap,* Knopf 2000

Hubbard, Barbara Marx. *Conscious Evolution: Awakening the Power of Our Social Potential,* New World Library 1998

Jacob, François. *The Possible and the Actual,* University of Washington, 1994

Kauffman, Stuart. *At Home in the Universe: The Search for the Laws of Self-Organization and Complexity,* Oxford 1995

Kuhn, Thomas., *The Structure of Scientific Revolutions,* University of Chicago, 1962

Luhmann, Niklas. *The Differentiation of Society,* Columbia 1982

Mayr, Ernst. *Evolution and the Diversity of Life,* Harvard 1976

Pirsig, Robert M. *Lila: An Inquiry into Morals,* Bantam 1992

Popper, Karl. *All Life is Problem Solving,* Routledge 1994

Smolin, Lee. *The Life of the Cosmos,* Oxford 1999

Surowiecki, James. *The Wisdom of Crowds: Why the Many Are Smarter Than the Few and How Collective Wisdom Shapes Business, Economies, Societies and Nations,* Doubleday 2004

Taleb, Nassim Nicholas. *The Black Swan: The Impact of the Highly Improbable,* Random House 2007

Williams, Howard. *Hegel, Heraclitus, and Marx's Dialectic,* St. Martin's Press, 1989

Printed in the United States
214576BV00004B/3/P